A LIFE *Not* EXPECTED

BUT A JOURNEY WORTH TAKING

VIOLET GRAYSON

ARPress

ILLUMINATING IDEAS.
EMPOWERING VOICES

ARPress
45 Dan Road Suite 5
Canton MA 02021

Hotline: 1(888) 821-0229
Fax: 1(508) 545-7580

Ordering Information:
Quantity sales. Special discounts are available on quantity purchases by corporations, associations, and others. For details, contact the publisher at the address above.

Printed in the United States of America.

ISBN-13:   Softcover   979-8-89356-170-8
             eBook   979-8-89356-171-5

Library of Congress Control Number: 2024914338

DEDICATION

To Dean and George for their support
and love and belief in me.

TABLE OF CONTENTS

INTRODUCTION

I THOUGHT I HAD TO have certain elements in my life in order to know real happiness.. I didn't realize I had all those elements in front of me but sometimes bungled my chance of creating happiness out of them.

I also learned during those times that happiness could lie just under the surface but you have to trust it's there and seek it out, even though you might have to change your idea of what you believe it will look like. If I had known that sooner I could have spared myself a sea of anguish, but isn't that the object of life? You live and you learn.

Along the way, I found that God doesn't always give you what you want but He never fails to gives you what you need, even if it's only a stranger's smile when you're feeling lonely or a cat's purr when you want to give up.

My story begins in Rhode Island where I was born and was fortunate enough to be raised by parents who gave me the basic tools of honesty, integrity, loyalty and faith. It was up to me to decide what to do with them. I've tried to use them well. At times, I've failed miserably but was given encouragement at the time I needed it to keep trying. That's all I can do.

The trek has been a long one, not only in years but in experiences. It has held joy, sorrow, adventure and sadness, but I don't wish it had been different.

GASPEE POINT

A HURRICANE BORNE IN THE subtropical heat of the West Indies howled up the east coast in September of 1938, a month before my thirteenth birthday, siring a tidal wave* that scoured clean the campground at Ocean Grove in Swansea, Massachusetts, where our family had spent summer weekends from the time I was six. Partnered with winds reaching one hundred twenty-one miles an hour, it demolished or swept out to sea the wooden floors and frames built by the campers to accommodate their house tents. Five hundred residents of southern New England lost their lives in its fury.

To my dismay and that of my sister, Ruth, our parents broke the news that the owner, after seeing the destruction, announced the permanent closure of the campground. We could no longer anticipate piling into the back seat of our old Plymouth on the weekend before Memorial Day for the drive to Ocean Grove to check our campground spot and greet our summer friends while my mother and father and the other families set up their tents for the coming three months. That first sniff of salt air as we drew near to Ocean Grove would become a cherished memory, along with our Sunday night goodbyes to our friends, part of our childhood that could no longer exist.

Gone would be the lazy days of lying on the beach or racing our friends into the waves or roaming the area surrounding the campground while our parents relaxed, knowing we would take care of each other. In later years, Ruthie confessed that although she loved me she also loved those weekends when she wasn't required to keep an eye on her little

---

* Tidal waves are also known as tsunamis.

sister. At Ocean Grove, she could enjoy just being herself. She admitted that she mourned the loss of her summer freedom.

That summer, not realizing our good fortune in having places to swim in Cumberland, we reluctantly adjusted to fresh water, splashing in a widened section of the Abbot Run river. At times, my father drove us to Hunt's Bridge which reached over Abbot Run in Adamsdale, Massachusetts, a village set on the border of both states. As a last resort we walked to New River, a bulb-out of the Blackstone River whose deep and swift-running waters had lured textile manufacturers in the 1800's. My mother frowned on that because the mill owners used the Blackstone as a sewer to wash away their waste, a common practice before Americans began taking care of the environment and before the Blackstone enjoyed a clean bill of health.

She had also heard rumors that farther up the river bank a group of boys had slung a rope over a tree branch which allowed them to swing out over the water and drop into it, stark naked and boisterous. Wanting to verify or dismiss the rumor, we crept through the bushes one day, peeked and hurried back, giggling all the way. We never confessed it to her but she was right about that, too.

It isn't surprising that we lunged at the chance, in the summer of 1941, when Aunt Betty** asked, "Would Ruth and Vi like to stay at our cottage with us next weekend?" Their daughter, Marian, a good friend to both of us, was an only child and a year or so older than Ruthie. The family cottage at Gaspee Point*** sat in a colony arrayed along a bluff overlooking Narragansett Bay, a few miles below Providence. Our pleading looks convinced our parents and they both agreed we could do it.

On the Friday night in July that our parents took us to Gaspee Point, Marian was waiting to greet us and we all rushed to sit on the beach.

** Aunt Betty wasn't actually related to us but in that era young people were discouraged from calling adults by their first names. She and Uncle Ted were related to my mother's sister-in-law.

*** See the History section at the back of the book.

After a chat to catch up on each other's lives, she remarked, "There's a family renting the cottage next to ours. They're from Cumberland." The last name wasn't familiar to us so she suggested we go to the cottage and meet them.

Besides their mother, Annie, and their father, Henry, the family consisted of three sons – Jack, 20, Tom, almost 19 and Don, soon to be 15. Their ages dovetailed almost perfectly with ours. Hollywood could not have improved on that set-up. Tom was smitten the minute he met Ruthie. Don gave me a big smile and Jack and Marian had already become good friends.

They had been about to go swimming which sent us back to the cottage to quickly change into our bathing suits. We all scampered down the wooden steps to the beach and splashed into the water, giving us a better chance to get acquainted and to learn that they had just moved to Cumberland from Seekonk, Massachusetts. That accounted for the fact that we didn't know them. When we were called in for our evening meal, Don asked, "Will you be back later?" I liked his looks – about five feet, eleven inches, with wavy light-brown hair and a nice build – so I nodded.

After supper, the others decided to take a walk. I met Don and suggested we go with them but he wanted to sit and talk. Alone with him on a darkened beach, I panicked, wondering what to do next. I needn't have worried. He took care of that by asking whether I liked to wrestle but gave me no chance to answer. Before I realized what was happening, he had wrestled me to the sand and was laughing, pretending it was a big joke.

At that point in my life, not much had come of the crushes I'd had on boys, except for a quick, shy kiss once in a while. None had reached this stage. Besides that, my parents, though kind and loving, were not overtly demonstrative. I'd been hugged and kissed as a small child but that ceased when I reached my teen years. This type of intimacy, especially with the opposite sex, scared me. I had never known a boy as aggressively familiar as Don and breathed a sigh of relief when someone called from the top of the stairs, "Violet, are you down there? We're going for ice cream. Do you want to go?" I pulled away and jumped up, making a dash for the stairs.

We didn't return to the beach that night. On Saturday, Marian showed us the tennis courts and taught us the basics of the game. Back at the cottage, we saw the boys and waved to them. They had company but yelled they'd go swimming with us later in the afternoon. That night, we all sat together on the beach, laughing and talking.

Sunday came much faster than we had hoped and so did our parents, it seemed. They visited with Aunt Betty and Uncle Ted, for a while, giving us a little more time to be with our new friends before we left for home. I waved to anyone in general who might be standing around, wondering when I'd see Don again. Since he'd be a sophomore and I'd be a junior in Cumberland High School, the chances were good that we'd be meeting again.

1941

NEW SUBJECTS, THE GLEE club, basketball games and the smugness of being a junior all occupied my mind in September at Cumberland High. As a junior, seasoned in the logistics of finding the classrooms and retrieving the right books from my locker for the next class, I felt somewhat superior to underclassmen such as Don and didn't make it my priority to look for him, assuming I'd see him at some point, maybe at a basketball game. Since it was our only school sport and Cumberland held the state Class C Basketball Championship for several years, it didn't surprise me to see him sitting in the stands once or twice that fall, but, as I told Ruthie the next day, "He left with his buddies before I could say anything to him." Actually, I had hoped when I saw him that he'd wait and talk a while but we were both unsure of ourselves and the opportunity slipped by.

In my sophomore year, I won an all-school essay contest with my entry, *Fun*. The win gave me a modicum of prestige and I was asked, as a junior, to be an at-large reporter for our school paper, *The Chronicle*, a position which held my attention as I listened and looked for stories to use.

The only puzzling part of winning the contest was that the teacher in charge of it took me aside to ask, tactfully, "Did you see this or read it somewhere?" Confused as to what she meant, I shook my head and told her I hadn't. That she was asking whether I had plagiarized it didn't occur to me. Years later, I could smile, flattered that the judges considered my essay good enough to make them suspect plagiary.

One other consequence of the win came when my English teacher asked whether I would be willing to switch from the Commercial to the College Course. "I can almost guarantee you a scholarship in Journalism," he told me, but he might as well have said he could send me to the moon. My goal was to get my diploma and find a job as quickly as possible. My father had lost his job during the Depression and been forced to apply to the WPA*, President Roosevelt's program to put America to work. It's highly regarded in today's world because of its legacy of public works projects, but my mother and father considered it welfare and even though it kept us from starving to death, their pride suffered. My mother hated standing in line at the library to receive free food but did it to keep something on the table. All of that ran through my mind when I declined the offer and didn't bother to tell my parents about it.

On October 11th, my birthday cake held sixteen candles, a major milestone in my opinion. "I'm old enough to drive," I crowed, "or get working papers and a Social Security number," both heady thoughts. I did get working papers and a Social Security number but learning to drive would have to wait a few years.

December showed up on the calendar. "I wonder what we'll sing for Christmas," I commented to my best friend, Louise, referring to the glee club and church choir. We gave no thought to the war in Europe. Television had not yet become a staple in every living room. We heard about the war on the nightly radio news or read of it in The Pawtucket Times or the Providence Journal, but only saw the catastrophic results in our local theater, watching The March of Time, or Movietone News or Pathe News. It only affected us in the way that a distant roll of thunder might, unsettling but not threatening. It was "their" war, not ours. Thousands of miles of ocean kept it far away from our shores.

On Sunday, December 7th, Louise and I lay sprawled on the living room rug at her house, reading the Sunday paper. "What happened?"

---

* Works Progress Administration, a New Deal program initiated by President Franklin Roosevelt in 1935, allowing the government to hire unskilled workers (mostly men) for public works jobs to help pull the country out of the Great Depression.

we asked in unison when the music of Kay Kyser that had been playing on the Philco suddenly stopped and an announcer said, "We interrupt this program to bring you a bulletin from the NBC newsroom in New York." Her parents came into the room to stand near the radio. The announcement continued, "President Roosevelt has said in a statement today that the Japanese have attacked Pearl Harbor in Hawaii from the air. This bulletin has come to you from the NBC newsroom in New York." That was it. That was all. The music resumed, but something had shifted. The faraway war had found us. What did it mean? "I think I'll go home," I told them. I needed the comfort and safety of our house and my family so I could fully absorb the solemn words of the announcement.

The following day, President Franklin Roosevelt addressed Congress and the nation. "Yesterday, December 7, 1941 – a date which will live in infamy – the United States of America was suddenly and deliberately attacked by naval and air forces of the Empire of Japan," he told us, in part, ending his address with, "I ask that the Congress declare that since the unprovoked and dastardly attack by Japan on Sunday, December 7th, a state of war has existed between the United States and the Japanese empire." In later news, we learned that two thousand, four hundred three people had been killed and one hundred eighty-eight planes at Hickam Field had been lost to strafing by Japanese pilots. Also, out of a total of eight battleships the Japanese damaged, four had been sunk.

The war was "ours" now! I wanted to *do something* but where would I start? Slowly, America began preparing for whatever lay ahead. A friend of my mother's told me, "We're folding bandages in the basement of the Universalist Church." I joined them for a few evenings to fold large gauzelike bandages to be put into medics' kits for field use. The government donated gray yarn to anyone who wanted to knit knee warmers, mittens and caps for the Ski Patrol who would be defending Alaska where the Japanese were expected to begin their invasion. My mother, who had knit all of our mittens and skating socks, immediately obtained a supply in order to start knitting. At school, a few students organized rallies to sell war bonds and stamps. We collected aluminum foil (which we called *tinfoil)* to toss into the collection bins set around town. We followed the directions to remove both ends of empty tin cans and step on them to squash them flat for our metal scrap collection. I asked one day, "How do these become ammunition or whatever for our troops?" No one seemed to know but we were willing to keep collecting them and we groaned as we told the story of the piles of scrap metal that sat for months on India Point wharf in Providence until the Japanese bought them up a few years before Pearl Harbor and probably recycled them into ammunition to be used against us. The first fumbling days of "what shall we do?" gave way to organization as our government issued pamphlets and aired broadcasts to help us fit into the war effort. Ration books entered our lifestyle.

We hummed new songs. "Any Bonds Today?" and "Let's Remember Pearl Harbor." Gas rationing meant no one would be teaching me to drive until after the war. One frigid morning the reality of the fuel shortage hit home when our school's allotment for that month ran out a day too soon. Our teachers allowed us to wear coats and mittens to class, but the absurdity of it didn't occur to us until we reached typing class. We all laughed, along with the teacher, when a few of the boys tried in a smart-alecky way to strike the keys with mittened fingers. As soon as Miss Roy, our principal, announced, shortly after that, "All students are excused for today," we scurried to our lockers to drop off our books, don our hats and boots and rush outside, chattering and shivering.

The good news of the season reached us fast. "The ice is in. Robin Hollow is safe for skating." We pulled our skates out of the attic, tied the laces together and flung them over one shoulder for the mile and a half walk to Robin Hollow. We could leave behind for a while the grim news of the war with its shortages and uncertainties to glide across the ice at Robin Hollow and pretend to be Sonja Henie for an afternoon.

THE BROTHERS

BEFORE THE PAWTUCKET WATER Supply Board dammed the river known as Abbot Run to form a sizeable reservoir in the late nineteenth century, the 40-acre area that dipped down into a hollow was home to a thick growth of hemlock, cedar and pine trees. The earth under the trees must have attracted a lot of worms because robins gathered in large numbers. Town residents dubbed it *Robin Hollow* and passed the name on to the reservoir that inundated it and which froze over in the chilly New England winter. Signs around the reservoir asked residents not to swim in it but nothing prevented us from skating on its surface.

The boys had already started their hockey game on the ice nearest to the dam and the bridge that spanned the water tumbling over the dam when Ruthie and I sat on the bank of the reservoir to put on our skates. "Wonder why they always play there?" I thought, but soon answered myself. It was near the road and easy to reach. It had an element of danger because of the thin ice close to the dam. Best of all, though, it left the rest of the reservoir open for the skaters, meaning that nobody would interfere with the game or vice versa.

I didn't have long to wait for an answer to my next question, "I wonder if the brothers are here?" Tom glided up to do a quick turn in front of Ruthie. "Is Don here?" I asked. He pointed to the hockey game. I laughed and skated off to find friends and enjoy the sunny winter afternoon.

Someone started a *whip* and a friend called out to me, "Come on." That meant catching up to the line of ten or so skaters flying over the ice and gripping the waist of the last skater. The *whip* was similar to a conga line, except that the leader picked his or her own time to suddenly veer, sending the speeding skaters arcing over the frozen surface. The last person in line ran the risk, if a grip was lost, of being flung across the ice. That turned out to be me but I was able to keep my balance and dig my skates into the ice to slow my momentum. I didn't see Don that day but on the way home, as we walked through the lengthening shadows, Ruthie said, "Tom asked if he could call me and I said he could."

"He seems like a nice guy," I said, adding, "I think I like Don." That word was used when a girl wanted to know a boy better and maybe become his girlfriend. I had *liked* boys in the past but nothing had come of it. With my meager skills, I had not attracted their attention. One boy, Billy, showed up in our sixth grade classroom when his family moved to Cumberland. I was smitten and told my cousin, Sam, who wanted to help. The next time he saw Billy, he put his fist under Billy's nose and growled, "My cousin likes you. You like her back, or else…" Needless to say, I was mortified, especially when Billy chose the "or else…" I was careful after that not to admit to anyone when a particular boy caught my eye, but I knew I could trust my sister and knew she would understand.

I could also trust Louise. I told her about Don. "I'll meet you at Robin Hollow next Sunday," she said, "And you can point him out to me, if he's there." On Sunday, we chatted as we put on our skates and were moving idly around the ice when Don suddenly appeared. I introduced him to Louise and we talked for a short while before he skated away. "He's cute," she said. "I think he likes you." I giggled and she and I watched discreetly for awhile to see whether he'd come back. He didn't and the afternoon passed while we skated and laughed together until she said, "I guess I'll go home. I'll see you in school."

Possibly that gave him the encouragement he needed. When Louise left, he came back to me and said, "I'll race you to the other end," pointing to the upper part of the reservoir where Abbot Run entered it. At that far point, reeds grew through the shallow water but it was possible to skate around them which took you out of sight of the other skaters for a short while. Thinking it was a serious race, I skated as fast as I could around the reeds and back to the open ice again, puffing and laughing when he outskated me, but he stopped in front of me and said, somewhat angrily, "You were supposed to let me catch you." Oh! My heart fell. Would I ever learn the art of flirting or teasing a boy?

To cover my dismay and humiliation, I turned and skated away, flinging over my shoulder, "I'm going to Massachusetts." Located in the northeast corner of Rhode Island, Cumberland shares a border with Massachusetts, a state-line that disappears in that area beneath the waters of Robin Hollow reservoir, making it possible to skate over it. We delighted in yelling that before heading to where we calculated the border to be. In the innocence of the era of the Great Depression, it seemed an exciting thing to do.

Soon after that, I decided to call it a day. He didn't attempt to talk me out of it. Once more I had lost in the game of the sexes.

A lot of snow fell in January, preventing us from doing much skating. The boys who wanted to play hockey cleared their space for it but the reservoir was too large for a general clean-up. We became busy with school activities but were able to make it to Robin Hollow several times during February and saw them once or twice but I didn't know what to say to Don and kept hoping he'd ask me to race again but he didn't.

My chance came unexpectedly when I bumped into him at our local pharmacy (*drug store* in those days). He smiled and asked whether I'd like to have a "cabinet" with him. I said I would since I had never had one. We talked and I drank my cabinet and he walked me halfway home, turning off when he reached his street. I was glad that we were friends, at least.

Rhode Island, by the way, is the only state where it's known as a "cabinet". Other states call it a frappe, a malted or a milk shake. It began as a mixture of coffee ice cream, coffee syrup and milk. One reason given for the name is that originally the coffee syrup was kept in a cabinet behind the counter. Another lesser known reason is blamed on the Rhode Island accent which doesn't include the pronunciation of the letter "r". That might have accounted for the name "carbonate" being pronounced "cahbonate" which eventually became "cabinet". I like that one.

March brought an early thaw that put an end to skating for that year, spurring Tom into finally asking Ruthie for a date. Approximately a year after they met at Gaspee Point, he came to our house in his 1930's Ford roadster. The fact that it had a *rumble seat* fascinated me. It meant that besides the two seats in the front, another two-person seat was set outside in the area where the back seat is usually located. A hinged cover could be closed when the seat was not in use.

One night, during the summer of 1942, Tom brought his brother along and asked me whether I'd like to go bowling. It was my chance to sit in the rumble seat and I jumped at it. By then, I had given up on thinking of Don as a boyfriend. I considered him just a good friend, Tom's kid brother, and often rode along with him after that, joking and getting to know him. One night when it began to rain, I squeezed into the front seat next to Ruthie. Tom closed the rumble seat cover with Don huddled inside it. We had a lot of fun during those months.

Ruthie, after graduating that June, immediately found a job in the Providence office of Brown and Sharpe, a machine tool builder whose factory lay on the outskirts of Providence. With young men leaving to join the service or being called up in the draft*, there was no scarcity of jobs. Tom who had turned nineteen by then, knew he was a prime candidate for the draft and most likely wanted to get to know Ruthie before he enlisted or was drafted.

In that summer of 1942, before entering my last year of school, I worked at my first fulltime job. Hassenfeld Brothers, who later shortened their name to Hasbro, made pencils and pencil boxes in an old textile

---

* Known as the Selective Training and Service Act, the draft had been enacted in September of 1940, the first peacetime conscription in our history. It required all American males between twenty-one and thirty-five years of age to register and become subject to military service. After Pearl Harbor and our entry into the war, that changed to all men between eighteen and forty-five. Those between eighteen and sixty-five also had to register.

mill in Central Falls, the city just across the Blackstone River from Cumberland. They needed packers for their shipments. I was one of a crew of six girls who stood on either side of a long table and filled the orders, setting various types of stationery products neatly into the boxes, with our forelady, Madeline, overseeing us.

At the "pencil factory," as we called it, I was thrilled to find an old schoolmate, Rita, a foster child I'd known in the fifth grade. I thought she'd been adopted by the family who took care of her because at that time I knew nothing of the foster care system and was puzzled and disappointed when she said goodbye in the sixth grade and moved away.

On the job, we occasionally sat on the shipping deck to eat our lunch together. Rita became my protector, telling the boys in the Shipping Department to leave me alone. Summer melted into fall and we bid goodbye to each other again, promising to keep in touch but we never did since our lives moved in different directions.

Don turned sixteen in September and chose to quit school and find a job in a local bleachery, putting an end to the rumble seat rides. I missed our camaraderie but my senior year proved to be full of challenges and activities. I was named Literary Editor of our yearbook, *The Reflector*, and asked to write the class history for the centerfold. We dedicated the yearbook to five teachers who had left to serve in the military – two in the Army, two in the Army Air Corps and one in the Coast Guard who also happened to be the English teacher who had been eager to convince me I had the talent to try for a scholarship in journalism and wanted me to transfer to the college course. His enlistment helped me to feel I had made the right choice. I'll never know.

The Chronicle was forced to cease publication because of a paper shortage. We seniors had to leave our yearbook cover a plain blue without any white trimming due to printing shortages. At home, my parents received instructions to cover the windows with black curtains at night to cut down on the glare that could be seen out at sea, making our coastline a target. We continued with the metal collections and my father became accustomed to dealing with gas rationing and coupons to get it. My sister and I learned to blend the little packet of yellow coloring into the white margarine to make it look like butter which was needed by the military. Speakers from the various branches of service came to recruit young men at school assemblies. As a member of the glee club, I sang solos at school gatherings, was part of the chorus for our senior play and stayed after school for the Socials where we learned to dance to big-band music.

In addition to that, Louise and I worked every Saturday in *Najarian's*, a five-and-ten-cent store in Pawtucket, earning the grand total of $2.50 for a day's labor. Our friends dropped in from time to time to heckle us so we enjoyed it tremendously.

Shortly before my graduation day in June of 1943, Don's father died unexpectedly. Ruthie and I went to the funeral and back to the house since she and Tom were going steady by then. Don showed up with a girlfriend – someone he had met on the job but I didn't care because graduation lay just ahead of me. I might possibly find a job in the city as my sister had done. All sorts of opportunities could present themselves as I stepped out into the world.

THE WAR YEARS

A T THE MIDPOINT OF World War II, June 11, 1943, one hundred and four Cumberland High School seniors walked solemnly down the aisle of the auditorium, keeping pace with the school band's brave offering of *Pomp and Circumstance*. Proud relatives and friends rose to honor the procession. Four years earlier we had begun with one hundred and six but lost one classmate to infantile paralysis*. The other was already on active duty with the United States Navy. Of the remaining young men, eleven had been classified as 1-A or fit for service. Five had already enlisted – one in the Naval Air Corps, two in the Navy V-12** program, one in the Navy and one in the Army Air Corps. Another was 2-A, a classification for male defense workers.

The basketball hoops drawn up and out of the way brought bittersweet memories, images of school plays and concerts in this hall and after-school socials, whispering and being reprimanded during study-hall sessions. Nostalgia filled me as I grasped my diploma but I soon consigned it to my beaming parents, told them I'd walk home and joined the festive crowd in the hallway

"Hey, girls, who wants to write to me?" It was Paul***, someone I'd been secretly *liking* in the year just past, a fact that erased the remnants of my disappointment at seeing Don with a girlfriend.

"I'll write to you," I blurted, overcoming my shyness in order not to miss the chance. He grinned and promised to send a letter as soon as he had survived basic training in the Army Air Corps. Floating on

---

*   Polio
** Navy College Training Program for high school seniors or graduates who passed a nationwide examination for acceptance at a college to become a commissioned officer.
*** Not his real name.

a cloud of joy, I mingled with my friends to ask about their plans, not really listening but nodding and smiling, my mind on what had just taken place. At last I had said the right thing at the right time.

On the way home, I wondered where I'd be working. Sure it would be in Pawtucket or Providence, I looked forward to taking a bus into the hustle-bustle excitement of the *city*, as Ruthie was doing.

That remained a dream. "Arthur called," my mother told me a few days later, her eyes shining as she spoke of the man who had been her boss at Berkeley Mill where she'd held a job for the few years my father couldn't find one. "He said they need a bookkeeper in the Carding Room." She smiled. "Just think," she went on, delighted at the thought, "You'll be working in the same room where I worked. Of course, you'll be in the office." She had been a *speeder tender*, monitoring a huge frame of equipment that spun cotton into thread. I didn't have the heart to tell her I didn't want to take it. Berkeley, a village a mile or so north of where I'd been born in Cumberland, was a far cry from the big city. At least I'd be taking a bus. I buried my disappointment and called Arthur and was hired.

As it turned out, I enjoyed the job and the people. Many of the men, married and too old for the draft or with physical problems that exempted them, liked the idea of a seventeen-year-old girl in the office. I often heard, "I brought you this from my garden." Many of them kept gardens during that period of shortages and set apples or peaches or a bag of vegetables on my desk as they ended their shifts and headed home. Sometimes they handed me a bouquet of flowers. Because I felt safe with them, I learned to trade jokes and laugh and even flirt. It occurred to me in later years that I might not have been as happy in the city.

Just before my eighteenth birthday in October of that same year, I read in the Pawtucket Times, "Canteen starting at the YMCA on Saturday night. Hostesses needed. Must be at least eighteen years of age." I told Louise, who had already passed that mark and the minute I qualified, we joined and became Junior Hostesses. A small band furnished the music in the lobby of the Pawtucket YMCA and the Junior Hostesses furnished the cookies. Due to an oversupply of Hostesses, the Pawtucket Times published a weekly list of the hostesses chosen for the Saturday dance which kept the ratio of sexes in balance.

Our real fun began when we realized we could get in without being on the list *if we had an escort.* Working out a system, we stood outside the YMCA, waited for two servicemen to come along and sweetly asked whether they'd mind walking in with us. We assured them they'd be on their own once we were inside. None of them turned us down. We had our bags of cookies and our escorts. The Senior Hostesses, who may have caught on after a while, always let us in.

According to the rules, we weren't supposed to make dates at the dance, but if we met men we liked, we surreptitiously slipped them our phone numbers or "accidentally" mentioned where we'd be waiting for the bus. Often, one or two showed up, we talked a little more and they asked us for dates. With several military installations along the east coast and an embarkation point on Cape Cod, a constant supply of young, lonely men passed through our area. Dancing with them and writing to them became my "war effort."

"You have a letter from Paul," my mother said, as I came through the back door one night, answering my unspoken question of whether I would actually hear from him. I snatched at it, thrilled just to see his handwriting. He told me of his disappointment at not being able to become a pilot.

"Uncle Sam has a glut of them right now. I may join the paratroopers and at least I'll be in a plane. That's what has kept me busy for the past few months." I answered immediately and in subsequent letters, we made a date for his first furlough. The picture remains in my mind. I had been to Pawtucket to do a little shopping and was wearing a hat, as was the custom. I stepped off the bus to find him waiting. He grabbed me and kissed me and my hat fell off, much to the delight of the bus passengers and I ascended to heaven. We only had two weeks but during that time, I met his parents and he met mine. To my delight, on a date when we saw a movie in Providence, he drove home with one arm around me. I felt lost when he returned to camp but the letters continued and became more loving.

We shared one more furlough before he shipped out to Europe in 1944. Before leaving, he gave me a Paratrooper wings pin and told me he loved me. I accepted it joyously but didn't say the words he expected to hear because they seemed too big, too important. I had never uttered those words to anyone. Besides that, they didn't flow out as easily in the social world as they would in later years.

I had another reason. Religion put up barriers in the forties and he was a Roman Catholic. If you married into the Catholic faith, you agreed to bring up your children in that faith. If you kept your religion, you married your love in a chapel, not at the church altar. I needed time to sort out my feelings about that. I set it aside to bask in the love and attention he showered on me, feeling safe in the fact that he loved me but unable to explain my reasons for not reciprocating.

Air-raid wardens began walking the neighborhoods to monitor compliance with the black curtains at the windows and to watch for enemy planes. I subscribed to *Flying* so I could learn the difference between the types of planes and feel I was closer to Paul. Nylon, introduced at the 1939 New York World's Fair, became the new stocking material, but we couldn't find any nylon stockings in the stores. Parachutes took first preference.

"Have you tried that new makeup on your legs?" a friend asked me. It could be smoothed on to imitate the look of stockings. Women wouldn't think of wearing high heels without stockings, even smeared-on, imitation ones. You could add a back seam which was also the fashion. If you left the make-up on for several days, though, you were forced to wash up at the basin, unless you could find a way to keep your legs dry; otherwise, you lost your stockings. I tried using the make-up for a while but soon gave up.

"Did you know you can get nylons at the mill on Exchange Street?" Word made its way around in whispers because it was *black market* (illegal) retail. If you went in through the back door of the mill, you could get a pair for $1.00. I did it once or twice, but felt guilty and waited until nylon became more available. Meanwhile, I made do with the ugly, saggy rayon ones available in the stores.

My letter-writing list grew to fourteen. In the rush of all that was happening in my life, Don slipped back into it. His eighteenth birthday in September of 1944 allowed him to join the Marines and his mother asked me to write to him. Tom, by then, had made the decision to become a fighter pilot in the Navy Air Corps and had attained the rank of Ensign. He gave Ruthie an engagement ring in 1944 before his orders put him aboard a train for California and the Alameda Naval Air Station. Since Don would be Ruthie's brother-in- law some day, I considered him to be a friend and added him to my list.

One night at the Canteen, Louise introduced me to Johnny, a young man from Wisconsin who was part of the ground crew on an aircraft carrier and stationed at Newport. She wasn't interested when I told her I was joining the Serviceman's Lounge and the Providence U.S.O. (United Service Organization, an entertainment group for the military) or riding a bus with a group of young women to Camp Edwards, an embarkation point on Cape Cod where the men left to fight in Europe. Armed guards posted around the dance hall that night prevented anyone from strolling away into the surrounding woods, but you could give your name to someone you liked and promise to write to him. I have a collection of souvenirs from the various young men I met and wrote to and sometimes dated – a Seabees pin, a Marine pin, a kerchief from Hawaii, a 6th Marines patch, four Paratrooper sleeve patches (the 82nd and the 101st) and a Navy V-5 patch.****

Paul's unit of the 82nd Airborne saw very little fighting. "Mostly, we're chasing the Germans back across Europe," he commented in one of his letters. He sent me a gold, heart-shaped locket and a bracelet

---

**** Naval Aviation Preparatory Program for seniors or high school graduates which gave them a deferment and an accelerated college education, plus flight training in the Naval Reserve and the rank of Ensign.

with Paratrooper wings on it. I put his picture into the locket. It's still there, taken in his World War II uniform. Both have been saved in a box of special items. I knew he had been in Switzerland when I received a tiny and lovely edelweiss (flower) pin carved out of ivory. A pair of ecru-colored gloves made of crochet thread and soft leather arrived soon after that. I continue to wear and cherish the pin and the gloves. In my memento album, I have several post-card pictures he sent of Berchtesgaden, Hitler's retreat in the German Bavarian Alps

Possibly it was an emotional immaturity or an inability to accept his declarations of love but in my mind my relationship with Paul had been suspended in mid-air until we could be together permanently. He was my boyfriend and I relied on the fact that he would come back to me when that time came. Meanwhile, I was having fun dancing and occasionally dating the young men I met, but not taking any of it seriously because I knew the war had to end some day.

BACK TO EARTH

WHISTLES BLEW, CHURCH BELLS rang, echoing along the Blackstone River Valley, and everyone, it seemed, came out to celebrate on August 14, 1945, when word came that the Japanese had surrendered. The war was over. My cousin Barbara raced up the road from her house. I met her halfway and we hugged and danced around, shouting, "They're coming home. They're coming home." The current love of her life, by coincidence a good friend of Paul's, had enlisted in the glider troops and would be among those returning. With perfect timing, the bus rolled into sight. "Let's go to Providence," she screamed.

We laughed and talked all the way into the city and stepped off into a milling, cheering crowd at Exchange Place where strangers hugged and kissed strangers and we were pulled into the pandemonium. We danced spontaneously or flung ourselves around in our exuberance, shaking hands, yelling "hoorays," doing whatever came to mind. To our delight, we somehow became the middle two in the first row of several lines of revelers forming in front of City Hall who urged us forward into a march through the streets, arms thrown around each other, singing lustily, "God Bless America."

When the march ran its course, Barbara yelled, "Let's go to church." I shouted back that we had no hats (another *must* in those years). On the steps of Grace Episcopal Church, we snatched the hats off two surprised sailors, promised to return them and dove into the peace and serenity of the interior to say a few quick and grateful prayers. The hush in the sanctuary calmed our over-stimulated senses and we lingered for a while. When we emerged, the sailors grinned in relief. We handed over their hats and attempted to join the boisterous crowd, but the church visit had subdued us. We wandered aimlessly for a few minutes before Barbara suggested, "Let's go to Pawtucket," but we couldn't get through the crowd to the bus. Two young men saw our dilemma and picked us up to pass us over the crowd and through an open window where we plopped into adjoining seats. By the time we reached Pawtucket, we decided we had done our celebrating and headed home.

The war was over but I wouldn't be seeing Paul until January of 1946, the date for the troop ships to sail into New York harbor where the Statue of Liberty waited to greet them. The YMCA Canteen closed as did the Servicemen's Lounge. Camp Edwards was deactivated as an embarkation point to be used later for other purposes. I didn't bother to check on the USO dance and found other ways to spend Saturday nights, looking forward to seeing Paul and grateful I had a job to keep my mind busy during the week.

By that time, the Berkeley Mill job lay behind me. Early In 1945, a friend alerted me to a job in the Personnel office at Narragansett Machine Company which wasn't downtown but closer to the city than Berkeley, lying on the line between Pawtucket and Providence. As the only "girl" in the Personnel office, I loved being the first contact for anyone visiting or seeking work. On payday, the employees lined up at my window to receive their checks. I posted the notices on the bulletin boards throughout the small machine shop, laughing, joking and flirting with the men as I had learned to do at Berkeley and they joked back. I felt I'd found my niche.

Unfortunately, the day after VJ-Day I also learned about government contracts. Narragansett Machine made gun turrets under a government contract. When I arrived at work, my boss told me, "You'll have to make out pink slips and pay checks for these employees," handing me a list that included most of the work force. Narragansett Machine had to convert to civilian contracts which meant scaling back. Taking care of the list swallowed up the day. The employees lined up and I regretfully handed out the pink slips and pay checks and wished them well. About an hour before closing time, my boss said, "Now type up your own pink slip and make out your pay check." Furious that he had used me in that way, I did it, paid myself and walked out of the office and through the shop to say a few last words to any friends who might still be around and I left.

Some companies had not relied on government contracts. I met no difficulty finding another job. By the end of the second week, the Fram Corporation hired me for their Purchasing Department in Pawtucket, in an office located a few miles from the center of the city. I gave up on the dream of working in the heart of a city.

Paul continued to write loving letters and described the victory parade planned for January 12th. The members of the 82nd Airborne had been asked to march down Fifth Avenue. "I want you to go to New York with my parents," he wrote. "They'll get in touch with you when the time comes." My heart swelled at the thought of seeing him again.

Two more letters arrived. In the first one, he asked a direct question, "How do you feel about me? You've never said. Your answer will decide what happens for the rest of our lives," words that turned out to be prophetic. In my reply I fervently poured out my love for him, but hesitated before sealing and sending the letter.

I longed to see him again, but love to me meant marriage and having children. Marriage was *forever* and the epitome of responsibility. I didn't know whether I was ready for that. I knew I was crazy about him and my heart filled with joy at the thought of being with him again but was that love? Couldn't we just be together for a little while, without the shadow of the war and its constrictions, take our time and learn whether we were right for each other? Did I truly love him or had I been caught up in the romance and tragedy of the war and carried away by his attention. I asked Ruthie who was two years older and in love with Tom, "What shall I do?"

"If you're not sure, don't say it," she advised me.

I wrote and discarded three more letters. In the fifth one, I felt I had explained my feelings and I mailed it. I can't recall the exact wording but it was along the lines of, "I'm crazy about you and have been very happy with you. I've been waiting for your return so we can be together and really get to know each other. I want to be with you. I can't wait to see you."

I received one more letter, his last, in reply. "Dear friend," it began and went on to say he was looking forward to seeing me and would call as soon as he arrived home. I did my best to ignore the feeling of doom that clutched at me, trying to convince myself I'd be able to explain when we were together, but the nightly news told me the parade had been spectacular. Where was he? When his call finally came, he had been home for two weeks. Tears stood in my eyes as we sat in our living room and he quietly said, "When I read your letter, it sounded like a *Dear John* letter and my love faded right then." I tried desperately to clarify my words but his love had plainly not survived my letter.

Somehow the sun came up and went down again and the days passed as I plodded on, struggling to deal with the first real grief I had faced in my twenty years, playing the *What if?* game, my life and my expectations shattered. Depression seized me and I asked for some time off from work. My mother made an appointment for me with a psychologist but his questions didn't seem relevant to the facts of the situation and it was difficult for me to talk about it. Counseling wasn't as available during those years as it became in later years. I couldn't explain to the psychologist about my deep hurt and broken heart. It had never occurred to me that Paul would leave me. He said he loved me and I believed him and trusted him in the same way I trusted my parents. I felt like a kicked puppy.

In the midst of my misery and confusion, Ruthie told me that Don had come home but it meant nothing to me. Toward the end of January, he called to say, "Thanks for sending your letters. I liked them," and to ask whether he could see me. I had no desire to see him or any other man, but I had no good reason to refuse. I accepted half-heartedly and out of courtesy, knowing he'd be my sister's brother-in-law.

Tom had been fortunate. With his plane on the carrier at Alameda Naval Air Station in California and his orders in hand, he had been spared when Japan surrendered. He was immediately transferred to Quonset Point, Rhode Island, to be mustered out of the Navy Air Corps. He and Ruthie had married on December 8, 1945. At the same time, Louise gave me the good news about Johnny. "He's staying here. He isn't going back to Wisconsin. He wants to study design and find a job so we can be married."

With everyone around me glowing and in love, my feeling of desolation increased and I rebounded to Don, consoling myself with the thought that I knew him and would feel comfortable with him and could come in out of the cold.

Another wedding added to my connection to Don's family. Jack married his longtime love, Betty, in January of 1946. Ruthie and I joined Don's mother and a relative, Lizzie, on the train ride to New York to be there for the ceremony in The Bronx, staying with a cousin of the family. We had a wonderful weekend together, softening once more my hesitation about dating him.

1946 TO 1949

THOUGH OUR TIME TOGETHER lacked the exhilaration of my moments with Paul, I continued to see Don and we drifted into being a couple. Hordes of young men no longer flowed through our state on their way to the war and the fortunate ones had gone back to their home towns. Don was available and seemed to enjoy my company. Dancing faded into a memory as he had never learned and had no interest in learning. My admiration grew for him as a person, though, when the gory and tragic details of his short-lived exposure to the war slowly emerged.

In the spring of 1945, he had been eighteen for about seven months when he was sent to Okinawa as a mortar-man and member of the 6th Marines, the first to go ashore to root out the entrenched Japanese. Don and his buddy, a full-blooded Native American known as Rainbolt, made their way up the hill together. A Japanese bomb dropped between them, bounced toward Rainbolt and exploded, killing him instantly while it took a chunk out of Don's back. He lay there beside his dead buddy, bleeding and in pain, until the medics found him, patched him up and put him on a plane filled with other wounded being sent to a hospital in Guam. He stayed in Guam, healing and waiting for re-assignment but the Japanese surrendered in August. Two months later, the 6th Marines were ordered to Tsingtao, China, to help Chiang Kai-shek's government carry out the surrender and disarmament of the Japanese.

The shock of Rainbolt's death still lingered with him. Occasionally, during down periods he'd say, "Rainbolt carried a bible and he read it every day," pausing before adding, "It should have been me." It showed me another side of him – the side that came to maturity on that hillside in Okinawa. I had no way of knowing what shadows it left in his mind.

Time passed and a gang formed, consisting of the newly-married Ruth and Tom, Louise and Johnny, Edna and Fred, who were two close friends of Ruthie, as well as Lester and Avis, two good friends of Tom. By default, we became part of it. The gang gathered for Hallowe'en parties in Edna's parents' basement and for hay rides, beach trips and various celebratory occasions. Don and I often dropped in on Louise and Johnny who was living with her parents while he attended the Rhode Island School of Design. We became a foursome, playing cards with them or just sitting together and talking and I was once more having fun.

Voice lessons also took up my time and soon Barbara decided to do the same thing. Together, we sang in the church choir, in minstrel shows and recitals or any other place where we could add our voices. I joined a group in Providence led by a man who dreamed of establishing a light opera company. At the same time, I took up piano lessons.

For a short while in 1947, Don and I broke up. Our relationship had been bumbling along, not headed anywhere, it seemed, and I felt a sense of relief that it had ended and yet I missed his presence in my life. One night he showed up at our house with Tom who was coming to see my father. We talked and soon after that he called to see whether we could date again and I, for whatever reason I used at the time, agreed to see him.

He must have thought things over because for my birthday that October he gave me a cedar chest. In the parlance of the day, it was called a *hope chest* and I was expected to fill it with linens, blankets or anything else a future bride might need. Actually, it was just a symbolic gift, assuring the woman that the man intended to marry her. He said he loved me and I said I loved him but neither of us spoke with great passion. He joked about the light-opera company and the piano lessons. Not having the confidence or the time to pursue both as well as continue with my voice lessons, I resigned from the light-opera company and gave up the piano lessons.

In 1948, Barbara announced, "I'm going to California. A friend of mine wants to visit her boyfriend. He's in San Diego in the Navy. Why don't you come with us?" It was in the same category as my teacher suggesting I change courses – simply not in the plans. Regretfully, I said I couldn't do it but looked back on it many times, wondering as I had with Paul – what if ?.

Other reasons kept me in Rhode Island. Louise and Johnny planned to marry in August and she told me, "I want you to be a bridesmaid and Johnny wants Don as his best man." Friends and commitments seemed more important than California and in October I was glad I stayed.

On my twenty-third birthday, Don slipped an engagement ring on my finger while we sat at the dining room table with my family watching – not a romantic scenario, but the ring was beautiful. I loved watching the prisms of light dance on the diamonds, especially when I moved my hand under the high ceiling lights in church. I had never owned anything so lovely. I felt happy yet unfulfilled at the same time. Where were all the thrills and chills? It seemed so perfunctory, making me secretly ask, "Is that all there is to being engaged?"

Edna and Fred married in January of 1949 and soon after that, Lester and Avis asked me to sing at their wedding. Friends began questioning me about the "big day" but we took it a step at a time, finally making the decision and setting the date for August 6, 1949.

The expanse of time allowed me to plan and save my money and I knew what I wanted - a white lace gown made exactly to my wishes. I invited the two brides-maids, Ruthie and Betty, and the matron-of-honor, Louise, to go to Providence with me. We found three pastel- hued, flowing gowns, two lavender and one pale green, with matching hats. The ushers, Tom and Jack, and best man, Johnny, looked handsome in tuxedos. My father escorted me down the middle aisle. We walked on a white carpet between pews decorated with sprays of flowers. My mother and Don's mother looked on, dressed in gowns. Don, handsome in his tux, waited at the foot of the chancel steps where we exchanged vows. My wedding ring had diamonds in it. I loved it even though in later months, Don reminded me it cost him a lot of money. Paul's memory lay somewhere in the recesses of my mind. I didn't miss him as a person but missed the tingling thrill of being with someone whose presence filled my heart with joy. We walked down the aisle together, Mr. and Mrs., smiling at our guests.

One little incident on the steps of Christ Church clouded an otherwise perfect occasion. We had to return to the minister's office to sign the register after the wedding. Don signed and stepped outside for a cigarette. Most of the guests, after congratulating us, drifted to the Parish Hall which was across the street. Once I had signed, I walked to the front steps and stood alone for a moment, apart from the sprinkling of guests laughing with Don on the area in front of the church.

As I lingered there, a cloud covered the sun for a second and a fleeting sense of doom caught at me, an unsettling portent that I had chosen the wrong path. I dismissed it as bride's nerves and the cloud darkening the sun and joined my new husband and our guests.

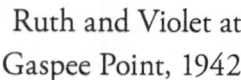

Ruth and Violet at
Robin Hollow, 1939

Ruth and Violet at
Gaspee Point, 1942

Violet coming home from
skating, 1943

Violet outside the Fram
office, Pawtucket, 1945

Ruth, Tom, Violet and Herman (her date), 1944

Ensign Tom, 1944

Ruth

Violet, the bride,
August 6, 1949

Violet and Don, with
nephew, Eddie, 1949

THE AFTERMATH

DON MADE NO SECRET of the fact that our honeymoon trip to New York's Lake George in the Adirondacks and the Allen "A" Resort and Hampton Beach in New Hampshire had fallen far short of his expectations. I wanted to explain my lack of passion and had no inkling of what held me back from doing that. In hindsight, it's easier to understand. Our marriage might have begun on better footing if I had said, "I'm adjusting to living intimately with someone twenty-four hours a day. I'm too shy to reach for your hand or casually put my arm around you. This is all new to me. Give me time to learn those things." Instead, I told him I loved him and tried to give him the attention and passion he desired and did my best to convince myself that the words were true.

I moved into the rented house, a few streets away from my childhood home, where he lived with his mother, Annie, and Aunt Ophelia, an aging and dying relative of Don's father, being cared for by Annie. My naiveté convinced me that all would be well once we were man and wife, but I had not taken into account the life he was used to living or what he would expect of a wife. My views were all based on the movies I had watched.

His mother made his breakfast every morning, for instance, and had his evening meal ready when he came in from work. Having no confidence in my cooking ability and afraid I might be late for work, I allowed that arrangement to continue. In later years. I blush now in embarrassment at my immaturity and unwillingness to take over as his wife. Though we had known each other many years and been a couple for three, we began life together completely without any real understanding of what each of us thought the marriage would bring. That isn't unusual, I'm sure, but it didn't help the fragile state of our marriage.

Shortly after our third-month anniversary, Aunt Ophelia died. As soon as possible after the funeral, Don's mother announced, "I'm going to California to visit my brother. They've been asking me to go out. I don't know how long I'll stay." Even though I liked her and she had been kind to me, I cheered silently at the news, hoping it would give us a chance to cement our marriage.

The second-floor apartment we found in Pawtucket lay close to the East Providence headquarters of the Fram Corporation where I had transferred from the Pawtucket office. "I'll be able to walk to work," I bubbled. I liked my job and the company and planned to work until we had saved enough to afford a down-payment on our own home and could start a family.

We moved in during December, just in time to invite the gang to a New Year's Eve party in our new home. I felt more confident after handling the details of the party and having everyone compliment me. All seemed to be going well except for the nausea that hit me every morning and prompted me to consult a doctor. Don wasn't happy to hear the news, "I'm pregnant" because I had promised to obtain information on birth control from my sister but had decided to try another method which had worked well for four months and lulled me into complacency

He grudgingly accepted his new role, especially when I left the morning sickness behind and gained a healthy appetite which helped me to become a better cook. At the same time, I was working on being a more loving wife.

One evening he asked, "Would you like to go out with a couple I know from work?" Actually, he only knew half of the couple. I agreed and we became friends with Dot, an employee at the mill where Don was a welder. We met her husband, Dick and we all watched movies together, enjoyed swimming at local beaches and went bowling. Don and Dot kidded a lot and traded insults and all of us had fun. I felt good and allowed myself to relax.

The change that occurred in the spring of 1950 didn't make itself known immediately. Don announced he was joining the company bowling league and I teased him. "We're becoming a typical couple." Something else added to my sense of well-being. One day toward the end of April, while I was talking with a co-worker, I felt a flutter inside me. I stopped, filled with delight. "My baby just moved," I told her.

A small someone was growing inside me. I longed to hold that small someone. Each time after that when I felt what I called the "butterfly wings" my eyes welled with tears and I couldn't wait to see my child.

It's hard to put a finger on the time it actually happened but we drifted away from Dot and Dick and I began spending more time alone at home. I didn't notice because we had a television set. They weren't standard equipment in everyone's living room which made us the envy of our old gang and made my alone-time easier to handle. Don, with my lukewarm approval, became part of the after-bowling crowd that stayed on to have a few drinks. Imperceptibly, his drinking increased, bringing on my concern. Nobody in our house drank when I was growing up. My parents weren't opposed to alcohol but it simply wasn't a part of their daily living. They accepted a drink if someone offered it but didn't keep any alcohol in the house. Dealing with it was foreign to me. I had no clue.

One night, after he had stumbled into bed, he muttered once more, "I should have died instead of Rainbolt." Another night, with liquor on his breath, he spoke of killing himself and said he had a gun in his car. I didn't believe it but thought I had better see for myself. I waited for him to fall asleep before tiptoeing downstairs and out to the car where, sure enough, I found a gun in the glove compartment. Trembling and not sure what to do, I decided to leave it there and ask him what it was all about. To my relief, he admitted that he was merely transferring it, as a favor, from a friend who had sold it to another friend.

I kept his strange behavior a secret because I believed we could settle our problems between us. In my mind, it was our business and just a phase he was going through. He had rarely picked up a drink in the days before we were married and had no history of drinking. He would get past it, I told myself, and we could look back on it and maybe even laugh about it someday.

LEARNING THE TRUTH

CCORDING TO THE UNWRITTEN custom in 1950 for young, working mothers-to-be, I left my job toward the end of my fifth month, before I began "showing" and could maintain my modesty. As our babies grew, we wore smocks and maternity dresses, not because we were ashamed but had been taught not to flaunt our "condition" and because they were more comfortable than tight clothes.

On an evening burned into my memory, a few weeks later, Don stood in front of me in the kitchen of our three-room apartment and told me his heartbreaking secret. "I love someone else and I want a divorce as soon as the baby's born." I didn't scream or pass out or hit him or anything and I still don't know why. It could have been because I didn't want to believe it. If I believed it, it would have to be true. Even though he wasn't the man of my dreams, he was my husband and the father of the child I was carrying. We had been married in front of one hundred people in a church and I had worn a white gown. He couldn't be telling me he loved someone else.

He added, "If you don't agree to give me a divorce, I'll leave and you'll never see me again or any money and I'll smash all the furniture in the house before I leave." I've never figured out why he added that unless he thought I'd fight to hold onto a marriage that had turned dismal during its short time.

No words came to me. What do you say to a confession that leaves you numb? I had no experience with yelling and screaming or calling other people profane names. I said nothing and moved away and sat down. "He'll change when he sees his child," I insisted to myself – the child that regularly kicked with life, sending a surge of love through me each time I felt the kick. He had never been curious about that or wanted to talk about the coming birth. He hadn't asked any questions or seemed at all interested in our child. It had to be a bad dream and I would wake up one day and breathe a sigh of relief.

I moved like a robot through the three and a half months remaining, not telling anyone, holding it inside me. I didn't dare speak it aloud for fear I'd go to pieces. I also felt I had to somehow solve it and make the marriage work but I had no idea where to start. I lay in bed each morning after he left for work, unable to face the day, feeling paralyzed, lost in an unreal world, unable to move forward or backward, until one special morning I tried something new.

Feeling awkward and embarrassed but with nowhere else to turn, I began praying, asking for help to get through that day. A tiny mustard seed had been planted, a seed that would falter at times and flourish at others, sometimes growing haltingly, sometimes in quick spurts, but would never shrivel up and die in later years. Faith had been sown, a faith that carried me through to the end of the nine months and well beyond that.

Things began to happen that had not happened in the past – or maybe they had and I had written them off as coincidences. For instance, I had a deep craving for a tomato but not just any tomato. I could buy those in the grocery store. It had to be fresh from a garden, warmed by the sun, just the way the tomatoes in my father's garden had been. I had no place to grow any which made no sense because I would have had to start in the spring, anyway. I decided to walk to our nearest store one day and get some tomatoes in the hope they would satisfy my craving. On the way, I passed the back yard of a woman I called "The Italian Lady," because she spoke very little English but always greeted me on the bus, patting her stomach and smiling, I'd hold up as many fingers as months that I had been pregnant.

Coming back from the store, I saw her beckoning to me. When I came near, she thrust out her hand to give me something – a huge, round, firm tomato, fresh from her garden and still warm from the sun.

I thanked her several times, wishing I could put together the words to tell her what it meant to me. I took it home, set it on a plate and cut it the way you'd cut a cake. Someone cared about me.

Don's mother, who had come back from California, was with us temporarily when the labor pains began early on the morning of August 29, 1950. She called Don who came home and took me to the hospital. At 5:30 that evening, I gave birth to a 6 lb. 2 oz. beautiful little girl. The nurse laid her on my stomach to cut the umbilical cord and I fell in love for the first time in my life, even though I had yet to see her. She was real, she was lying on my stomach, she was healthy and she was mine. The nurse cleaned her and allowed me to hold her for a second. I looked at that perfect little face and a powerful surge of emotion, protection and pure love flowed through me. I felt at that moment that I would gladly kill anyone who hurt her.

Alone in the delivery room, I relaxed and whispered, "Thank you." My baby and I had come through it. The soft hum of activity outside the room lulled me rather than disturbed me. I wanted to lie forever on that hard surface, softened by a peace I had never known in my life. Still drifting between a dream and reality, I wondered, "Is this the way real love feels?"

Apparently, Don had been sitting in the waiting room. He came in and awkwardly tried to be kind and to sound concerned. He may have felt as relieved as I did, but he couldn't possibly know the depth of the love I had just experienced.

New mothers stayed for eight days in the 50's. My friends and relatives visited, bringing gifts for my new daughter. Don came in again, bringing Ruthie and our friend, Dot, who gave me a sweater for my daughter. Once more during my stay, Don showed up and asked when I'd be going home. I told him and his only comment was, "Well, make it snappy. I have a clambake in the afternoon."

Ruthie came to the apartment to help and asked about Don. "He's at a clambake," I said, flatly, without emotion. She loved me and knew something was wrong but also knew I'd tell her about it when I was ready. By that time, I had come out of my torpor. A human being needed me, a tiny piece of humanity who depended on me and who would always be attached to me in some form.

I concentrated on caring for my newborn for six weeks, not ready to move out, living in the little world I had created for the two of us until the day Don reminded me of my promise. I made the arrangements for the mover to come the following Saturday to pick up my cedar chest, my clothes, other miscellaneous articles and, at Don's suggestion, the new refrigerator we had bought and the television set. Most likely, he was attempting to salve his conscience a little. On the Thursday prior to the move, I called my mother and father. My father exploded. "I'm coming right over to get you." In my emotionally fragile condition, I couldn't handle the upset so I talked him out of it. Also, I wanted to be sure I moved my personal possessions out before I left. In later years, I wished I had let him come and express himself so that he and I could feel we had fought back somehow and it would have allowed him to show he loved me.

MY GIFT

O N A GOLDEN DAY in October in 1950, standing at the window of my old bedroom, I stared at the green grass and the trees with their gorgeous, multi-colored leaves and wondered why they looked so beautiful when they should have been black. The sun was shining when it should have been overcast. Coming out of my make-believe world had plunged me into deep grief for the loss of our marriage. I didn't grieve for Don but for the collapse of the life I had expected to live with him.

Fortunately, my tiny daughter, Darcy*, kept my mind and my heart busy. A relative, trying to be understanding, commented that it was a shame I'd had a child since the marriage had failed. I assured her my daughter, my gift, made it worthwhile.

Working my way through the shock of the loss, I felt an urge to find an answer. "I'll go to church," I decided. As though guided by someone, I put Darcy in her carriage and walked to Christ Church where I had been married just a year and two months earlier, the church where Darcy had been baptized and I had taught Sunday School and listened to the hymns, prayers and sermons.

Churches, in those years, remained unlocked during the week. At the front door where I stood on my wedding day and felt the warning hint of unhappiness to come, I pulled her carriage up the steps, wheeled it inside and set it beside a pew.. This time I didn't feel awkward as I knelt on the prayer stool and prayed, "Dear God, I don't know what

---

* Her full name is Dorothy Louise but my oldest niece, Jan, as a small child, pronounced it "Dotsy" which became "Darcy" and it stuck.

to do now. Please help me." The tiny mustard seed was expanding and growing.

In the comfort of the healing silence, I glanced at the choir stalls where I had sung so lustily and innocently, happy in my trust of life. Sunlight made plain the figures in the stained glass windows. I felt again the peace that had enveloped me in the delivery room and didn't look around wildly when I heard the words, "It will be all right" because they didn't come to me in the same manner as though someone had spoken them. Holding my body very still, I listened and heard them again, clearly sounding in my mind. "It will be all right." When they repeated a third time, a cloud filled the chancel area. I froze, my gaze fixed on it, but not through fear. I didn't want to destroy the atmosphere of love it brought. In a few seconds, it lifted and the chancel area cleared. I sat still and tried to stare in the same way in order to bring it back but the moment had passed. I remained in the pew, awed by the experience, feeling more serene than I had for months, knowing instinctively that I wouldn't have to travel alone on the journey ahead of me.

The walk home gave me a chance to take it all in – the message and the cloud in the chancel. Again, I didn't tell anybody but kept it inside me, to relive and to make me feel safe. It was mine. It had been given to me at the very moment I needed it.

After the church message, I poured my attention into taking care of and bringing up Darcy. It hit me one day that I would have to learn to drive, something I had ached to do for a long time. Don tried to teach me before we were married, but I couldn't overcome my nervousness. One day I backed up, putting a dent in the bumper of his Pontiac convertible and that was the end of the lessons. He took it surprisingly well but I didn't want to chance any more lessons.

The most sensible thing to do was call a driving school. The instructor I talked with told me to meet him in Pawtucket in front of the Memorial Hospital where Darcy had been born. I left her in my mother's care and took a bus to within walking distance of that spot and found him sitting in the passenger seat which forced me to sit behind the wheel. After introducing himself, he asked whether I had ever driven and I told him of my meager experience to which he said, "Take me to Providence. I need to check in at the office." I looked at him, stunned and uncomprehending. .

"Don't worry," he assured me, pointing to the dual controls. I let out the clutch on the manual transmission and we moved away from the curb. Nine lessons later, I was ready to apply for my license and he accompanied me to the building next to the State House where an employee of the Department of Motor Vehicles tested me on a drive around the State House. The instructor cheered when he saw my newly-acquired license.

With the help of Tom and my father, I became the owner of a 1941 Plymouth Club Coupe being sold by a man in Pawtucket for $250. Its only fault, a rusty radiator, meant it had to be drained whenever it was left overnight, but only during the winter months. By the time cold weather arrived, I'd had the radiator flushed out so I could put in anti-freeze for the winter months. I began to feel that I wasn't a complete failure and could move on with my life.

Don's drinking diminished after we separated, telling me that I had been right about it being a temporary condition. As to his new love, I hadn't asked for her name, not wanting to know because that would make her real, but it didn't take long to figure out that it was my "friend," Dot, who was sharing his bed and had left her husband, Dick, for him. They had no children. Good Will gladly accepted the sweater set she had so brazenly given to me in the hospital. At a later date, I met Dick in Pawtucket. He asked how I was doing and was glad to hear all was well with me. "It wasn't Don's fault," he said, surprising me. "She went after him." I haven't seen him since and have hoped many times that he eventually found happiness.

My happiness lay in the precious gift I had been given. From the time she was born in 1950 until early 1952, I was with her fulltime and could shower her with love and proudly show her off. Rhode Island offered maternity benefits which meant, as a mother, I would receive an allotment which, along with my unemployment benefits, allowed me to stay at home. Also, in the divorce settlement, Don was required to pay alimony until I found employment. He also paid support and we divided up our savings account to give me some security.

While we lived with my mother and father, Barbara came back into my life. In southern California, she had met Bill, the love of her life. They married in October of 1949, two months after Don and I married.. As we had done when we were growing up together, we continued to do things almost simultaneously. Barbara and Bill had their first child, Suzan, on November 4, 1950, slightly over two months after Darcy's birth.

She wanted to see and live in New England again which made me happy. They rented an apartment and Bill landed a job in Pawtucket so I was able to visit them from time to time, using my new license and driving my car. California called them, though, and they moved back while our babies where still toddlers, settling eventually in Downey in their own home.

Darcy learned to walk during our stay with my parents, delighting all of us with her first steps. It took me awhile to realize my good luck in having a family who stood behind me and supported me while I made my way through that period. I was also fortunate in not having to immediately seek employment, giving me time to be with my precious gift.

THE COMMONWEALTH
OF MASSACHUSETTS

*T*OM, MY BROTHER-IN-LAW, MET *Pete from Mansfield, Massachusetts, in 1950 in a bait shop when they were both entering the annual Striped Bass Tournament in Narragansett, Rhode Island. That meeting led to a friendship, sealed by a mutual love of fishing. When the conversation turned to their jobs, Pete asked Tom, "Where do you work?"*

"In Haskell's Machine Shop in Pawtucket." "Do you like it?"

Tom shrugged, "It's a good place to work but I don't see myself moving up any time soon — too many people ahead of me. My uncle and cousins work there so I feel comfortable but..."

"Why not try The Foxboro Company?"

"Foxboro?" Tom looked puzzled. "All I know about Foxboro is there's a race track out on Route 1 — a trotter track — sulkys pulled by horses. I went there once with my brother, Don. I've never been to the center of town. What do they do at The Foxboro Company?"

"They make precision instruments. That's where I work. It's right next door to Mansfield."

Tom thought about it, talked it over with Ruthie and decided to invite Pete and his wife, Rita, to dinner to find out more about The Foxboro Company. That's the way Tom became an employee of The Foxboro Company and Darcy and I moved to Massachusetts.

* * * *

Early on the evening of October 31, 1951, my father, in the family car, waited patiently behind my Plymouth in the middle of Mansfield, with Darcy asleep in a car-bed in the back seat of my car and both of them stuffed with my clothes, Darcy's clothes and a few other things I felt I needed. My bedroom set and her crib had been brought up from Cumberland earlier in the week. Ruth and Tom had invited me and Darcy to live with them and I was starting a new life in a new state, with the hope of finding a job at The Foxboro Company. Pete and Rita had located an apartment in Mansfield big enough for all of us. Unfortunately, we arrived on Hallowe'en at the same time as the annual Horribles parade. I didn't care. I would be living in Massachusetts, not just crossing the invisible line at Robin Hollow.

As we waited, a pleasant memory slipped in, one that backed up the message, "It will be all right." Shortly after he was hired, Tom said to Ruthie, "I don't mind driving to Foxboro every day. Let's take our time moving so we don't grab the first place that comes along and regret it." The delay meant I'd be staying in Rhode Island with my parents for as long as it took, but I'd need a part-time job to augment the support and alimony I was receiving from Don. My maternity and unemployment benefits had run their course. The night I learned we wouldn't be moving as soon as I had expected, I opened the classified section of The Pawtucket Times. Directly in the center of the page, as though it had been placed there just for me, was an ad, "Do you need a part-time job?" I applied the next day and was hired by a Pawtucket industrial caterer known as Coffee An' to keep track of their inventory. I stayed until the first of October.

In Mansfield, the parade ended, I turned right on North Main Street with my father following and soon I shouted to no one in particular, "There it is." Several hours later, Darcy and I fell asleep for the first time in our new home.

I was glad I had a car. Except for the Boston train which stopped in Mansfield, no local transportation system existed, but even the idea of being able to drive and having a car amazed me. I had a new life. It all seemed magical.

I found a part-time job at Letty's, a dress shop across the street from the apartment. That gave me extra money. Pete and Rita made good neighbors, helping when we needed help. Rita took me to St. John's Episcopal Church. I enrolled Darcy in Sunday School and, as soon as possible, joined the choir. I drove around to learn about Foxboro and the surrounding area, feeling free for the first time in a long time.

With the income from the job at Letty's and the support payments and my desire to be with Darcy as long as possible, I put off looking for fulltime work until early in 1952 when the divorce would be final.. The alimony payments had stopped once I had a paying job. Rita and Ruth decided I should do something for myself before I went back to fulltime work. Louise and Johnny had left Rhode Island for his hometown of Oconto Falls, Wisconsin. "Go out and see them," Rita said. "I'll go with you to Boston to buy the ticket." Air fares were still reasonable and I had half the bank account money. Darcy, at a year and a half, didn't require a ticket.

In February of 1952, she and I boarded a plane at Logan Airport. It had four propellers and a stairway which was accessed from the tarmac. Carrying Darcy and a bag full of bottles, diapers and whatever else I needed, I climbed the stairway, unable to believe I was going on my first long-distance flight. At various fairs, I had flown in Piper Cubs but had never been on a long commercial flight. My excitement built as we taxied down the runway. Darcy slept for part of the four- hour trip from Boston to Chicago and didn't fuss. In Chicago I sent telegrams to my parents and Ruth and Tom while we waited to continue on.

At Milwaukee, we took a taxi to the train station where a challenge awaited us. I called Louise and Johnny to tell them, "The train is four hours late because there's a snowstorm." We sat in the waiting room and I chuckled at a memory. The driver of the taxi, wanting to amuse us, said he could guess where we all lived because of our accents. He told one man he was from the southwest but didn't name a state. He continued in that same vein with the other four fares until he came to me. "And you're from Rhode Island," he said. I still laugh when I think of it. The accent gave me away and still does and that makes me proud.

The ride to Oconto Falls, once we were actually on the train which was a local, took several more hours through the storm, making me nervous but not sorry that I had set out on the adventure.

Even in the cold weather and snow, I enjoyed Wisconsin, Louise and Johnny and their daughter, Donna, who had been born shortly after Darcy. They showed me what Johnny described as the "best trout stream in the country" and Darcy and Donna played well together. I met Johnny's relatives and friends and admired his home state. At the end of a wonderful two-weeks' visit, they helped me arrange a flight from Green Bay Airport to Milwaukee airport to avoid repeating the train ride.

Back in Massachusetts, I knew the time had come and applied for fulltime work at three different places - The Foxboro Company, S. W. Card Manufacturing Company which was a machine shop in Mansfield and The Mansfield Chocolate Factory whose aroma greeted you from a distance. The Foxboro Company called first, followed closely by Card's and The Chocolate Factory. I couldn't believe I had three offers for a job, but the choice was easy. On April 21, 1952, a year and eight months after Darcy's birth, I walked into The Foxboro Company building. "Thank you," I said to the unseen guide who had turned my steps in the right direction.

THE MERRY-GO-ROUND

ESIDES THE FACT THAT it would give me a steady income, the job offered a stability I desperately needed in the confusion of the fast- moving events in my life. In less than three years I had married Don, given birth to a daughter, become a divorced single parent, taken both of us on our first commercial plane ride and moved to another state. Added to that was the uncertainty of not knowing where I fit into a society whose stereotypical family in 1952 consisted of a mother who stayed at home to take care of the children and a father who earned the wages. Mine was made up of me and my daughter. I felt I had wandered onto the wrong path but as I drove into the parking lot of the Foxboro Company on the 21st day of April, 1952, I felt I knew what I was doing. The job had substance to it, a reality I could grasp.

All twelve brick buildings taking up both sides of Neponset Avenue belonged to The Foxboro Company but the office building, with its four floors to their three, stood out, especially in its place at the front of the complex. The company name etched into a granite block above the double doors of the main entrance reflected the 1890's style for manufacturing plants. Neponset Avenue, a short and tree- lined street between Chestnut and Mechanic Streets, was also home to several private residences and had a view of Neponset Reservoir at the Chestnut Street end. Freight trains occasionally rattled through on the track that ran behind the buildings. The whole effect could not have been more of a microcosm of small-town New England if it had been painted by Norman Rockwell.

Factory offices lay scattered throughout the buildings but the heart of the company beat in the main office building which held, at that time, Purchasing, Sales, Accounting, Engineering, Personnel, Payroll and the Mail Room as well as the Corporate offices. The two young women in the first-floor Purchasing Department where I had been assigned took turns training me. At noon we crossed Neponset Avenue to the company-owned cafeteria which was next door to the garage where the company-owned cars were repaired. They listened with interest when I talked about Darcy. "Don't you want to stay home with her?" one of them asked.

"I'd give anything to be home with her," I answered, holding back tears, "But I have to work." I explained the situation and they nodded in understanding. I enjoyed their company as we chatted and they told me about themselves but somehow, in the days that followed, I felt uncomfortable with the work and the office atmosphere.

A few weeks after I had begun my job I was sent on an errand to the third-floor office of the Manager of the Accounting Department where sunshine filled the area and I longed to stay. "I'd love to work here," I blurted. Flattered, the Manager smiled and said he might be able to arrange that. In a few days, I was reassigned to a group consisting of two women, Barbara and Mary, who posted the debits and credits on the customers' accounts, and Dave, the head of the department.

To orient me with my new surroundings, Dave pointed out, on the first day, three men occupying the offices at the front end of the third floor. "That's Ben, the President," he said, "That's Rex, the Treasurer and that's Corey, the Vice-President." Unwittingly, I had stumbled into the nerve center of The Foxboro Company.

It felt good and yet strange at the same time to be back in a routine – get up, get ready, have breakfast and get to work. Ruth and Tom's first child, Janet, had been born in April of 1949 while they were living in Pawtucket and Ruth was, at the time I began working, seven months pregnant with Marilyn. She planned to take care of Darcy and Jan during the day and I took over Darcy's care at night and on weekends.

Over the next few months, the social life of the third floor drew me in which raised a conflict. "How can I be having fun when I have to leave Darcy every day and let Ruthie take care of her?" As was my habit, I didn't talk to anyone about it but buried the guilt as far down as possible, rationalizing that I'd make it up to her some day when I remarried and could leave my job. I had no doubt I would only be working temporarily, even though I had no desire to date for almost a year after my divorce.

Control was taken out of my hands when I became friendly with another Barbara in Accounting who was my junior by six years. I knew nothing about the annual company Outing until she asked one day in October, "Are you going to the Company Outing? It's at The King Philip*, naming a ballroom in the next-door town of Wrentham. When I hesitated, she added, "Why don't we go together. Do you mind driving?" She explained she had lost her license. I politely didn't ask why and she didn't furnish details. The Outing was actually a dinner/dance given to the employees by The Foxboro Company. It included a full-course meal, prizes and an orchestra, all of which dazzled me.

Barbara loved both night life and liquor, neither of which, as I've mentioned, had a prominent place in our family. At the Outing she suggested we get drinks. I fell back on the one I had been introduced to at eighteen by my co-workers at The Fram Corporation who insisted we go to the Biltmore Hotel in Providence so they could buy me my first drink – a claret lemonade. I could count on one hand the number I'd had since that first one. "I'll have a claret lemonade," I told the bartender. I took a few sips and my life looked a lot better to me.

Gradually, Barbara's enthusiasm swept me along. Although it wasn't the life I had envisioned living, I joined in the social whirl of the office. A few of the women started a pot whose money could be used for buying tickets for stage shows in Boston. I put in my contribution and six or seven of us drove in for dinner and a show. In that way, over a space of months, I was able to see Oklahoma, South Pacific, Stalag 17 and Guys and Dolls, to name a few, and I was also accompanying Barbara to cocktail lounges.

---

* See the History section at the back of the book.

I always made sure Darcy was tucked into bed before I left. One half of me wanted to be Darcy's mother while another half felt a heady excitement at having a social life different from any I had ever known. With boundless energy, I was tasting and testing and wondering when my real life would begin – the life at home with a father for Darcy. Meanwhile, the office group decided to go to New York for New Year's Eve and be in Times Square when the ball came down to announce 1953. Slowly, each one dropped out but Barbara and I decided to go by ourselves, with me driving my old Plymouth. My mother was always glad to have Darcy for a few days. I don't remember all of the details of that weekend, except driving along the old Merritt Parkway before I-95 had been built. Somehow we made it there and back and saw the ball drop in Times Square, an exhilarating experience but not one I was anxious to repeat.

I stayed on the merry-go-round, convincing myself I was having the time of my life, aware that it had been a very short time since my first day at the Foxboro Company. It isn't hard to understand the reason. I was a prime candidate for a new life. All through 1953, I danced and drank, graduating to new drinks. I liked their effect, especially daiquiris and vodka collins. Drinking, as it has for millions of others, allowed me to overcome my shyness and inhibitions but I wasn't meeting any men I wanted to date. On the other hand, it seemed the antidote to the past few years. I told myself I deserved it and that I wasn't neglecting Darcy, which was true, but it caught up with me on New Year's Eve. I spent it at a ski lodge in New Hampshire with three other women. I missed Darcy dreadfully that weekend and vowed I would never leave her again. To show her I cared and to overcome my guilt, I bought her a little wooden Noah's Ark set in the gift shop.

The excitement had worn thin. I longed for my own place, a home for me and Darcy and I wasn't enjoying the drinking any more but I hesitated to tell Barbara. I thought she'd be hurt that I no longer wanted to live her life.

I told her of my decision to change my lifestyle and get off the merry-go-round. It took her all of two minutes to say, "Okay," and start looking for another patsy to drive her around. By then I knew that she lost her license because she had driven under the influence too many times. I was hurt briefly but glad to be away from her and away from that life.

It had not been a completely negative experience, though. In the eddying of crazy times and false friends that followed the divorce, I learned what was most important to me and that was my life with Darcy.

SQUARE ONE

FROM MY CHILDHOOD HOME I moved to one I shared with Don only to bounce back home again and now my daughter and I lived in Ruth and Tom's apartment. I believed that being a mother meant making a home for me and my child.

The first unit we looked at, with Don's mother joining in the search, didn't turn out to be a good fit, but I was far from discouraged. My friends suggested I try nearby towns. "No," I told them emphatically. "It has to be Foxboro." Though I didn't realize it, I was obeying a guiding voice. My future lay in Foxboro. I felt that instinctively.

A few days later, I heard of an apartment on Rockhill Street, near the center of town. I visited by myself. "I love it," I told Ruthie as soon as I could call her. "It's three rooms and it's on the first floor. It has a tiny kitchen, a combination living-dining room, one bedroom and even a porch which opens onto the back yard. The best part is the owners both work for The Foxboro Company. Oh," I added remembering something else, "They have a four-year-old son so Darcy will have a playmate."

My excitement grew as I told my parents about it. "I can get my pans and dishes out of your attic and whatever else I have up there," I burbled in my happiness. "Also, the rent is only $50 a month."

Darcy and I moved into our new home in April of 1954. Tom and Johnny helped move the bigger furniture and my father and I brought up my cartons from their attic. Alone in my apartment that evening, I looked around and knew my life was moving in the right direction.

After a few weeks of taking Darcy to Ruthie's every morning before I went to work, picking her up at night, making our meals and keeping the apartment clean I also knew it wouldn't be easy but it would be worth it. I settled into what I expected to be my routine for the next few years, not missing my former life at all.

As it turned out, somebody else had other plans. Two months after my move, on Saturday, June 26th, my sister called. Struggling to talk between sobs she gave me the news, "Daddy just died. I'm going down right now." I told her I'd be there as soon as possible. My landlady, on hearing the news, offered to take Darcy and keep her overnight.

We heard the whole story from my mother. "I made our lunch and took it out so we could eat outside. Your father had just finished mowing the lawn but hadn't put the lawn mower back in the garage. He said he felt a little sick so I told him to go inside and I'd be right there. I put the lawn mower away and took the sandwiches back into the house." She had difficulty finishing the story. "When I came inside, he was sitting in his favorite chair. His face was as red as a beet and he was having trouble breathing. I ran outside and yelled to our neighbor, Pete, and he came running but it was too late. Pete called a doctor but by the time the doctor came, he was gone." The doctor gave it a name – coronary occlusion, better known as a blood clot.

My father died four months short of his seventieth birthday, still working at his mechanic's job, trying to hang on for three more years until my mother became sixty-five and could collect her full Social Security. We had just begun to understand each other. His loss seemed ill-timed. I felt cheated as I stood with my mother and sister during the visitation at the funeral home and the funeral itself.

Through all of it, I gave no thought to the future but my sister put it into perspective once we had returned to Foxboro and tried to pick up our lives. "It might be a good idea for you and mother to live together." I recoiled inside. I was Darcy's mother. I didn't want to go back to being *someone's daughter* and sharing a house again. I loved my little place and Foxboro.

"No," I cried silently, heartbroken at the thought, but promised aloud to think about it.

Financially, it made sense to combine our small incomes. To have any income at all, my mother would have to apply for Social Security payments, probably my father's, which would give her a small income for the rest of her life. If she stayed in the house, she would need financial help from both of us and other help as well with the structural upkeep of it. Also, I had to consider what was best for Darcy. As much as I fought against the reality of the facts, one stood out. She wouldn't have to leave home every morning, except to go to school. I cried and sighed but made the decision, apologized to my landlady and moved back to Cumberland, my grief for my father compounded by the loss of my dream.

"I'm back at Square One," I thought, sadly, ignoring the fact that a crib sat in the corner of my old bedroom and that Square One no longer existed As I commuted to Foxboro every day after that, my role slowly became apparent to me. "I'm the wage-earner," I told myself in amazement. I didn't consider myself a pioneer but wasn't sure once again where I fit into society. At the time, divorced parents were thought of in negative terms. Many of our society's ills were blamed on *juvenile delinquents,* children of divorce who came from *broken homes* The catchword, *single parent,* had not yet been coined. I did the *man's work* around the house. Somehow, that thought gave me an odd feeling of pride. Whether I liked it or not, I was taking care of my family.

MY OWN RULES

THOUGH I HAD INWARDLY rebelled against it and even cried in my frustration, combining my household with my mother's worked out well for both of us and certainly made it easier for me as far as Darcy was concerned. Also, having her in the house may have helped my mother through her grieving process. She didn't have to adjust to living alone after forty-two years of marriage. Of course she missed my father, as we all did, but seemed to accept it more readily than I had expected. It's possible she did a lot of grieving in private but her English "stiff upper lip" attitude didn't allow her to speak of it. She had never been the helpless, dependent type who was lost without someone to take care of her. She readily pitched into the physical work, especially when a job became too big for me.

Though I realized it was the best arrangement for both of us, I had difficulty feeling happy about it and hated the idea of leaving my little apartment and relocating which may have pushed me into the uncharacteristic adventure that followed. It's possible, too, that I had another lesson to learn.

One night a friend asked me to substitute for her on the Foxboro Company bowling team. I explained to my mother about having to drive back to Foxboro and she didn't seem to mind. "I'm not a particularly good bowler," I warned the team captain but that night, for whatever reason, I couldn't seem to miss and the captain wanted me on his team. "It was a fluke," I kept insisting but he didn't believe me and talked me into joining. Deep in my heart I may have wanted to join because it meant I'd be spending more time in Foxboro.

I don't remember that I ever repeated my initial performance once I was actually on the team. That led to a lot of teasing from one of the men and we laughed together about it. A short time after I joined, he suggested coffee one night but I declined. I wanted to get home, for one thing, but the other reason was more important – he was married and spending time with him was against the rules in my opinion.

On the way home, though, a thought insinuated itself into my reluctance. "You've followed the rules. You've been a dutiful daughter and mother. You've done what was asked of you and where did it get you? Maybe it's time to make up your own rules." I put the thought aside but it continued to taunt me.

He persisted until the night I said, "Yes," ashamed and yet a little excited about this new adventure. What would it be like? I had never strayed outside society's rules. I called my mother to say the gang was going out for coffee.

We had music in common. He was a musician, ten or fifteen years older than I was, quiet and intelligent, with a deep voice and rugged good looks. I didn't fall madly in love with him but felt happy in his presence, though guilt always lay at the bottom of my happiness.

At first it seemed romantic and I felt that I was somehow getting even with Don but the glow slowly dimmed and I started to question my motives. It didn't make me deliriously joyful and its shabbiness nipped at me.

At Christmas, in the bowling alley, he mentioned the gifts that his two children wanted that year. The thought of Christmas and his family together brought me out of my dream and I stood face-to- face with the reality of the situation. I was an intruder in someone's marriage and I didn't belong there.

Being with him had satisfied my need to do something outside the moral code I had learned at home and from society, but I suddenly wanted to get as far away from him as I could. "It isn't for me. I can't live this way any longer. I deserve better. He's somebody else's husband. She deserves better than that," I told myself, setting in cement a moral code that I had personally tested and could call my own. From that day on, any man I met would have to be free and clear of marital ties, not just unhappy in his marriage or separated from his wife, but totally available and untethered. I couldn't be happy in a love that was built on someone else's heartbreak.

I didn't miss him or fall into a depression but accepted the guilt that came with my actions, completely aware of what I had done and enormously thankful to be able to step away from it, especially when I learned something else about him. Through a friend who knew nothing of our relationship, I heard that he had cheated in his marriage several times. I was just one of several others. It didn't erase my guilt or make me feel any cleaner but at least I hadn't been the only fool.

Having that behind me opened my eyes to my surroundings. At my old home, some things hadn't changed. Two propane tanks still furnished gas for the stove in the kitchen. We depended on a big black range in the middle room for our central heating. An electric pump brought water in from the well dug by my grandfather and uncles and it ran cold out of the faucets since we had no hot water heater. The stone path leading to the outhouse remained in place even though the structure had been dismantled after being blown off its foundation by the 1938 hurricane.

On the other hand, some things had changed. My mother, without realizing it, showed that to me the day she introduced me to a neighbor. "This is Pete. He's the one who came to help me the day your father died." Pete and his family lived in one of the four houses built in the field next to our house – the field where my friends and I had played baseball. Buried somewhere beneath the foundations lay the shortcut path I used each day as I returned from school.

On the other side of the yard, beyond the privet hedge that separated it from my grandfather's orchard, another house stood, occupying the section of the orchard sold by my mother and father. The tree my grandfather had given to me and Barbara still stood, devoid of its tree-house and looking rather forlorn. In front of the house, Lilac Street had finally been paved and, as an official town street, was plowed every winter.

A strong reminder that Square One had blended into the past came in November when the cooling temperature warned me to do the yearly ritual known in New England as *putting up the storm windows*. That meant individually lugging each heavy wooden-framed window from the shed near the garage and climbing a ladder to hook it onto the hardware fastened to the frame on the house for that purpose. Aluminum combination windows, permanently attached to the house, were in their early stage of acceptance in 1954, but that made no difference because we couldn't afford them, anyway.

"I guess I'm the man of the house," I mumbled as I hung the first storm window and managed not to fall backwards. "Thank you, daddy," I added, grateful that he had allowed me to tag along when he did repairs, even when it meant crab-walking across the roof. Society, not my parents, had come up with the labels, *men's work* and *women's work*. My mother and father never felt that my sister and I couldn't do certain chores because we were girls.

Maybe that's where I came up with the idea for establishing my own moral code. I know they would never have approved of my method of doing it but would have agreed with the conclusion I reached.

MOVING ON

USING CHRISTMAS AS AN excuse, I told the team captain it had made me realize I wanted to have more time with my daughter. I offered the lame promise that if I ever moved back to Foxboro, I'd think of rejoining the team. He understood and said they'd be able to find someone to fill my spot. Possibly it gave him a good excuse to bring in a better bowler. Either way, it would relieve me and my friend the awkwardness of seeing each other at the bowling alley. I had already told him of my decision. He wasn't happy but knew he couldn't do anything about it.

In truth, I didn't mind the twenty-mile commute and played a little game with myself each morning. At the juncture of Lilac and High Streets, I had a choice. Turning left meant, when High Street became Diamond Hill Road, following it to Wrentham Road which would take me, after I passed through the town of Wrentham, right into Foxboro. Lovely scenery with gentle hills and tree-bordered lakes and ponds, as well as sparse traffic made it a pleasant drive. I enjoyed it, especially when I passed the entrance to the old ski run at Diamond Hill State Park where Ruthie and I had spent some happy winter afternoons.

The other option – a right turn on High Street - led me eventually to Route 1, the commercial four-lane highway that stretched from Florida to Maine and had not yet been replaced by Interstate 95. I picked up Route 106 in Plainville which led me to Foxboro but meant descending a hill between two lakes, climbing back up again once I was past the lakes and continuing on to South Street in Foxboro.

The whole trip, though not as scenic, was possibly a little easier, except for the snowy winter day when Route 106, though plowed, still had a layer of snow on it. Knowing the slope was ahead of me, I touched the brakes, sending the car fishtailing toward a telephone pole and forcing me to desperately work on pulling out of the skid. The car and I stopped about two inches short of the pole. "Whew! Thank you," I gasped to whatever guardian angel was watching over me and sat still for a few moments, thinking about what might have happened. In that brief time, I matured a tiny bit. "Thank you," I repeated. "My mother and daughter depend on me." It was as though I had received a message.

Okay. I've allowed you to indulge yourself. Now it's time to take on your responsibilities. I squared my shoulders and drove on to Foxboro, more confident that I could handle whatever lay ahead and certain I would never tell my mother about the skid.

No handy magazine articles existed in 1954 to give me helpful hints as to what the responsibilities of a single parent might include. I would have to face them as they came along. That was especially true the night I arrived home from work and my mother told me, "One of the propane tanks ran out. We have to replace it." She had more good news. "The cesspool is full. We'll have to have it emptied." I asked how much each would cost. "Well," she said," We paid $12 the last time we had a tank replaced and the cesspool was $20 but that was quite a while ago."

I barely slept that night, wondering where I could fit the unexpected $32 into my budget. My pay plus the support payment from Don had to cover food, gasoline, heating costs and whatever Darcy might need. Anything extra threw off my careful planning. I brooded all day on the $32. "I'll have to ask each of them to take half and give them half next month," I thought. I didn't have a credit card as they weren't used as liberally as they would be in later years. That night, at home, I stepped through the door, took a deep breath and asked, "Did we get the propane tank and is the cesspool empty?"

My mother smiled. "The propane tank was only $6 because we've used a certain number of them this year and the cesspool wasn't as full as I thought and it was only $10."

It was just the beginning of a lesson that would take me a long time to learn. *It will be all right.* That was the promise. In the years ahead, similar precipice moments came along and I allowed myself to worry instead of trusting that a solution would present itself..

One of my concerns centered on moving back to Foxboro before Darcy was ready for school, not because I didn't trust the Cumberland schools but I didn't want to subject her to a change of schools if it wasn't necessary. I needn't have fretted.

In the summer of 1955, a year after my move to Cumberland, when the skidding on Route 106 had become a memory, my mother said, with no prompting from me, "Let's move to Foxboro. It's time. I'm ready and I don't want you to go through another winter driving all that way."

Joyfully, I agreed and agreed again when she suggested checking to see what was available in Foxboro first before jumping into the selling process. We talked with a real estate agent who showed us a house being built off Mechanic Street. I liked the location and it would be new. The price of $10,000 seemed doable since we'd have the down payment from our house. We didn't promise anything as we hadn't yet advertised our house which we did the next day.

Our ad in the Pawtucket Times caught the attention of a real estate agent. He called to say, "I have someone for your house. He has the money and is ready to buy whenever you're ready to sell." We had trouble believing our good fortune and made arrangements for him to visit and see our house. His name slips my mind but since I didn't like him from the moment we met, I'll leave it that way.

The contract he brought only needed my mother's signature. Though I wasn't comfortable with the agent, the offer seemed a good one. He set the contract on the dining room table. My mother sat down and picked up the pen, but set it down again. 'I can't do it," she said, looking at me and obviously close to tears. Forty-three years of calling Cumberland her home lay behind the simple act of signing her name. "You and your sister were born in that bedroom," she said, pointing to it. "I didn't want to move into this house when grandma left it to us but it's my home now." I didn't press her but let her sit quietly, wandering back over bittersweet memories. "Your father died in this room." She had seen her children leave it to marry and become mothers themselves. It held other memories, I'm sure, that only she could remember. After heaving a deep sigh, picked up the pen.

As soon as she had signed, the agent, or whatever he was, began a spiel to convince us to lower the price which was already ridiculously low. We had not started high, asking only $5,000 because we knew the limitations of the property. For one thing, it had no cellar. Before placing the ad, my mother had advanced herself enough money from her small bank account to have city water piped in which allowed us to install a hot water heater in the kitchen. That soothed our fears about leakage into our well from our neighbors' cell-pools. A contractor removed the pump and tank from the bathroom, allowing us to install a new tub, washstand and toilet. We considered $5,000 a reasonable price.

"This guy has a wife and child to support and doesn't make much money," the agent added. "He could pay cash if you're willing to cut $2,000 off the price."

"I have a mother and child to support," I told him, angrily, "And I don't make much money."

He couldn't grasp the comparison. Women, in society's belief, occupied a separate category from men, the accepted heads of most households, and didn't require as much income. His mind could only hold the image of men working and he had obviously promised his client he'd get "these woman" to lower the price.

My mother and I both shook our heads. He stood up, thanked us and said, "Well, think it over and I'll call again in a few days."

We weren't sure what steps we needed to take since my mother had signed the agreement, but we knew somehow we would not sell the house for $3,000. Help arrived, as it usually does, in a totally unexpected way.

The day after his visit, when I walked in the door from work, my mother blurted out, "Rose and her husband want to buy the house and they'll give us our price." Rose, the daughter of a neighbor, and her husband shared a very small house with her widowed father. Ours would be perfect and she would be near her father.

We put in a call to the agent to say we wanted to discuss something with him. He gave us directions to his house in Pawtucket where we sat down with him and explained, "We have a buyer for our house who'll give us the full price so we'd like to cancel our agreement. We're willing to give you a portion of the fee."

As expected, he wasn't happy. "You signed the contract," he reminded my mother.

"You tried to get us to lower the price," she shot back but he was adamant and I asked him whether he was working for us or for his client. I almost accused him of being dishonest in his dealings with us and at that point, his wife ordered us out of the house.

In the car, we decided to talk with a lawyer and stopped at the office of a local Cumberland attorney whose family we knew well. "Where did you find this guy?" he asked., when he heard the story, promising us, "I'll take care of it." We didn't ask later what he said to the agent but the contract was torn up and we sold the house to Rose. We were free to buy one in Foxboro.

BRIDGES TO CROSS

IN AN ODD QUIRK of fate, the person who led us to the house we eventually bought was my old "friend" Barbara. "It's diagonally across the street from our house," she told me. "The woman who owns it is a widow. She's asking $9,000." During the hassle with the real estate agent we had been forced to walk away from the new $10,000 ranch house but had toured several others after Rose bought our house. We drove to Foxboro, viewed the widow's house and snapped it up with a down payment of $3,000, leaving my mother with $2,000 that made her feel more secure..

The next step, once our loan of $6,000 had been approved, was to sign papers in Boston. With all the signatures in place, the loan officer commented to me, "If you hadn't had $3,000 to put down we wouldn't have given you the loan."

"Why?" I asked, completely befuddled. I had a steady income which would easily cover the mortgage payment of $42 a month.

"Because you're a woman," he said, seeming surprised that I hadn't guessed the reason. Women weren't considered good risks in the 50's because women had the *bad* habit of becoming pregnant and leaving jobs. The relatively few single working mothers weren't apt to do that but women were all lumped into the same class. I added it to my list of *things I'm learning about being a single, working mother.*

In Cumberland, we waded into the arduous task of sorting through what we'd take, what we'd throw away and what we'd give away. A neighbor helped us by tending a large bonfire in our dirt driveway. Outdoor fires had not yet been banned. That took care of some of the unusable items. We sorted though my father's tools, keeping those that had sentimental value and those I knew I could use, spread the rest on a tarp in the driveway and asked a tool company representative to look them over. We accepted the price he gave us for all of them.

In the attic, among other relics, we unearthed my grandmother's old picture frames and the bells that jingled on old Bill on winter sleigh rides around the area. Some decisions proved to be difficult, such as which furniture to take and which to give away, making it a long and exhausting process, but on a day in August of 1955 we felt we were ready to move.

The loan officer in Boston apologized as he explained it would take time for the paperwork to travel through all the channels, prompting my mother to suggest we take a week off. "Neither of us has had a vacation in a long time so let's do it." I had used a few of my vacation days but not all of them.

She made plans to stay for a week at the Allen "A" Resort in New Hampshire with Lizzie, the same relative who had accompanied us to Jack and Betty's wedding. Darcy and I rented a very inexpensive room in a weathered-shingled cottage near the beach in Hyannis on Cape Cod for a week.

"What will we do about Trixie?" my mother asked. Trixie, my dog, had to be left with my parents when I married Don and had become known as "the family dog". We decided to lodge her in a kennel in Pawtucket and off we went.

As Darcy and I drove over Cape Cod Canal on Sagamore Bridge, it occurred to me that my mother and I had crossed a bridge into a future that neither of us had foreseen or expected.

Darcy, not quite five at the time, loved being near the water, splashing and playing in it or searching for tiny crabs or anything else she could find in a stream that trickled down from somewhere to empty into the bay. One day, as we were walking to the beach, she cried out, "Look at the boats, mommy," gazing at all the sailboats moored at a marina. We moved closer and one of the owners noticed us and gave us a short tour of his boat, which pleased her immensely. On another day, we drove to Provincetown where we had lunch, meandered along the narrow streets and I took a picture of her standing at the foot of the Pilgrim Monument.

My mother's suggestion hadn't cost much and gave us a welcome rest. One slight dark cloud was the forecast of Hurricane Carol blowing its way up the coast on the day before we planned to leave for home. Fortunately, it did little damage on the Cape and I cheered when we felt we had escaped it. What we didn't escape was a problem with the brakes which began shortly before we reached Sagamore Bridge. I panicked and stopped at the first gas station in sight.

"I can't help you," the attendant told me, "but there's a garage on the other side of the canal."

"You mean I'll have to cross Sagamore Bridge without brakes?" I couldn't believe him.

Two bridges, Bourne and Sagamore, which carries the Route 6 traffic over the canal, connect Cape Cod to the mainland. Both are four-lane arch bridges with suspended decks and Sagamore has a ship clearance of one hundred thirty-five feet. That means it isn't completely flat but rises in the middle and descends toward the mainland, an incline I would have to negotiate without brakes.

I had no choice. After grimly climbing up one side, I set my old, standard-transmission car in second gear and kept a slight hold on the handle of the emergency brake all the way down the other side. At the bottom of the slope, we left the bridge and careened around the old rotary* which was still in place at that time. Luckily, we had decreased our speed when I saw the garage ahead. We rolled into the driveway and I yanked up my emergency brake. A quick look assured the mechanic that nothing serious affected my brakes and he announced,

"You've lost all the brake fluid." I breathed a sigh of relief. That was easy to fix.

---

* A rotary is also called a *roundabout* and is used where several streets meet or cross. Traffic is routed in a circle, allowing motorists to join or leave the circle without having to stop.

He put in the fluid and we started off, making it back to Cumberland without any mishaps except for a short drive through an overflowing brook on Route 140 in Taunton, a gift from the hurricane. Most of the damage was water-related since the hurricane had produced a sizeable rainfall.

At home, I dropped off our suitcases before starting out again to pick up Trixie. Our path lay along old Route 1 on Broadway and to the Division Street bridge across the Seekonk River in Pawtucket.

That's where we learned that Carol had produced a sizeable rainfall, dropping twenty inches of rain over a two-day period. The Blackstone River which rises in Worcester, Massachusetts, and flows through northeastern Rhode Island, was running at twelve feet above the flood stage of 9.0 feet. Dams broke in Woonsocket, Rhode Island, causing extensive damage. By the time the Blackstone reached Pawtucket Falls where it becomes the Seekonk River, it had mutated into a rushing, angry force, endangering the old Division Street bridge. Traffic being monitored to avoid a tie-up on the bridge in case it didn't hold was in turn causing gridlock on Broadway.

Unable to move ahead, I shut off the engine and turned to Darcy, "Would you like to see the river?" It flowed through a shallow valley so I knew we'd be safe when we walked the short distance to where we could look down over a fence at its viciousness. Darcy, enthralled at the sight of the brown, writhing water carrying debris and smashing against the banks, like a living thing in its rush to the bay, remembered it in later years, asking from time to time, "Can we go see the river again, mommy?"

At long last, we were allowed to cross the bridge and I turned left toward the kennels. Soon, we picked up a happy, tail-wagging Trixie and headed home, wisely using a different route. My mother came in the same day, with lots of stories and undeveloped snapshots and as happy as Trixie to be home.

Rose called soon after that to tell us the mortgage had been approved. We had crossed our final bridge.

Trixie and our family cat,
Nehi 1954

Grandpa Grayson with
Janet and Darcy, 1954

First car, 1941 Plymouth
Club Coupe

Grandma Grayson at
Allen "N' Resort, 1955

Violet with Darcy

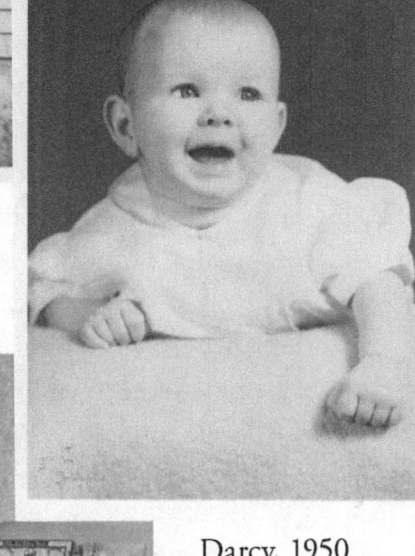

Darcy, 1950

FOXBORO

F ROM THE FIRST TIME I drove around the Common* in the center of town, I wanted to live in Foxboro - to walk its streets, stroll across the Common and bask in the safe feeling of its small-town coziness and typical New England village appearance. Cumberland, just as pretty and historic, held my past. Foxboro** held my future.

The house we bought at 5 Vernal Avenue sat almost on the Foxboro/Mansfield line which led to my one big disappointment. In 1955, phone exchanges bore names, not numbers. Our Cumberland phone had a *Perry* number. "Now we'll have a *Kingswood* number," I gloated to my mother. My bubble burst when I learned we'd have a Mansfield number due to our proximity to the town line. I had nothing against *Mansfield* but wanted the lovely-sounding *Kingswood* 3-2893. Oh, well. At least I was in Foxboro but it would cost us fifteen dollars to have a phone installed, a deposit the phone company requested because the phones we had in the past were under our husband's names. It would be returned in a year if we paid our bills on time.

The house itself, a snug, five-room bungalow, had a living room, dining room, kitchen and two bedrooms. I loved the small sun porch at the front of the house and the large yard in the back with its stone wall and towering trees behind the wall. I was pleased to see that someone had built a small brick fire pit in the back yard for cook-outs. That would certainly be used by us. An old cow path, now overgrown, also

---

* A grassy, fenced-in area, usually in the middle of a town, with walkways and benches, used for public events and gatherings and often having a bandstand.
** See the History section at the back of the book.

lay behind the wall. It had been used in the past to walk the cows from a farm in the area to Robinson Brook which flowed through the woods at the bottom of our dead-end street. From our front steps, we could see a large expanse of land that bordered Vernal Avenue and stretched to the Mansfield line with nothing on it but an abandoned farmhouse. It made a wonderful spot for me to help Darcy learn to fly her kite.

To get to work, I just had to turn left from Vernal Avenue onto Central Street, which was also known as Route 140, and follow it to the Common, as many Foxboro Company employees did who lived in Mansfield. As I told a friend who was visiting from Rhode Island, "Before I reach the Common, I pass a row of stores which is the center of town and then I veer right to continue around the Common. Almost immediately, I see Bird Street which swings off on the right, just past the post office and takes me directly into the Foxboro Company parking lot. The whole trip probably takes about ten or fifteen minutes, plus I have the luxury of calling a fellow employee for a ride if I can't start my car on a cold day or something else keeps me from using it".

We were one of about seven houses on the street, plus two that faced onto Central Street. Though Barbara lived diagonally across from us, we didn't resume our friendship but were pleasant to each other. My mother gradually became acquainted with the neighbors and had a lot to tell me over our evening meal. She did the cooking and I bought the groceries. We cleaned the house together. I took over Darcy's care at night. The neighbors were glad to see the place occupied and the lights on at night.

As soon as possible, I transferred our membership from Christ Church in Rhode Island to St. Mark's Episcopal Church in Foxboro and enrolled Darcy in Sunday School. It seemed that all roads, similar to a rotary, led out from the Common, including South Street where the church was located. I liked the ride around the Common to access South Street. After I passed the Orpheum Theater, I could glimpse the Congregational Church spire which rose just off the Common on Rockhill Street. The fire station fronted conveniently on the Common, next to the Baptist Church. That church, whose spire had been weakened by hurricanes, was later razed and the congregation built a new one on Mechanic Street, outside the center of town.

In time, as the congregation increased, St. Mark's also built a new church on a lot which lay farther down South Street, near a back road, eliminating the need to swing around the Common to get there. The back road led through a woody, scenic area but I still enjoyed the swing around the Common for other trips through Foxboro center.

Though the change in states could not alter my status, it provided me with a fresh perspective, a feeling that my new future had begun. When Don surprised me by starting the practice of driving to Foxboro every two weeks to bring the support payment instead of mailing it, I had no objections since it would give him an opportunity to be with Darcy. As far as my personal feelings were concerned, he had no part in my life. He belonged in my past, but I was grateful that he had in no way attempted to evade his financial responsibility to his daughter.

I tried to stay out of the way during his visits, but he kept asking. "Can I do anything to help?" and I finally decided to put him to work.

"You can help me cut down the tall grass and bushes in the back yard," I said. They had grown while the house was on the market. He also helped me set up a swing set I bought for Darcy and did some heavy lifting in the basement. In hindsight, I can picture him offering to help as his way of trying to make up for the breakdown of our marriage.

I sometimes did housework during his visits in my efforts not to be in the way. One night in 1956 as I stood at the ironing board and my mother was working in the kitchen, he quietly said, "I'm going to be a father again in August."

I almost dropped the iron as I blurted out, "Are you married?"

"Of course I am," he huffed but I learned in later years that the marriage involved a secret trip to Connecticut for a quick ceremony. After revealing his news, he continued to visit like clockwork to bring the support payments, greet me and my mother, offer to help and smile and talk a little with Darcy.

BRINGING UP DARCY

DESPITE THE POSITIVE THINGS happening in my life, sadness and tears of frustration caught up with me several times over the fact that I couldn't give Darcy a father. One sleepless night, I turned to the Higher Power that watched over us. "What can I do for my little girl?" I asked in desperation.

My answer came on a cold December day while we were driving to Mansfield and saw smoke rising from the chimney of a house. "Why is the smoke going up, mommy?"

Whew! Help me, somebody! I searched for the words and somehow found them. "The air is still,' I explained, "And there's no wind to blow the smoke so it has to go straight up."

She seemed satisfied but that was just the beginning - Question No. 1. She had reached the inquisitive age of five. If I didn't know the answer, together we looked it up in our old encyclopedia which she soon learned to do by herself. Grateful for the guidance I had received, I said a silent, "Thank you," and the truth hit me. "I can't give her a father but I can give her curiosity." A rush of joy filled me, making me impatient to start.

I set up a bird feeder and bought a Golden Press book, *Birds of North America,* to help us identify those who came to feed. In company with an interested pet cat, Snagglepuss, we watched from a bedroom window. "Look, mommy, there's a chickadee," she'd shout, delighted that she could identify it. We both held our breath and watched on the evening in early spring when a hungry pheasant found its way to the feeder and wandered under it, looking for dropped seed. It never came back but we always remembered it.

The Golden Press, beginning in 1949, also published a *Golden Nature Guide* series that included *Stars* and *Rocks and Minerals*. When warmth at last returned to New England in the summer of 1956, I suggested on a clear night, "Let's take our *Stars* book and a flashlight out with us, spread a blanket and lie on our backs and study the stars." We didn't have as much luck naming those as we'd had with the birds, but at least she became familiar with the Big and Little Dipper and Cassiopeia and found the pleasure of searching the skies. She didn't seem as interested in *Rocks and Minerals* so I waited to let her discover some things on her own.

During that summer, I hammered together four six-foot boards to make a square frame on the ground in the back yard. A dump truck brought in a load of sand and she had a sand box next to her swing set. It pleased me that I could give her as normal a life as possible.

The day I found her scrunched down on the front sidewalk studying ants scurrying around in the cracks, I said to myself, "I'll make her an ant farm." With helpful hints from various friends, I filled an empty bottle with sand from her sand box, punched holes in the lid and dropped in several ants. It fascinated her to watch them in their tunnels and to feed them with bread crumbs. When she eventually tired of her ant farm, we returned them to the sidewalk and disposed of the sand.

I know I had unseen help in my quest because I couldn't have come up with all the ideas by myself but was led to more ways to whet her curiosity. In the five-and-ten-cent store, I spotted a toy microscope. She became obsessed with studying everything and anything that would fit on the tiny slides, including sugar from our bowl, enthralled by the enlarged crystals. It thrilled me to see her intensity.

In time, her curiosity spread to other areas. She surprised me by asking, "Is it all right if I bring home some pollywogs from Robinson Brook?" I said she could but would have to also bring brook water, to keep them in their natural habitat. We found a large enough container and she took care of them, replenishing the water when necessary and showing me their progress. When they began growing legs,, she decided, "I think I'd better take them back to the brook." I agreed with her.

"Mommy," she exclaimed, running into the house one day. "Come see the cows."

They browsed in a field to one side of the farmhouse and driveway across Central Street. "Do you think they go down the path?" she asked. I explained that they had water troughs and didn't need to go to the brook for water. Even though the cows no longer used it, I liked the idea of the old path behind our house. She and I often wandered along it to the brook, stopping to smell and admire the flowers, bushes and trees. *Field Flowers, The Red Book of Trees* and *The Blue Book of Trees*, published by Whitman Publishing, helped tremendously.,

Darcy and my mother gradually reached out to other families on Vernal Avenue while I was working. They made friends with the mother of two boys whose yard bordered Robinson Brook. Bobby, the youngest, was Darcy's age and his brother, Billy, was two years older. They enlightened us about the field where we flew kites. The abandoned farmhouse, one of the casualties of the growth of that area, belonged to their grandparents, Billy told us.

With her two new buddies, Darcy, as she grew older, roamed the woods and fields behind our house in an imitation of my life in Cumberland. I met their mother who told me, "This area is known as *Foxvale*. We have Paine School just up Central Street and she can walk with Billy and Bobby." *Foxvale*. I liked its comfortable sound. We had come to a good place.

SCHOOL DAYS AND BEYOND

GARVIN MEMORIAL, A MODEST but handsome brick building on a large lot on Diamond Hill Road in Cumberland, where I entered school in 1931, combined two grades in each of its three rooms, ending with the sixth grade. Paine School, fittingly located on School Street in Foxboro, also combined grades in a small, wooden building on a large lot, but stopped at the fourth grade and used the extra room for everything else. Besides being pleased that Darcy's first school experience would mimic mine, it comforted me to know she wouldn't be faced with a multi-storied, bewildering building.

On her first day in September of 1956, I went to school with her to meet the teacher, Mrs. R. Darcy cried and clung to me, "Mommy, don't leave me." Mrs. R., who was also the principal and had probably been through that scene many times, gently convinced her to stay. I left for work, full of anguish, tearfully watching the clock. At noontime I dashed back, positive I'd find her standing alone and ready to rush into my arms. I found her - running and laughing with a group of girls. I called to her. She waved and went on with the game, leaving me to slump onto the seat of my car, tears welling again, but for myself. My little girl had entered the world.

She enjoyed the challenge of learning, her fertile mind soaking up the new knowledge. She chatted about her broadening group of Foxvale friends, "I walk to school with Judy and the twins, Jean and Joan, and Elaine and Tommy and Bobby."

She visited their homes and they came to ours, encouraged sometimes by the peanut butter cookies that my mother baked.

The school year passed quickly, with no upsetting incidents, as did the summer of 1957. August arrived, bringing Darcy's 7th birthday. Just before she and her friends entered second grade, I invited Judy, Jean, Joan and Elaine to a birthday party. Darcy's cousins, Janet and Janet's sister, Marilyn, came with Ruthie. She and Tom's growing family also included baby Ann, a month and a half and too young to attend the party.

"I'll invite Donna," I decided. Louise, Johnny and their daughter, Donna, had moved back to New England. Johnny had joined me and Tom as an employee of the Foxboro Company and they bought a house in North Attleboro, a town south of Foxboro. Louise and Ruth helped with the backyard picnic and games, but the highlight of the day came when I told the girls, "Okay, your parents have given permission for you to go to Foxfield Plaza." They all had nickels and dimes to spend on whatever gems they could find in Woolworth's, one of the stores in the tiny mall. They came back, giggling and ready to go home to tell their parents about the party and their trip to Woolworth's.

Foxfield Plaza, a minuscule shopping center, had taken over the abandoned farm area where I taught Darcy to fly kites. We missed the space, but as I said to my mother, "We have a First National Supermarket within walking distance and a five-and-ten-cent store."

Our joy increased with the news that a laundromat planned to open. Our old washing machine died shortly after we moved to Foxboro which had no laundromats, forcing me to drive to Mansfield every Monday night. Once the new one opened, Darcy's little red wagon came in handy. "I'll set the laundry basket in it and pull it around the corner to the plaza and use her sled in the winter," I told my mother. My system worked fine until The Foxboro Reporter ran the story, "Laundromat in Foxfield Plaza closed by complaints!" Our town, with no municipal sewage system except a limited one in the center of town, required residents to rely on backyard cesspools. The laundromat owners had quietly laid pipes to Robinson Brook, sending suds and anything else downstream to Mansfield ponds where the residents objected. Odors from the brook had also brought questions from the Vernal Avenue neighbors.

We lost our laundromat but a new Shell station and garage opened across Central Street from the Plaza, making up for the loss. "What problem have you brought us this time?" the co-owners, Gordon and Ed, asked whenever I left my car for some sort of repair, but they always reassured me they'd find a way to fix it. Their good humor and mechanical expertise helped lift the cloud of worry each repair brought. If they weren't able to perform their magic and I needed to replace the car, Tom helped me scout the back areas of used car lots to find another gem that would take me through a few more years. Ed and Gordon, my angels of mercy, kept each used car in running order for as long as was legally possible, making me extremely grateful.

They even fixed the problem in the car that had a hole in the floor under the passenger seat. The salt spread on the winter roads had taken its toll and worn away the metal to open a hole about the size of a grapefruit. Darcy could see the road from her perch on the front seat. Otherwise the car and its motor were in good shape. Gordon and Ed found a thin sheet of metal and somehow attached it to the floor to cover the hole, making me realize my good luck in having them nearby.

Another angel of mercy blessed me during Darcy's second year in school. A mumps epidemic sweeping through town caught up with her. My co-workers, laughing, asked whether I had ever had the mumps. "No," I told them. We all joked about how funny it would be if it happened.

It was no joke when it did. Thirty-two isn't a good age for anyone to be when it comes to having the mumps but that wasn't my biggest concern. Being on hourly pay meant I would have no income while I was sick and at home. Whatever health insurance the employees had at that time didn't kick in for two weeks. "What will we do?" I worried silently, lying there with swollen glands and praying in desperation, "Please help us."

On the third day of my confinement, my mother brought in the mail. "There's a letter from the phone company," she noted. I opened it, *You have paid your telephone bill consistently since having your telephone installed a year ago; therefore, we are returning your deposit.* With exquisite timing, the phone company had returned the $15 deposit, which went a long way in 1957.

"Look," I held it up, emotions constricting my throat, hurting my jaws, but I didn't care. *It will be all right.* I settled back on the pillow and relaxed.

The following Monday, well again, I cashed a savings bond left over from World War II and we made it to the next payday. You don't always get what you want but you certainly get what you need.

NOT YET

OCCASIONALLY, DEPRESSION CLAIMED ME that I had not yet found a new mate. At those times, I pounded my pillow when I couldn't sleep, releasing my anger, loneliness and frustration. "When will it be my turn, God?" I demanded to know.

During the day, I sat by the bedroom window, watching but not really seeing the birds nibbling at the seeds in the feeder. After our beloved Trixie succumbed to old age, we acquired a kitten, Snagglepuss, now grown, who sought my lap to lend his brand of comfort, seeming to sense my need. We'd linger together until the mood passed. Even his name, borrowed by Darcy from a Saturday morning cartoon character, made me smile. "Good old Snagglepuss," I'd murmur as I stroked his velvety back and felt his purr.

Though the low spots saddened me, I could handle them much better than I could the high ones – the proud moments, for instance, when I ached to share my happy news with a husband and tell him, "Darcy's teacher says she's a joy to teach," or "Isn't she beautiful?" I pictured him beaming with pride along with me in our pride at Darcy's accomplishments.

The hard labor of maintaining our house and yard, though it absorbed my after-work and weekend time, provided immediate and gratifying results to give me a sense of worthiness. I especially enjoyed landscaping. Our back yard needed a fence to "make good neighbors" as Robert Frost suggested but I opted for a privet hedge. It flourished and I was pleased even though it had to be trimmed. Trees grew tall behind the stone wall and in our neighbor's yard but, as I commented to my mother, "We have no trees in our back yard. I think I'll plant an apple tree." That led to putting in two other saplings – a red maple in the front of the house and a birch at the side. Fond memories of my grandmother's peony bushes prompted me to set in some bulbs under the birch tree outside the dining room window, with a bird bath amidst them..

Having visitors was always a pleasure. Ruth and Tom and the three girls joined us during the summer months for cookouts in our back yard and Darcy's school friends – Judy, our next-door neighbor, and Gail who lived a short walk up Central Street - dropped in at other times. Uncle Bobby, my mother's brother, and his wife, Aunt Nellie (Aunt Betty's sister) drove from South Attleboro, near the Cumberland border. They had no grandchildren and he loved Darcy. As a young child, she had climbed on his lap and told him what she'd been doing, making them buddies. His sister, Aunt Alice, who was also, of course, my mother's sister, occasionally stayed a weekend with us. She lived in Seekonk, another town south of Foxboro, with my cousin Lucy and Lucy's husband, Joe. Lucy always called ahead. "I'll bring my mother if Vi can bring her home." I loved both Uncle Bobby and Aunt Alice and welcomed their visits.

At the encouragement of Ruthie, a Girl Scout leader, Darcy, Gail and Judy joined the Foxboro Girl Scouts which led to an incident that still brings a teary smile. In the summer of 1959, they spent several days at Shady Pines Girl Scout Camp in South Attleboro. Judy's father offered to pick them up on the last day and Darcy told me the story. "The leader invited the fathers to go stand next to their daughters for a picture," she said. "Judy's father stood between me and Judy and put one arm around her and one around me." I thanked God for taking care of her even when I didn't know about it.

Our life, though good, was far from idyllic. Foxboro had no transportation system which made my mother, who didn't drive, feel trapped in the house. Typical of her generation of women, she had not learned to drive but, in Cumberland, lived within walking distance of a bus, a convenience she didn't have in Foxboro. That led her to decide, in her seventies, that she would learn to drive. I tried teaching her but she had difficulty mastering the car's standard shift. An automatic one would have helped tremendously. Undaunted, she signed up for lessons but her teacher became sick toward the end of them and also made a few remarks about my mother's ability to learn. Discouraged, my mother didn't resume the lessons when the instructor recovered. I offered to contact the driving school to find another instructor but she had lost her will and berated herself for not being capable enough to do something that would have easily solved the problem of her isolation.

Life could have been much fuller and happier for everyone if each of us had been able to clearly see the many blessings in our lives - the house, the quiet and peaceful neighborhood, good schools, a loving family, our stable health, no tragic addictions and an income that paid the bills and bought the food.

Other reasons to be grateful escaped my attention in those years. Ruthie never minded having Darcy come to visit and included her in the family's camping or fishing trips. In the summer, I occasionally drove to one of the sandy, lovely beaches along the east coast and my nieces were always happy to go with us, giving Darcy company. I also recall the trips to the Orpheum Theater. Usually, I took Darcy and stayed with her if none of her friends planned to go. I recall the day we were waiting in line to see a popular movie and several school buddies asked whether they could sit with us. Mothers who knew me drove up, saw me, and asked whether I'd mind if they left their children in my care. We ended up occupying the whole middle row of seats in the theater. I felt like Mother Goose and loved it.

After the movie, I waited until all the girls were safely with a parent and I thanked my guardian angel for the experience. That same guardian angel also took care of other things. As children do, Darcy kept growing. In the winter of 1960, when she put on her coat for the first time, I saw that the sleeves had crept up above her wrists, Dismayed, I knew she needed a new one but worried about where I could find one that I could afford.

A few days later, right on cue, the phone rang and Ruthie, without knowing Darcy needed a coat, asked, "Can Darcy use a winter coat?" I almost shouted in joy that she could. "Well, Janet has one that's too small for her." It turned out to be a perfect fit and much nicer than any I could have afforded to buy. *It will be all right.*

DATING AND WAITING

ON A SUNDAY IN the early 60's I came across an ad in the Boston Sunday Globe, "Saturday night dancing to live music at the Norwood Elks Hall." That appealed to me since Norwood is just a few miles north of Foxboro. From then on, each Saturday night I put on a pretty dress and high heels and, unless something more important had been scheduled, went looking for someone to dance with or possibly get to know better.

It brought new men and new dates into my life, but for one reason or another, none clicked with me or vice versa. I complained to my friend, Louise, "I have no trouble finding men and dating them but I can't seem to keep them."

She laughed. "Maybe you're too picky, or maybe you need help." Soon after that, she called to ask, "Would you be willing to go on a blind date?"

"Yes," I answered, "Do you know someone nice?"

"Well, we have a neighbor who's a widower with two young children. If it's all right with him, we'll make arrangements for all of us to go out so you can meet him and that will give him the directions to your house." With the passing of time, I've forgotten his name, but I remember that he was tall, fairly good-looking, seemed pleasant and the evening together gave me hope. He said he'd call me and he did.

He picked me up for our date and met my mother and Darcy which also went well.

"Where would you like to go?" I asked since it was 8:00 P.M. and nothing had been said about dinner.

"I'll leave that up to you." he said, "but I don't want to be away from my children for too long. My mother is baby-sitting and I promised I wouldn't be late."

I hadn't frequented any cocktail lounges in years, but reasoned that if he wanted to see me again, that would give us an opportunity to become acquainted. Shortly after we sat down and ordered drinks, a thunderstorm rolled in. He shivered a little with each flash of lightening and worried out loud about his daughter, "I hope Sally is okay. She's afraid of thunderstorms." Due to his concern about his daughter, we left early. He dropped me off and thanked me but didn't make any plans to see me again. He also didn't call again but Louise did.

"Where did you take him?" she asked, in a dumbfounded tone. When I told her it was the one in the Holiday Inn, she confessed that he had described the cocktail lounge as a *dive* and apparently had not gone home with a good impression of me. She said he sounded angry when he said, "I'll find my own girl." That was the end of that.

I recounted the story to a fellow choir member from St. Mark's church. "That's funny," she said, "Because I was thinking about introducing you to someone. Are you willing to try again?"

"Sure. Why not?" I answered.

"My husband and I have a friend who attends the Seventh Day Adventist church here in Foxboro," she said. "He's divorced and has two grown children."

A few nights later, he called to introduce himself and set up a date. Again, the name slips my memory. He came to our house and met my family and turned out to be fairly tall, not bad-looking and pleasant. In the car, he asked, "Would you like to hear a concert?" I said I would, expecting we'd head up Route 1 to Boston but he turned west and drove to Harvard, Massachusetts, a town in the middle of apple country and a long drive.

I knew nothing of Harvard or the Seventh Day Adventist Atlantic School located there whose chorus sang for us that night. I enjoyed the concert but the long drive offered more opportunity than I really wanted to hear my date's views, which I doubt he had learned in church. "I wouldn't let my daughters work at the swap shop," he told me early in the drive, referring to The Foxboro Company. "All they do is change partners." My ire rose. I told him I hadn't seen much of that in my eight or so years working there and changed the subject to Boston and St. Patrick's Day which was just around the corner and asked whether he had ever been to the parade in Boston.

"I've never been to the St. Patrick's Day parade," he bragged, going on at great length to tell me of his animosity toward anything Irish. As it turned out, that was only one of several biases. I had difficulty keeping the conversation on a subject which didn't provoke a comment on his views, both driving to Harvard and on the way back.

At last, we pulled up in front my house in Foxboro. He turned off the engine and said, "I'd like to see you again," but I'd heard enough and wasn't anxious to spend another evening listening to him. I tried tactfully to decline, but he pressed for a reason, giving me no choice but to tell the truth.

"I'm not sure I could deal with your prejudices," I said. He seemed surprised but didn't attempt to change my mind. I thanked him for the concert, thinking I would never hear from him again.

Possibly my words had affected him after all. A few weeks later, he called to specifically tell me he had gone to the St. Patrick's Day Parade and had watched the whole thing, adding proudly, 'And I stood right next to an Irishman." I told him I appreciated his call and thanked him, doing my best to suppress my giggle, but sincerely glad he had taken that step.

Around that same time, two friends of mine from The Foxboro Company, a married couple whose wedding I had attended, also joined the act. They arranged a date for me with another widower who had young children at home and whose name escapes me. We all drove to an outdoor movie to see "Where the Boys Are," and had a wonderful evening, so I thought. He was also fairly tall, good-looking and I enjoyed his comments about the movie, hoping to see him again, but heard nothing until my friends invited me to visit so we could *talk*. I didn't like the sound of that. "He likes you," they told me, "but senses you're ready to settle down and he isn't." Well, I couldn't argue with his reasoning and once again, that was the end of that.

My friends stayed out of the matchmaking game after that, but the minister at St. Mark's tried. "Ted would like to get to know you better," he told me one Sunday. "He asked me whether I thought it was a good idea. I told him it was but wanted to see how you felt about it." Ted sang in the choir. I knew he had never been married, had a degree in engineering and was very intelligent. I also knew we really didn't have much in common outside of enjoying singing, but decided to give it a try.

We went to dinner, saw a movie, talked a little and he took me home. I respected and admired him but knew it wouldn't work. I think he sensed that also and didn't ask to see me again. We remained friends. One day, a choir member told me the news, "Ted's getting married!" I cheered heartily at the news. I liked him and hoped he'd be very happy and that was the end of that.

At least my professional life was active. The Foxboro Company sponsored the Ten-Year Club for those employees who had been with them for ten years or more. In April of 1962, unbelievably, I became eligible to join. The Club had officers and to my surprise, a member contacted me to ask whether I'd be willing to run for the office of Financial Secretary. I would be an assistant to the Treasurer who was one of our Security Guards. Since he and I were good friends and I liked the responsibility, I ran for office and was elected. One of the duties of the board was to plan the yearly Ten-Year Club dinner dance, a sister event to the Outing and to meet monthly to discuss any questions or business that had to be settled. I stayed in the office for two years and truly enjoyed the experience.

Darcy by 1962 had proven to be an excellent student. It didn't surprise me because I knew she had the talent and intelligence, but it certainly made me proud. She had long known about the library located on the Common and often asked, "Will you take me to the library?" That pleased me immensely. The time I spent driving back and forth or waiting for her to decide which books she wanted to check out or waiting while she browsed through several others was, in my opinion, well spent. I laughed in delight the day, carried away by youthful exuberance, she vowed, "I'm going to read every book in the library."

Her words stuck with me. "Well," I thought. "She just might do it. She'll be twelve in August and she's been coming since she learned to read," which prompted another thought. "I'll be thirty-seven in October. That's three years short of forty. They say life begins at forty. I hope it's true."

TWO BUSY YEARS

RUTHIE BROUGHT UP THE idea in May of 1962, "Let's take the girls to New York for a weekend. We can go by train. It'll be fun." I agreed and we made plans before telling them. Once they knew, they had trouble waiting until the Friday morning Tom took our group of five – Ruthie, me, Janet, 13, Darcy, 12, and 10-year-old Marilyn, to Providence. The train came in, huffing and chugging to a stop. We boarded amidst their chattering and excitement to be heading for the biggest city in America. Ann, not quite five years old, stayed at home with Tom.

The ride to New York held the attention of all of us as we tried to name the cities we were passing through. At Grand Central Station, we stepped down into the din of the Friday crowd and lingered on the concourse, taking in the panorama of the terminal, awed by its vastness and energy.

"Let's find a cab and go to the hotel," Ruthie said finally, "We can drop our bags in the room and go eat at an automat".

"What's that?" Marilyn asked

"You'll see," we promised.

They loved the automat, grinning as they viewed the sandwiches, salads and desserts in their little glass cubicles and chose what they wanted. As soon as we had eaten, we headed for the Empire State Building. The elevator ride to the 102nd floor and the 360-degree view from the glass-enclosed area fascinated them. Darcy pointed, "Look at the cars down there, like little bugs."

When they had seen and exclaimed over every view on the horizon or down below, I said, "Let's go to the United Nations Building."

The flags fluttering outside the building, the aura of world-wide business being conducted inside and actually being in the room where it all took place thrilled all of us. The girls kept a respectful silence which surprised and pleased us until we realized it might be coming from tiredness. "We have a big Saturday coming up," I suggested. "Let's eat and go back to the hotel."

On Saturday morning, we found our way to Battery Park and the ferry to the Statue of Liberty, a fun trip in itself. At the base of the statue, reading Emma Lazarus' poem brought tears to our eyes, "Bring me your tired, your poor, your huddled masses yearning to breathe free."

The spiral staircase inside the statue threatened, for me, at least, to induce vertigo and claustrophobia but I made it to the crown and its breathtaking view of New York harbor and the city itself. "Look at the boat. It looks so small," Janet shouted, pointing to the ferry we had taken from Battery Park. Reluctantly, we descended, an easier trip on the straight stairway.

On the mainland, we headed to Times Square to see the ticker tape, walk along Broadway a little bit and go inside Rockefeller Center. A massive gold curtain stretching across the stage told us that no shows were about to start, but we didn't care. We just wanted to be there and see it.

"Central Park is next," Ruthie said. On Park Avenue we all smiled at the horse-drawn hansom cabs and their passengers. Children screamed in play and parents lounged on the grass or the benches in Central Park. We gazed at the tall buildings visible through the trees and marveled at this oasis in the midst of such an active city. At last, we headed back to the hotel.

On Sunday, our last day, we found transportation to the Episcopal Cathedral of St. John the Divine, up above Harlem. The heavy carved door and the glowing colors of the stained glass windows, the hush of the interior and the high pulpit brought a beautiful close to our weekend.

That afternoon, tired but satisfied, we returned to Grand Central Station to board the train, full of memories we'd relive for many years. Tom picked us up in Providence and the girls talked all the way home, telling him of the wonders of New York city.

The break in our routine and the fact that the girls were old enough to take the trip woke me up to the fact that Darcy was no longer the baby of six weeks that I had carried into my parents' house. A year earlier, when she still seemed to be my little girl, I had struggled through *the conversation* with her about sex, her physical expectations as a woman, dating and boyfriends. Now she was asking me to drive her, Judy and Gail to a dance at the high school auditorium. I thought it was cute until she asked, "Can we pick up Paul, too?" and I did a mental double-take. All sorts of worries entered my head.

My uneasy thoughts disappeared as I watched all four of them walk toward the door of the school. The three girls stood at least a head taller than Paul, a phenomenon caused by girls growing faster than boys at that age. I giggled at the image of couples on the dance floor – not a romantic picture – and I relaxed.

Work began that summer, in the woods beyond Robinson Brook, on our portion of Interstate 95, part of President Eisenhower's American highway plan and scheduled for completion in 1963. It would replace Route 1 which meandered through various cities on its route up the Atlantic coast from Miami, Florida, to Portland, Maine. In our curiosity, Darcy and I often walked to the site to view from a safe distance the gradual emergence of the Foxboro cloverleaf.

With the exception of the green and white signs on the completed highway that indicated the north and south Foxboro exits, no drastic or heartbreaking changes hit our little town. One section of High Street was cut off but an access road from Central Street solved that. A new bridge to carry the traffic over Central Street meant several houses had to be put on wheels and moved to new locations. Our small section of Central Street which had also been Route 140 morphed into a local road after Route 140 was relocated for access off and onto I-95. "Well, it'll make going into Boston and Providence a lot easier," I told my mother when we discussed losing our state road.

Once again, though my love life stayed stagnant, at least my professional life improved. From my start as a clerk and assistant to Barbara and Mary, I was now working with them on the Sensamatic[*] bookkeeping machines, making more money and enjoying the change.

We each had been assigned a section of our customers' alphabetical card files and were required to balance the books at the end of each month. That appealed to me, an October baby born under the sign of Libra, the Scales. Each time I balanced my accounts, the Libran personality smiled.

Things had improved at home, too. "Will you drive me to Mansfield on Friday night?" my mother asked one day in 1963 and explained. "I can take the train to Pawtucket and play bingo. I just heard about it. There's a big hall on Times Square. I can walk from the Pawtucket depot." That became a Friday night routine. She boarded the train to enjoy the short ride to Pawtucket. I drove there at 10:00 with a sleepy Darcy beside me, happy that my mother had found an outlet for her restlessness.

Also, in 1963, I heard about an opening in the Credit Department that sounded interesting. Having reached the top of the wage scale in my old job, I knew I couldn't make any more money so I applied for the job and was accepted. I'd be back doing secretarial work but not dictation and I would still be on the third floor, not far from Mary and Barbara and Dave. It was a lateral move which meant I wouldn't be given an immediate raise but its higher pay scale opened the possibility

---

[*] The Burroughs Sensimatic Accounting Machine of the 50's looked like a large adding machine with an oversized typewriter carriage. The carriage allowed each customer's card and statement to be fed into the platen side by side so that the data entered would print on both while the carriage moved to the left and back to the right and released the card and statement so that another customer's card and statement could be inserted. The action made a "clunk, clunk" sound as the carriage traveled back and forth.

of future raises. I'd be working for Cy, the Credit Manager and Fred, the Assistant Credit Manager. I knew and was fond of both of them.

The Foxboro Company, growing and expanding, had opened offices and was selling control instruments in foreign countries. In the Credit Department, I looked forward to learning a lot about approving and exporting orders. I had a feeling things were turning around for me and wondered, "Could it be that Darcy isn't the only one in the family who's growing up?"

CARL

FOXBORO'S RICH COLLECTION OF large old houses caused a lot of discussion at several town meetings during the 60's. New residents complained, "I'm paying a tax rate based on the appraisal done when I bought the house a few years ago. My neighbor has lived in his house for thirty years so it hasn't been appraised or re-assessed in thirty years. I think it's time to update the tax code." Eventually, the tax assessment system was overhauled but that didn't stop the complaining. This time it came from the longtime residents.

"I no longer need a big house but if I sell it and buy a smaller one, I'll be paying a lot more taxes at today's rate." Some made the decision to remodel the upstairs, rent it out and live downstairs. Others decided to bite the bullet and sell the whole house to someone who would cut it up into apartments. That brought Carl into the picture..

He asked me to dance at Norwood in June of 1964. At the end of the evening, he invited me to have coffee with him and told me some of his history. "I'm originally from Winnipeg, Canada, but met some Americans during World War 11 when I was in the Royal Canadian Air Force. I wasn't having much luck finding a job after the war so decided to try my luck in America and moved to this area because it sounded like a good place to start. I found a job, met my wife and stayed." He quickly added, "We're divorced now. I have two daughters, Bonnie and Lesley. They're twelve and ten."

I reciprocated with my story and added, "I live in Foxboro." He smiled.

"I'm a bricklayer by trade," he said, "but these days I'm buying old houses in Foxboro and making them into apartments," and I smiled at the coincidence.

He was tall, good-looking and liked to dance and we began dating. In August, my mother, Darcy and I left for a long-planned vacation with my sister and her family, traveling in our Plymouth station wagon to Lake Anasagunticook in Canton, Maine. Carl asked for the address so he could write to me which he did, saying, in part, "I miss you. Please call me the minute you get back."

After our wonderful week of swimming, lying in the sun, rowing a boat around our small cove and visiting with a friend who was staying nearby, we headed home. "I guess I'll call Carl," I commented the Sunday night we arrived back at Vernal Avenue.

"I'll be there to take you out tomorrow night," he said.

I had missed him and enjoyed seeing him, flattered that he had been so anxious to be with me again. On our date, we finished our meal and were having coffee when he reached into his pocket and pulled out a box, "I have something for you." He opened it and astonished me by putting a diamond ring on my finger.

All I could mumble was, "Thank you," stunned into silence. Word of my ring spread quickly. Over the next few weeks, I moved in a fog of confusion, thanking friends who called to say, "I'm thrilled for you, Vi. You deserve to be happy." I used my mother as an excuse for not having set a date. That allowed me to say we had to sell our house and either find one that would hold all of us or find a senior citizen apartment for my mother.

Carl still hadn't said he loved me or wanted to marry me and I wondered whether he realized the promise that lies behind a diamond ring or whether he just thought it would make a nice gift. If so, I didn't want to make him feel like a fool. I liked him and wanted to continue dating him and see where it would lead us.

The members of St. Mark's church choir showed their love and took both of us totally by surprise with a bridal shower that included Carl. Pleased but unprepared for such an event, I did my best to fend off questions about the wedding date, even wondering, "Does he love me," and more importantly, "Do I love him?" Carl looked very uncomfortable and admitted later that the whole affair had embarrassed him. That nagged at me, but the overall excitement swept me along.

He talked about a park in Westwood where Darcy and his daughters could become acquainted. The idea worked well. He picked us up at home and introduced us to Bonnie and Lesley who invited Darcy into the back seat. They liked her and teased her, a new experience for an only child. At the park, they tossed a ball around and found other ways to intermingle. It gave me a warm feeling to pretend I was with my family on an outing.

"Bring your daughters to a cookout," I told Carl soon after that. One incident marred an otherwise pleasant afternoon. At a chance comment about our engagement and possible marriage, Lesley looked stricken and began to cry. Carl took her aside and quieted her down, but it stirred up my uneasiness. Apparently, it was news to her.

Carl had, by then, taken me to see his cozy Cape Cod style house which sat on a large, heavily-wooded, somewhat isolated lot in Westwood, an upscale town north of Foxboro and closer to Boston. His only comment was, "I want to see whether you like it," another confusing comment which sounded as though he expected me to live there. I liked it but had serious doubts about leaving Foxboro, moving Darcy and settling my mother where she'd have no close neighbors. Too many questions lay unspoken and unanswered and I had not yet been able to shake off my old habit of keeping my thoughts to myself. A good, open discussion was due but neither of us wanted to launch it. "Let's go see Westwood," I suggested to my mother and Darcy one Sunday afternoon. Instead of taking them to Carl's house, I headed toward the center of town which was on Route 9 which ran parallel to Route 1. We found stately old houses, a well-built high school with a large athletic field and a town where I felt I could be happy. It didn't have the coziness of Foxboro but its charm appealed to me. "I might like living here," I thought, and added out loud, "I'll show you Carl's house."

His property, I realized, was located on the other side of Route 1, a distance away from the center of town and not easily accessible to the rest of Westwood. To make matters worse, as I was turning in the narrow road something happened to my transmission, preventing me from shifting out of first gear. I crawled along, praying I could find a service station on Route 1. Fortunately, Darcy spotted one as soon as we reached the highway, but the experience made me more aware of the remoteness of the house.

With excellent timing, the Foxboro selectmen, the elected leaders of our town, announced plans to build senior citizen apartments in a field at the end of Centennial Street which was just off the Common.

My mother immediately applied for one. "I've been accepted," she told me, as soon as I came in the door one night, adding with a big smile, "I'll be a charter member and can move in whenever they're ready." That settled the question of where she'd live.

The time sped by. "Carl and I have been together a year," I realized in June of 1965. Two months later, my mother was thrilled to receive an award which confirmed her status as a charter member of the Centennial Court Association, the name given to the senior complex which was scheduled for completion in August of 1966.

The year-long wait for her to be in her own apartment turned out to be beneficial. I had been noticing gradual changes in Carl. The time he didn't show up for a date in 1965, for instance, I had visions of him lying in a hospital somewhere after having had an accident or worse still, trapped in his truck. I called his house. "What's wrong?" he asked. I told him we had a date. He seemed bewildered. "I guess I fell asleep," he mumbled, slurring his words as though he were drunk. "What time is it?"

"It's too late now," I said, "but I just wanted to be sure you were all right." The disappointment and doubt about his dependability stayed with me but I didn't confide in anyone. I wanted to be sure before I drew any conclusions or took any action.

The disturbing signs continued. Over time, his clothes assumed a rumpled, not-too-clean look and he was sometimes late in arriving. Another time, he showed up with a strange man and the man's daughter in his truck. The only explanation he offered, without saying who they were or where they had met, was, "His car broke down and I told them I'd take them to the bus station in Dedham," It was an awkward ride, with both men drinking beer and the woman barely speaking. I questioned him some more when we dropped them off but he found nothing unusual in having them in the truck. Oddly, I didn't go into a depression or feel cheated. Somehow, the course I was taking seemed the right one and I felt certain I'd find my answers in time.

"The apartments will definitely be ready in August," my mother announced in the spring of 1966. "I saw it in the Foxboro Reporter. Let's put the house on the market. It might take a while to sell it. If worst comes to worst, I can live with Ruth and Tom for a while."

Carl surprised me by volunteering to paint the outside of the house for us. We accepted his offer. He also assured me not to worry. "You can live in one of my apartments, free of charge," he said, sounding like the Carl I had been attracted to originally. The house sold fast. A young couple with two children bought it. I asked Carl about the apartment he had promised us. He acted surprised and bristled. 'I can't afford to let you live free of charge," he said, dashing my hopes and yet, oddly, setting me free. Quietly, I made up my mind. Once Darcy and I were in our own place, I'd confront him and find out exactly what was in his mind.

We found apartments but were told we couldn't bring Snagglepuss with us, an unthinkable idea. We continued to search and found a three-room third-floor apartment on short and hilly Maple Avenue, where Snagglepuss was welcome. "Look," I told Darcy, pointing out the kitchen window, "I can see almost the length of Neponset Avenue. I can walk to work. I love it." I peeked into the huge bedroom. "I can use screens to sub-divide this so we can both have privacy."

We had a living room, an old-fashioned, spacious kitchen, the large bedroom and a good-sized bathroom. The apartment, built into the attic of the house, had slanted walls in some of the rooms which added to its off beat ambience and gave us lots of storage space under the eaves. The rent, $65 a month, appealed to me.

The landlady said she'd waive the first month's rent and furnish the paint if we wanted to freshen up the walls ourselves. Five of Darcy's school friends – Gail, Judy, Frankie, John and Jan - joined us with brushes, keeping me laughing and grateful for their presence.

"How about a lavender bathroom?" someone joked but we decided to do that, even painting the bottom of the claw-footed bathtub in a Bohemian salute. Fortunately, it was a pale lavender. The apartment looked cheerful with a light green kitchen, a soft yellow bedroom and an off-white living room.

On moving day, the same friends brought lunch to our old house, amazing us with their kindness. As soon as we had eaten, we all drove to Maple Avenue, our cars filled with boxes. At the apartment, they formed lines, carrying the boxes on their heads, safari-style, up the three flights of stairs. Carl, who had not offered to help, was nowhere in sight.

"The perfect touch," I thought, "would be if I could have a Kingswood number, but it's too late." Phone numbers had become just that – numbers – without the exchange names.

A lot had changed, including my feelings for Carl, during the two-plus years we had been together. It was time to confide in someone. I talked with my minister who advised me to date him a few more times. "He may have felt left out during all the moving," he said, "or he may have been waiting until you were on your own. Give him another chance."

On our next date, Carl took me to a lounge in Wrentham where he promptly ordered a large pitcher of beer. I asked for ginger ale and he seemed surprised but ordered it. He paid little attention to me but drank his beer, smiled a lot and continually glanced around at the other people, obviously very much at home in that environment. "This is not the man I met at Norwood," I told myself. "This is a stranger I don't know any more."

At the apartment, I made an excuse for not inviting him in, kissed him and said, "Good night. It's late so I'll go up by myself. I'll call you." He didn't argue. A few days later, we talked on the phone and I came right to the point. "It isn't going to work between us," I said, adding, "You've never mentioned marriage and I'm still not sure why you gave me an engagement ring." He offered no explanation; in fact, didn't seem to know himself why he had done it and even seemed surprised that I had mentioned marriage. He didn't beg me to stay or try to change my mind. "I'll keep the ring if it's all right with you," I said. Again, he didn't argue.

Once more I had struck out but had seen it coming and wasn't left with a heavy heart or under a cloud of despair. The sliver of doubt that had nagged at me all along transformed into a suspicion that he had an alcohol problem and had met me during a period of attempting to stay sober. My impression that he had gone back to drinking seemed to be fairly accurate. Once more, I had been saved a lot of heartache.

I took the ring off my finger and put it into my jewelry box. "Well, that's the end of that."

ME AND MY CAT

NO, IT WASN'T MY imagination. Something had changed. In the frenzy of selling the house, moving my mother into her apartment and breaking up with Carl, my search for a husband had lost its grip and slipped away along with any depressing disappointment in the loss of Carl. Instead, I felt gloriously free, not harboring the need to start the search again. Instead, a totally fresh thought glowed in my mind. "Why not volunteer somewhere – give my love in that way – to many people instead of just one?" I felt lighter and reveled in the new way of thinking and the relief of having set down a long-carried burden.

The hardest part came in convincing friends that I was all right. Even harder was having to face choir members who had given me a wedding shower and numerous gifts. How could I close the door to the past without reconciling that part of it? The choir made the decision for me when I revealed, lying a little, that Carl and I had cancelled our wedding plans. "Keep the gifts," I was told. Gratitude filled me for their loving response. Over time I was able to explain the situation, relieved when they understood.

Shortly after the breakup, Snagglepuss also helped by unwittingly passing on his wisdom to me. I kept him in for a month after we moved, before allowing him to make his way step-by-step down the three flights of stairs and out into the yard. On that busy Saturday, I didn't call him until the rays of the late afternoon sun slanted across my kitchen floor. He didn't come running, as usual. I panicked, calling and searching, checking the railroad tracks that ran through a small grove of trees just beyond our backyard to make sure he hadn't had an accident of some sort. No Snagglepuss. Heartsick, I checked the veterinarian who took care of him. "Nobody's brought him in," he said. Darcy searched the neighborhood, positive she could find him but came back looking downcast.

We tried not to picture him sick or hurting somewhere. "I'll post pictures of him around town," I decided, "and put a notice in The Foxboro Reporter."

A long and agonizing week passed before the phone rang. The woman who had bought our house asked, "Do you have a black and white cat?" Delighted, I said we did. "Well, he keeps trying to jump into one of the bedroom windows," she said. I laughed and told her I'd be there shortly.

I found a skinny, bedraggled-looking cat and snatched him up immediately to hug him while I explained to her, "He was trying to get into that window because in the winter, I left the storm window open a little to let air into the room. He'd jump down into the snow, prowl around and jump back up when he was ready. In the summer, I left it open so he could sit on the sill and peer through the screen at whatever fascinated him in the outside darkness. It was his window."

The fact that he was able to do it amazed me. He had to walk at least two miles, cross Robinson Brook and Mechanic Street as well as Central Street and wander through woods and fields he had never visited in his life. His instincts had served him well. He wanted to be back at the only home he had ever known, to jump through his window, to watch for the toad that lived in one of the drains.

Darcy was as thrilled as I was to see him. Again I kept him in for a month but the minute he was let out, off he went. In all, he made the trek four times before he let go of his former life to accept the new one and explore its advantages.

"Aha," I thought. "If he can do it, I can, too. That inspired me to examine the pros and cons of my life.

For starters, though she liked him, Darcy didn't appear to be upset that Carl would no longer be in our lives. There would be no move to

Westwood which I can only surmise pleased her as much as it pleased me and no adjustment to a new school and new friends. Also, she had no sense of what it was like to have a live-in father which meant she wasn't losing something that had always been a part of her life.

To my delight, she had matured into a young lady who made me proud in every way. At sixteen, as an excellent student, she brought home report cards showing numerous A's. She sang with the Foxboro High School a capella choir, a musical group well-respected for their talent and versatility. She cheered and marched with the high school drill team. She had her license and had proven her driving skills so I allowed her to take the car to school.

Her friends – Gail, Judy, Richard, Jan, Frankie, Sandy and John – visited often. When I came in from work, I'd find them sitting in a circle on the living room floor. I loved them all and they respected me.

In addition, I had a dependable job and two good bosses. The Credit Department was slowly expanding as the Foxboro Company grew and so was my paycheck. Besides singing with the St. Mark's choir, I belonged to the Neponset Choral Society, a well-established group of about seventy-five singers who offered three concerts a year, singing Broadway tunes and sacred songs.

"What more do I want?" I asked myself, not bothering to look for the cons. "I have my own place and my mother has hers." As Snagglepuss had done, I accepted my surroundings.

After a few months, Darcy asked whether she could have a party and I agreed, "As long as I'm in the house somewhere and there's no liquor," I told her. On the night of the party, which she and her friends planned without any help from me, the boys moved my television set into the bedroom so I could watch my favorite programs. Occasionally, one of Darcy's friends popped in and sat with me for a while, taking a break from the party.

At 11:30, John, the tallest, stuck his head in the room to ask what time I wanted the party to end. We agreed on 12:00 and he called out to the party-goers, "Okay, we have another half-hour." The crowd cleaned up and everyone was gone by midnight.

One of my top memories from that time still brings a smile. Darcy and her friends played guitars as everyone did in the sixties. Each night, in the slowly darkening living room, she picked out tunes and sang softly. I loved the pleasant sound as I worked in the kitchen. Even now I can close my eyes, picture the kitchen, hear the soft music and let the nostalgia claim me.

Another happy memory returns from time to time. As I said, it was the sixties. St. Mark's formed a bond with St. Stephen's Episcopal Church in Roxbury, a neighborhood close to Boston and made up mostly of African-American residents. We sponsored a program within that church to bring students from Roxbury to attend Foxboro High School. They stayed with host families and were taken back to Roxbury each Friday to spend the weekend at home. We decided to invite those young people of St. Stephen's who were not in the program to Foxboro for a weekend. I volunteered to have Paula with us. Darcy took her to a high school dance. At mealtime, we shared our hopes and dreams. Paula wanted to work in the medical field. My only regret is that we lost touch with each other after that weekend so I can only hope she reached her goal.

Both Snagglepuss and I were branching out, living life differently and accepting new ways of thinking. I liked it and it appeared he did, too.

OUT OF THE RUT

UNLIKE HER SMALL-CHILD QUESTIONS, the one Darcy asked early in 1967 stumped me. As a junior looking forward to her senior and final year at Foxboro High School, she wanted to know, "Where do you think I should go to college?" I had to confess that, as a high school graduate only, I knew nothing about choosing or applying for colleges.

"Okay," she said, "I'll ask the Guidance Counselor." A few days later I was told, "She'd like to talk with you." I made an appointment.

"You're in a perfect position," the Guidance Counselor explained, "to choose any college Darcy wants to attend. Her grades are excellent and your income qualifies you for all kinds of help, including scholarships," but even with her assurances, the question overwhelmed me. I could handle physical challenges and all the emotional letdowns I'd had over the years, but was woefully ignorant of the complexities of seeking higher education. My boss, Cy, suggested visiting campuses but where would I start and what should I do to take advantage of the help available? It was easier to procrastinate by telling myself we had another year to think about it.

One thing I knew for certain - I was tired. *I need a break before she goes to college because that's a four-year commitment.* Another thought hit me. *She might not want to come back to Foxboro permanently. It won't matter where I live when she's in college. Maybe I should have gone to California with Barbara when she asked me to go back in 1948.* As in the comic strips, a light bulb of an idea appeared above my head. *Maybe I should visit Barbara and find out whether I like California.*

I didn't tell anybody until I had all information and a plan. *I' ll go by bus so I can see the country and not just fly over it. Besides, a bus ride will be cheaper. I have three weeks' vacation. Might as well take it all.* For reasons only I could understand, I decided to go alone, to be away from the responsibilities of being a parent.

Barbara was thrilled when I called. My family urged me to do it. "Darcy can stay with me," Ruthie said. Darcy didn't seem to mind which pleased me because I couldn't explain, without hurting her, why I wasn't taking her. Snagglepuss, who was getting old, could stay with our local veterinarian.

Amazingly, the day in October of 1967 arrived and the whole family saw me off at the Providence Greyhound terminal. The driver climbed aboard, revved the idling engine and I was on my way to California! Of course I had to sing silently, *California, here I come.*

We stopped at Greyhound "Post Houses" where we had thirty minutes to eat and use the facilities. Passengers on short trips traveled between cities meaning your seat partner changed from time to time. A lady several years my senior, heading back home to Iowa after visiting relatives in Illinois, boarded at Great Lakes, our first stop. She told me many stories of the history of Iowa before saying goodbye in Chicago, where we stayed for forty-five minutes. If you could both eat and take a shower in that amount of time, the rest room had showers. I opted for a quick wash-off at one of the numerous sinks.

A senior gentleman boarding in Chicago removed his black Stetson for the ride as he sat down next to me. "I'm heading home to the Black Hills," he told me. "My grandparents left Illinois in a covered wagon to settle there." Wide-eyed, I listened to his tales, occasionally glancing out the window, overcome by the vastness of America. New England's charming abundance of trees had gradually given way to rolling open fields that encircled farmhouses and stretched endlessly as we traveled through Iowa and Nebraska. The words to *America* came to mind. *Oh, beautiful, for spacious skies, for amber waves of grain…"*

In Nebraska, three men on horseback urging one lone steer toward a herd caught my attention. *Cowboys.* There was so much to see. "Entering Wyoming," a sign read. I turned back to my seat partner when he said, "I'll be leaving the bus in Rock Springs." Silently, I tasted the name. *Rock Springs, Wyoming. Little Violet will be in Rock Springs, Wyoming.* Tears filled my eyes at the thought. Soon I spotted low, long hills. *Mesas.* Eagerly I looked for other signs, thrilled to see one for Laramie, even though we wouldn't be stopping there.

Soon after that, the bus pulled over to the curb. My seat partner stood up, put on his hat, bowed to me and said he had enjoyed my company. "Have a great trip home," I said, adding that I had enjoyed his company, too, and that I wanted to say I had actually set foot in Wyoming. I trailed after him and strolled around the corner before returning to the bus.

A young Native American woman heading home to Los Angeles took the empty seat. She seemed quiet and shy. We didn't talk much but she told me she had been back to the reservation visiting her relatives. I forgot to ask which tribe.

Shortly after nightfall, we entered the pitch-black Wasatch range and I fell asleep. The driver's voice woke me around midnight. Speaking in a soft southwestern accent, he announced we would soon be outside Salt Lake City. *Salt Lake City.* At that moment I briefly regretted not having left at a different time. *I'd have gone through here in the daylight and could have seen the Mormon Temple and the lake itself.* My regrets faded when I caught sight of the city lights strewn like sparkling diamonds in the valley below us as we descended into the city and circled the lake. I strained to catch sight as much as possible of the city, before the darkness closed in again. "I can see why Brigham Young stopped here," I commented to the young lady, but she just smiled. The comfortable seats lulled me to sleep until the morning sun woke me. I found the unfamiliar dry desert landscape interesting, but the sentinel mountains held my attention. The history of the valiant pioneers flowed through my mind and I understood more fully the challenges they must have faced.

We stopped in Nevada. *Las Vegas. I'm in Las Vegas. Wow!* I scrambled off the bus, anxious to call home. It wasn't hard to find a store where I could exchange paper money for quarters. Naively, I didn't at first realize that's what everyone does in Las Vegas. The clerk smiled. I tried to explain, "I want to call home," but she just smiled some more.

Ruthie answered. "Where are you?" Choked by my emotions, I couldn't speak for a second.

Finally I was able to squeak out, 'I'm in Las Vegas." She put Darcy on the other phone. There was so much to say that I tried to crowd it all in, telling them, "I wish now that I had gone by way of San Francisco, but it's been a wonderful trip." We talked some more before I checked my watch, said a regretful goodbye and hurried back to the bus.

Our route lay through Bakersfield where I took a picture of a small house with a horse standing just outside the front door. I laughed. *I'm not in New England any more.* Another thought struck me as we drove in our air-conditioned bus through Death Valley. *How awful it must have been to do this in a covered wagon, walking beside it or bumping along inside it, tired and probably thirsty and wondering when it would end.* Once more I silently saluted them.

Four days after leaving Providence, we pulled into Los Angeles. I marveled at the thought, gazing out the bus window like a curious child. A dry cement runway which ran under the highway puzzled me. I didn't learn until later that it was a riverbed. The rows and rows of palm trees and encircling mountains looked the same as they did in all the photos of Los Angeles but seeing the real thing thrilled me. When the bus stopped, I stepped out into the vibrant atmosphere of southern California.

Barbara was waiting with her teen-aged children, Suzan and Gary. We hugged and chatted excitedly. On the way to their house, I heard giggles from the back seat when I mentioned our *cellar.*

In the whir and whirl of my visit, Barbara and her husband, Bill, took their country cousin to Disneyland where I rode in a teacup, climbed an artificial Alp and sang "It's a Small World" in a tunnel.

I watched "Lincoln" give a speech on a stage and heard the sounds of the swamp on a ride through a jungle. At Universal Studios, I had my picture taken in "jail" and posed with two stunt men. We visited the Universal prop area high on a hill above the studio where I lifted a "boulder." At Knott's Berry Farm, I had my picture taken sitting next to a "prospector" on a bench. At a live television show, I heard Pat Boone sing. Outside the studio, Barbara and I walked to the corner of Hollywood and Vine where I saw the Hollywood sign standing tall up in the hills. Barbara and Bill had just installed a pool in their back yard, teasing me by saying, "It's a present for your 42nd birthday" which was on the 11th of October.

For thirteen magical days, I lived in a totally different environment but by the 17th of October, I had suffered through a bout of homesickness and was ready to see Foxboro again.

I thanked Barbara and Bill for their wonderful hospitality and bid them a tearful goodbye. The driver pulled out onto the freeway and we headed toward the distant mountains.

One particularly steep one seemed to be blocking our way but to my delight, we didn't go around it but climbed it, laboring up to where I could see clearly deep into the canyon and could also notice that we had no guard rails. The ride down the other side turned wild as we zipped around curves and once more I stared into the abyss and also observed white crosses at the side of the road. Later, when I asked about them, I was told, "Oh, that's where cars went over and people were killed." I'm grateful I didn't know that.

In Flagstaff, Arizona, I boarded another bus in order to visit the Grand Canyon. We arrived at Bright Angel Lodge on the east rim and I walked through the lobby mesmerized by the breathtaking view ahead of me, tears again streaming down my cheeks. At the edge, I just stood and drank it all in before wandering along the rim, trying to capture it on camera before boarding a sightseeing bus for more spectacular views. I wanted to stay longer but had to get back to Flagstaff to pick up the cross-country bus.

We passed through Albuquerque at night. Outside the city, I settled in the seat for a rest just before the bus broke down. The driver went inside a restaurant to call for another bus and left the door open. That's when I discovered how cold the desert can be at night, another new experience.

An hour later, on the replacement bus, we rolled through Amarillo, Texas, a pretty city with tree-lined streets. Signs along the way told us we were traveling on portions of the old Route 66 with its motels and diners left over from the 30's and 40's. The driver still announced the high points in an easy-to-listen-to accent. On a bridge over the Mississippi, he suggested we look down and later said we were heading north toward Columbus, Ohio, before we reached our last stop before Providence which was Pittsburgh.

Those of us crossing the country had become a "family." I bid goodbye to the last of my friends at Pittsburgh and changed to another bus and another driver. I found myself crammed up against the window in a three-passenger seat and heard nothing from the driver until we had passed through Pennsylvania and New York. "Next stop, Providence." His short announcement and familiar nasal tone made me chuckle. *I'm home.*

The sight of my family waiting at the terminal brought a lump to my throat and another one arose when I saw the sign, "Entering Foxboro." My trip had shown me the opportunities and grandeur of our country, but it had also opened my eyes to the blessings in my life. I could handle graduation and college. This was my home, the right place for me and I planned to stay for a long time.

Grandma Grayson's
senior citizen
apartment, 1966

Violet and Darcy,
Maple Avenue, 1967

Snagglepuss at Maple
Avenue, 1966

Gary, Suzan, Barbara,
Bill, October, 1967

Barbara and Violet in the
pool, October, 1967

Violet at Universal Studios
Prop Hill, October, 1967

Bus in Columbus, Ohio, October, 1967

DEAN

H E CAME TOWARD ME as I waited on the sidewalk to cross Neponset Avenue to the Foxboro Company cafeteria. I stared. *I know him.* I turned to speak but he looked right past me and I shook my head slightly to clear it. *No, I don't know him,* but it was too late. I had mutated into a forty-two-year-old teenager with a tremendous crush on the stranger-yet-not-a-stranger on the sidewalk. Each day for two weeks, in that fall of 1967, I lingered at that corner in order to "accidentally" run into him. My plan was to smile and speak and ask casually where we had met, but I waited in vain as he didn't show up again. Toward the end of the two weeks, I didn't wait but walked along the sidewalk, heading to another Foxboro Company building to meet a friend for lunch. There he was, coming toward me, making me giddy in my anticipation. *Now's my chance to ask where we met.* He didn't slow his pace or acknowledge me. I could have been invisible. The crush left my body and I returned to mature-woman status.

Several weeks passed before someone at St. Mark's church asked, "Have you met our new member, Dean? He works at the Foxboro Company and comes to the 8:00 A.M. service." Aha! I attended the 11:00 A.M. service and besides, I had been in California for three weeks. No, I had neither met nor seen him prior to that day on the sidewalk. *Strange.*

Following my return from California, in my search for a new path, I heard about a newly-formed group of Parents Without Partners. Many of the members had children younger than Darcy but I enjoyed the conversations, hearing of new ways to deal with my single-parent state and offering my own suggestions for problems others might be having. I volunteered to hold a meeting at my house. By then, even though we had not become acquainted, Dean had lost his mystique. In bits and pieces, I discovered he was divorced, had two teenage sons and was a recovering alcoholic, sober in Alcoholics Anonymous for three and a half years. He made no secret of his addiction, sharing his story in the hope he could help others. . He also, to my surprise, lived across the street from our apartment on Maple Avenue. We were neighbors. *I think I'll invite him to the meeting.*

One night after work, I waited near the exit that most of the employees used. He appeared in the crowd, walking with a woman. "Hello, Dean," I said, "I'm Violet. You don't know me but we both go to St. Mark's Church." I told him about the meeting. In a deep and pleasant voice, he replied, very politely, that he was sorry but much of his time was taken up with A.A.

"This is Ann," he added. "She just began working here." She smiled and stared for a second. I smiled back and left it at that.

Our church sold Christmas trees that year as a special project. When I stopped to look them over, I saw Dean helping with the sales and waved to him. Several months later, in the spring of 1968, I arrived at church just as he was leaving and had to pass my car. He smiled and asked, 'How are you?" catching me at a time when I felt particularly exasperated with some personal setbacks and my life in general. I spilled out my frustration, considering him a friend. He pulled out a business card and said, "Call me if you'd like to talk." I thanked him, tucked the card into my purse and hurried into church.

I let the card sit in my purse for several weeks but, alone at home on a Sunday night in May of 1968, I felt the need to talk with someone about a small problem, remembered the card and called Dean. "I'll be right over," he said. I had barely hung up before he was knocking on my door.

He gave me little chance to explain my problem before launching into the story of his alcoholism. "I lost my family, my job, everything and ended up in Foxboro State Hospital with just the clothes on my back but I'm grateful to be alive and sober." he said, adding that his whole life revolved around Alcoholics Anonymous, which included the responsibility of making sure the A.A. meeting continued at the hospital. He made the coffee, set up the chairs and saw to it that a group came in to put on the meeting.

"I have a car now but didn't for the first year." He smiled at the memory. "I walked all over town. I felt safe here and free. There were no bars that I could walk into – just package stores which made it a little more difficult to get a drink. It was wonderful. My brother, Jack, moved in with me and found work with The Foxboro Company as a draftsman." I asked about Dean's own work. "I'm in Plant Accounting," he explained. "We keep track of the cost of manufacturing the instruments. I started out in the factory but when this job came open, Personnel suggested I apply for it. I like it."

Conversation flowed easily between us. I shared some details of my story but didn't mention the original small problem that had prompted the call. It no longer seemed important. As he stood to leave, he asked, "Would you like to go to an A.A. meeting on Tuesday night?" Assuming I'd just be one of his passengers, I said I would.

I told him I'd meet him outside on Tuesday so he wouldn't have to climb the stairs to the third floor. We were halfway to the meeting place, just the two of us, when I recognized it as a *date*. Oh! At the meeting, he introduced me to his friends who all smiled and said they were glad to meet me. He brought me a cup of coffee from the pot that seemed bottomless. I soon learned it was the life-blood of every meeting. No matter whether the group consisted of two or twenty, the coffee had to be made and the cups set out. An atmosphere of hope permeated the stories and pervaded the room as the speakers revealed what had brought them there. Each one expressed gratitude for having "come to the doors of A.A." I could, even as a non-alcoholic, *identify* with that feeling of having stepped into a new life. I immediately felt at home and knew I had made the right decision to get to know

Dean better. Listening to the speakers' stories taught me a little about alcoholism. I liked the positive way they spoke of being sober and doing things they never thought possible. Some were professionals with college degrees, some were blue-collar workers and some were housewives but the "anonymous" part of the program took care of that. In that room, they were all alcoholics.

On the way home, Dean filled in other parts of his story. "I left college just short of a degree in Accounting because I wanted to get married but mostly because studying got in the way of my drinking. My wife, Edith, filed for divorce some time before I sobered up." He paused slightly before admitting, "I don't blame her."

He asked whether I'd like to go out for dinner on Friday night and I said, "Yes." I had no qualms or nervousness about seeing him again.

No unanswered questions lay between us, as though we had known each other a long time.

After dinner, we attended another A.A. meeting. That night he strongly suggested I attend the Al-Anon meeting being held in a separate room for families of alcoholics. I dutifully listened at the meeting but thought, "I'll never need this." He kissed me when we returned to the car and said, "You're wonderful." I knew I'd be seeing more of him and I welcomed the idea. It held no qualms or fears or doubts. It just felt right.

In another area of my life, Darcy had been receiving and reviewing replies from the colleges she contacted with the Guidance Counselors' help, plus suggestions from high school friends. Oberlin College in Oberlin, Ohio, made the most promising offer which included an almost full scholarship. The University of Massachusetts also gave her a generous offer. When I read the letter from Oberlin, I commented, without asking what she wanted to do, "I don't see how we can pass that up." She replied to it and we began planning what needed to be done before she left for college.

With the wisdom of hindsight, I can easily understand what a confusing time it was for both of us. I was losing Darcy but Dean had walked into my life. I've chastised myself many times for not being of more help to Darcy and not allowing her to make up her own mind but mine was doing somersaults.

For the next two weeks, I attended more A.A. meetings with Dean and also filled him in, one night as we sat on the couch in my living room, on my experience with Carl and the "engagement ring." I had already told him about Paul and he knew the story of my first marriage as well as the various letdowns I had endured through the years. He didn't make any comments but asked, "When will Darcy be home for her first holiday?" I guessed it would most likely be Thanksgiving. "I'll be right back," he said and left for home, mumbling that he had to look at a calendar.

A short time later, he returned and with no hesitation, knelt in front of me. "I love you," he said. "Will you marry me on November 30th?" I remember so well that I wanted to shout, "Yes! Yes! Yes!" but said it quietly, having no trouble whatsoever in assuring him I loved him and would marry him. No undercurrent of doubt held me back. For the first time in my life, I truly loved a man. It had nothing to do with wanting a father for Darcy or of being tired of being alone. I just knew he was the one I had been seeking.

He told me later that he chose November 30th because it would give us six months to get to know each other and Darcy would be home on her first break from college. His other reason was to save me from embarrassment and having to make excuses when anyone wondered about the "big day." He loved me and wanted to marry me. He also explained that he urged me, on our second date, to attend Al-Anon because he had already decided he wanted to marry me and thought Al-Anon would be a big help to me.

It still thrills me to remember the miracle of knowing him before I met him. Some friends tried to convince me I must have seen him at church, but I knew I hadn't and never doubted that I was given a glimpse of my future but a happy glimpse, unlike the one I had as I stood alone on the steps of Christ Church in 1949.

Incidentally, he told me that his friend, Ann, his girlfriend at the time, said, as soon as I walked away. "You're going to marry her."

1968

DARCY, WHEN I GAVE her the news the next day, wasn't as thrilled as I had expected but shrugged and accepted the news, confessing that it seemed too late and it would have been more welcome news to her when she was younger. I have to assume, too, that she reasoned she'd be leaving for college in the fall, anyway. She wandered into bedroom and flopped on her bed. I followed and sat at the foot of the bed, no words crowding in my throat for several minutes but finally coming to me. "Just give him a chance," I asked. She reminded me years later of those words and thanked me for saying them.

As soon as possible and before we told our friends, we broke the news to our minister, Walter, to be sure we could have that date. With that settled, we immediately told my family and our friends. My sister, brother-in-law and mother all greeted the news joyfully. At last, Violet was getting married and they'd no longer have to worry about her being alone and, besides that, they liked Dean. We all laughed at his comment to my mother. "We've already met." She hadn't remembered his name but recognized him and agreed that they had met. In order to become part of the St. Mark's Church family, in the fall of 1967, he had been part of the Stewardship campaign. The practice in those days was to visit each member of the church to talk about pledging an amount for the following year. Although my mother wasn't a member, she was on Dean's list as a possibility. Before we had our first date, he and my mother sat in her apartment and talked.

Also, Dean confessed to me that Frank, our former minister, told him about a woman in church who was a single parent with a daughter.

Frank felt we might make a good couple. The day we met and I invited him to the Parents Without Partners meeting, he realized I was the woman Frank had discussed. By then Frank had been called to a church on Long Island but was working as a chaplain at a summer camp in northern New England before joining his new church. We asked Walter whether he had any objections to sharing the ceremony with Frank and he graciously said he'd enjoy it. Dean and I drove to the camp to tell Frank and his wife, Barbara, who were overjoyed to hear our happy news. He promised he'd be there to help officiate.

Darcy's graduation day arrived on June 11, 1968. As I watched her, solemn in her cap and gown, move with her classmates down the aisle to take her assigned seat and await the awarding of her diploma, emotions welled up in me – pride in her, that she had come to this point, for one, and that this lovely young lady was my daughter. I knew I'd miss those moments when she played her guitar in the living room while I prepared our evening meal in the kitchen and I grieved for that. I'd miss the moments of pride when I watched her, along with a friend and my niece, Janet, playing and singing in the concerts occasionally held on the Common. I thought back to the day she and her friends went shopping for dresses for graduation night, to show off when they removed their robes. She called to tell me the price of the one she had chosen and I told her she could buy it.

I'd miss the lively chatter of her friends coming in to visit, calling out, 'Hi, Auntie Vi," a name they'd picked up from my nieces who also attended Foxboro High School. I'd miss those patterns, yet the new ones dazzled my senses, making it difficult to concentrate on what still lay in front of us.

I planned a small graduation party in our apartment and invited friends and relatives, including Don and Dot, not expecting that they'd attend. They surprised me twice, once by coming and again by giving Darcy a check for $100. We all laughed and congratulated Darcy on the fact that her life had moved into a new phase.

Immediately after graduation, I forced myself to consider what she'd need for college – a portable typewriter, a foot locker for her dorm room, a small lamp, a suitcase and a clock, as starters. I consulted A A A for directions to Oberlin, Ohio. I was given a map with the route plainly marked on it - the Massachusetts Turnpike out through the Berkshires, Route 90 at the New York border, a drive across the top of New York to Buffalo and Erie, Pennsylvania, a turn south toward the Ohio Turnpike and another turn south near Cleveland to find Oberlin and the college. My boss at The Foxboro Company suggested that Darcy and I tour the campus first to know what to expect but doing that twice in that particular year was way beyond anything my mind could grasp. I thanked him but didn't even consider it. I'd done all I could to prepare her, I told myself, yet worried that I should be doing so much more. I needed to reassure her I was still her mother and that Dean would make a good step-father, but couldn't find the way to put that into words, especially to a teen- ager on the verge of leaving home for an extended stay for the first time. On the other hand, I wanted to let go of my responsibilities and turn her loose and let her establish her own path. I had my own path to follow and convinced myself I had fulfilled my motherly duties. I was tired. I'd been a single parent for almost eighteen years.

I felt I was looking through a kaleidoscope, its patterns wild and changing. I recall that Darcy found a summer job working at a motel on Route 1. I knew Craig, the boyfriend she'd met during her junior year at Foxboro High, was home for the summer from Slippery Rock College in Pennsylvania. He had been in the Foxboro High School Class of 1967. I liked him and liked the family and felt she'd found her future, but just before she left for college she confided to me that she wanted to start college feeling *free*, with no entanglements and had broken the news gently to him. Despite that, he would be riding along with us to Ohio. From there, he'd hitchhike back to Pennsylvania.

Sometime during the summer, another turn of the kaleidoscope took us to Northwood, New Hampshire, so I could meet Dean's two sons, Peter, fifteen, and Mark, thirteen, who lived with their mother and step-father. The introductions went well and confirmed to me that I'd made a good choice. I liked Peter and Mark and their mother, Edith, and was glad I'd be seeing the boys at our wedding. I had already met Dean's best man, his brother, Jack. Two other brothers and their wives lived in Binghamton and Schenectady, New York, but wouldn't be at the wedding. Though I felt I was watching images in a kaleidoscope, I didn't feel frightened at the pace of the changes in my life. All of the pieces fell into place as though they had been planned for a long time.

On August 29th, we celebrated Darcy's 18th birthday. A few days later, I kissed Dean goodbye and promised to call as soon as we arrived in Oberlin. With Darcy's bicycle securely strapped to the new roof rack and with Ruth, Craig and Darcy in the car, I backed out of the driveway and headed for I-95 and Ohio. Her other belongings had somehow been stashed in the trunk. A grown-up Darcy was leaving and I hadn't had time to absorb all that was happening.

Finding the college and getting Darcy settled there still had to be accomplished, plus welcoming her home for her first college break just before our marriage and moving on to begin our own adjustment to a new life as husband and wife. The kaleidoscope had not yet stopped spinning.

MORE OF 1968

W ITH THE IMAGES ON the kaleidoscope dazzling me, I lost sight of the changes swirling through Darcy's life, taking it for granted that she would welcome the adventure that lay ahead for her. She may have been apprehensive or she may have been looking forward to living in a different state, miles away from her life in Foxboro. I don't know and have often regretted that I didn't tune in to that excitement or that I failed to answer any questions troubling her because I was caught up in my own blissful world.

On the other hand, communication can be a problem during the inconsistent teen years. That added to the stress I experienced at being torn between my concern for my child and my duty to myself. I clearly remember the relief that flowed through me when I saw Oberlin College for the first time and felt she had come to the right place.

It's described in brochures as "a four-year, highly selective liberal arts college and conservatory of music. Founded in 1833 by a Presbyterian minister and a missionary, it holds a distinguished place among American colleges and universities. It was the first college to grant bachelor's degrees to women in a co-educational environment and, historically, was a leader in the education of African Americans". I knew none of that at the time but only perceived that it looked safe and appealing.

We found Darcy's dorm room and carried in the foot locker and all of the other things that had been stuffed in the trunk. She looked around, "Well, it's small but it's nice," she said, adding, "I guess she hasn't arrived yet," referring to the student who would share the room with her. We piled everything in one corner next to one of the built-in desks and nodded in agreement that it was a pleasant room. Once more, the comfortable feeling washed over me.

Darcy said, "Let's check out the campus." Except for the dormitories and other campus buildings surrounding the square in the center of the campus, it reminded me of Foxboro Common. Pathways crossed from all of the four corners and sides of it with shade trees and benches adding the finishing touch. "Darcy can sit on one of the benches and study for the next test," I commented, noting at the same time that the climate felt similar to the New England climate. She wouldn't have to adjust to different weather conditions.

We all agreed that calling Oberlin a city seemed overambitious because it's more like a big, small town or was in 1968. We didn't see any high rise buildings or other typical city sights. Ruthie remarked that Darcy's bicycle would come in very handy.

We found the city center and stepped into a small restaurant to have something to eat and sit for a while to review the day. I thought about Craig. He said goodbye to all of us when we stopped on the outskirts of Oberlin to ask for directions. I gave silent thanks that the parting had been less dramatic than I had anticipated..

After our meal, we browsed around the campus. Darcy pointed to a building just outside of the campus. "I wonder what's in that?". It turned out to be the library. We attempted to see as much as we could before Ruthie and I started back to Massachusetts. For some inexplicable reason which came out of the jumble of thoughts in my mind, I had decided not to stay the night in Oberlin. It was tied in with my fear, during the years of single parenthood, of running out of money, plus my need to get back to Dean and the security he represented. We hugged Darcy and said our goodbyes. As we drove out of Oberlin, I glanced back. A stab of pain and guilt shot through me. She stood alone, next to a tree, waving forlornly, an image I've never been able to erase from my memory. I looked quickly away and concentrated on driving and the road ahead that would take us back to Foxboro and Dean and my new life.

As soon as possible, I immersed myself in preparing for the wedding. "Let's go shopping," I suggested to Ruthie who would be my matron-of-honor. At the South Shore Mall in Braintree, I found a rose-colored knit suit, the style at the time. We both smiled when Ruthie found a light blue one, similar in style. "I want to wear a small hat, maybe something that's mostly a veil," I told her, "and I'll carry a prayer book and a tiny spray of flowers."

In an effort to include everyone, Dean and I agreed not to send out invitations but to depend on word-of-mouth and to welcome anyone who wanted to attend. He had friends in A.A. and several from his younger years, besides his sons. I had friends from church and childhood buddies and relatives. We shrugged and said we'd manage somehow if more people showed up than we had expected.

Just before Thanksgiving, we picked Darcy up at Logan Airport. She had a lot to tell us but I confess that I barely listened, my mind consumed with the wedding. At home, I told her, "I've put out your yellow dress. It looks very nice on you," Although it had been one of her favorites, it was the 60's and she wanted something different. With no time to go shopping with her, I let her choose her own. She settled on a navy dress with slim white stripes which looked good on her but I'd had a brighter color in mind. Thanksgiving must have come and gone and I imagine we had a family dinner but I have no definite memories of it.

I do, however, have a clear recollection of every detail of the Saturday after Thanksgiving when I walked up the aisle of St. Mark's Episcopal Church on the arm of my brother-in-law, Tom. I heard Mary, our organist and choir director at St. Mark's, who had graciously donated her time, playing "Here Comes the Bride." Behind me was the brief time of anxiety that preceded the wedding when I kept checking my watch and the door because Dean hadn't arrived. "Sorry," he said as he rushed in a few minutes before the designated time. "I was showing my boys around Foxboro."

At last, the ceremony began and I was actually marrying a man I truly loved and feeling the joy of it. Tom gave me away. I repeated the vows and heard Dean repeat his and smiled when Walter said, "You may kiss the bride." As husband and wife, we walked down the aisle, bonded forever by our vows, smiling in our happiness.

Our guests lined up in the area we called the Common Room, to hug us or shake our hands. "I've set out the cupcakes and the tea and coffee," my niece, Jan, told me, "and I'll make sure everybody gets a piece of cake." Among the seventy-five guests were Darcy's old gang, most home from college for the first time. Suddenly, through the hum of conversation, I heard music. Tears rose in my eyes. The gang, who had sung along with Darcy in the high school a cappella choir and had helped us move into our apartment, did an impromptu chorus, as their gift to us, of a sacred song that had been part of their repertoire. I didn't think I could ever be happier in my life.

Among the guests were my Aunt Alice (who was actually my father's first cousin), who lived about fifty miles away in Lowell, Massachusetts, and her daughter, Hilda, and two grandchildren. Ruth, my childhood friend, and her husband, were there to help us celebrate. My heart swelled when I looked around at the people who wanted to be there on our special day. Dean and I did our best to greet and chat a little bit with all of our guests and had the first piece of cake so that Jan could pass it out to the others.

Around 1:00 P.M. Dean commented, "We should start soon." Our family offered to clean up the Common Room. We thanked them, hugged them all goodbye and hurried home to change clothes. Darcy planned to stay with Ruth and Tom and I had boarded Snagglepuss with the veterinarian.

We stopped for lunch in a restaurant on Route 1 before covering much of the same route that Ruthie, Darcy, Craig and I had followed in August, but were headed to Binghamton, New York, to meet Dean's brother, Bill, his wife, Doris, and their two daughters. I stroked and admired the gold band on my left hand from time to time, feeling its strangeness yet also feeling its assurance. I was married. I had in-laws. Darcy had a step-father.

We didn't talk a lot on the drive, feeling at home in each other's presence and knowing we had years ahead of us for conversation. In Binghamton, we called Bill from the lobby of the hotel. "I'll be right there," he said. We met and hugged and he invited us to dinner that night. I immediately liked him and the rest of his family and was glad we had included that visit on our honeymoon. Their cozy house and hospitality gave me a secure feeling.

The next morning, we gazed down into the lovely Shenandoah Valley in Virginia from the Skyline Drive and the Blue Ridge Mountains, a trip that Dean had planned for our honeymoon. The magic of the trip stayed with me all the way to Waynesboro, Virginia, our next overnight stay. In the morning, heading north once more for a hotel in Bridgeport, Connecticut, we encountered a snowstorm but it didn't dim our happiness. Dean ran out of cigarettes. I strolled through the snow with him to find a drugstore, enjoying the role of being his wife.

On our return to Foxboro, he lost no time in carting his few belongings across Maple Avenue to what was now "our" apartment. "This is my dowry," he laughed, plopping down a box which held twelve *Women's Day* cookbooks. He had collected them, one by one, when they were offered by the now defunct magazine, and were crammed full of marvelous recipes. His mother had taught him to cook years earlier, a skill he utilized in the army and in his last job as a cook before he found sobriety. "I'll take care of our Christmas meal," he offered, much to my delight. It became our first tradition and one that allowed me to relax every holiday. The cookbooks, though looking time-worn and ragged, are still with me and I continue to use them and treasure them.

OUR FIRST CHRISTMAS

ITH THE PERMISSION OF Home Life magazine, I'm reprinting a story published in their December 1988 issue. It describes the first Christmas Dean and I and Darcy shared and tells it more eloquently than I could if I tried to re-write it. After that first Christmas, life settled into an easier pattern, our love deepened and we lived through what I call The Golden Years as a family that consisted of me, Darcy, Dean, my mother, Ruthie, Tom, Janet, Marilyn and Ann. I thought it would last forever and be my way of life until I died and I was fine with that.

I've never forgotten that stroll through the cold, peaceful night.

IN 1968, TWENTY-FOUR days before Christmas, I received what I believed to be the best present possible when I married the man of my dreams. The following year, another gift proved to be even more meaningful, one that would last a lifetime.

I met this man, my second husband, when my daughter was seventeen and I'd been a divorced, single parent for sixteen years. We worked for the same local firm, attended the same church, and lived on the same street. During the course of a year, we became friends. I learned he also was divorced, was a recovering alcoholic, and had two teen sons living in another state.

One day in May of 1968, he asked me to accompany him to a meeting of the self-help fellowship he attended. That turned out to be our first date.

Two weeks later, he asked me to marry him. Six months later, on November 30, 1968, we were married. I felt as though I'd known him all my life, yet I scarcely knew him. I *did* know he was a kind and compassionate person. I knew he'd do his best to be a friend to my daughter. I didn't know about his moods at Christmas. I learned of them three weeks later when he descended into a deep depression.

This is not uncommon for

Christmas Comes Again

A wife learns the difference between support and interference

by Violet Grayson Lawton

recovering alcoholics, but that was something else I didn't know. It was eventually explained to me that my husband felt profoundly inadequate when faced with the "season to be jolly." Especially during that period in his developing maturity, he felt unable to love enough or give enough to be worthy of the whole aspect of Christmas. Even though he did everything in his power to make Christmas happy and meaningful for other persons, it wasn't enough to satisfy himself.

She Tried to Cheer Him
On the other hand, my Christmases usually had been joyful and family oriented, with much hugging and kissing. I was therefore confused,

© 1988, Jim Har[...]

naturally assuming it was up to me to *do* something. That consisted of following him from room to room in our small apartment, trying to cheer him up, and wringing my hands when it didn't work. I blamed myself for his silence, even while he continued to assure me it wasn't my fault. I felt helpless and hurt, but didn't give up. After all, I was his new bride, and I loved him. Who else could bring him out of it?

On Christmas Eve, prior to the midnight service at church, we attended a meeting of the alcoholic self-help group. He became himself again during the meeting, laughing and joking with his friends. I was devastated. I'd tried everything—me, his loving wife—and I had been unsuccessful. A few minutes with other alcoholics and he was out of his depression.

I couldn't handle it. On the way to church, I cried hysterically, pouring out my hurt and jealousy, accusing him of being selfish and uncaring. Somehow we struggled through the midnight service and the following day, maintaining a facade for our family's sake. The Christmas season passed, we made up, and our life together continued.

It wasn't until the following May that I also joined a self-help group to learn about myself and alcoholism. I

discovered that people cannot be made happy simply because of another's love. Happiness must begin inside a person. What I could do was express my love, give encouragement, and place my husband in God's hands.

I learned I had to allow my husband the dignity of being responsible for his own peace of mind. With guidance, I found I could care deeply but remain serene, even as he appeared to be suffering. In the past, I had only added to his burden by insisting on suffering with him. I was told that two drowning people can't save each other.

Another Christmas Scene
I continued attending meetings while life with my new husband improved daily. The Christmas of 1969, just after our first anniversary, I watched my love sink into his yearly depression. This time I said a prayer for him and assured him of my devotion. I went on to have a glorious Christmas, laughing and talking with friends, writing cards, wrapping presents, and enjoying every minute.

On Christmas Eve, our small New England town was picture-perfect under a glistening blanket of snow and a bright moon. I suggested a walk to see the Christmas display in

the center of town. My daughter was busy wrapping last minute presents and my husband declined, so I went alone.

I've never forgotten that stroll through the cold, peaceful night. The spirit of the season was all around me—in the lights, the snow-laden trees, the silent adoration of the figures in the creche, and in my heart. A perfect touch would have been a chorus singing, "Glory to God."

On my return walk, uplifted and awed by the experience, I knew I'd done something wonderful for myself and my family, giving us an unparalleled gift of respect and space. The day after Christmas, my husband confirmed my feeling when he thanked me for being patient with his mood and for loving him.

Seventeen years later we celebrate Christmas in our individual ways, even while trimming the tree together or unwrapping gifts. He isn't able to share my childish delight in the season, but he is quietly joyful just watching me. His depression appears to be a thing of the past. At any rate, they no longer dominate the Christmas scene. He worked his own way through them, with my *support*, not my *interference*. There's a world of difference. □

MY FORK IN THE ROAD

ANY LONG-HELD, TREASURED IMAGES of walking hand-in-hand down Lovers' Lane with my beloved faded into the mists of reality after that first Christmas. At least it had not discouraged me or caused me to think we had made a mistake. We still loved each other but it had been easier when we could do it from the distance of two separate apartments. On-the-job training to be a happily married couple would take time but I had no idea where to start, even though I had no fantasies about it immediately happening once we had declared eternal love for each other.

On our first venture as a married couple to Fernandes supermarket, Dean grabbed a cart as soon as we entered and began tossing items into it while I walked "six paces behind," stunned and wedged between anger and disbelief. When my voice returned, I said, a little more angrily than I had intended to do, "We need milk."

He paused as though he had forgotten I was with him, but caught on fast. Glancing toward the tiny coffee shop in one corner of the market, he asked, "Would you rather do this while I have coffee?" In answer I reached for the handle of the cart and he retreated to the coffee shop. I had taken it for granted that I'd do the grocery shopping, even though I wouldn't have objected if we had done it together, with him pushing the cart and me filling it with groceries.

During his drinking years, in order to support his family and his habit, he had controlled the income which included the amount spent on groceries. Due to my mother's meager income and the fact that she didn't drive and my limited income, I had done the food buying which gave me control over our budget. Clearly, Dean and I had stumbled upon our first adjustment prior to the Christmas debacle, but had worked it out it before it became troublesome.

The next one proved harder to handle and never really became a closed case. Dean didn't avoid social encounters and was well-liked but labeled himself a *loner*. In Newton High School, he preferred to be the disc jockey for their after-school dances while at the Cumberland High "Socials", I danced with the boys and had fun. "When we lived in Newton," he told me, "I liked to take the *T* (the Massachusetts Bay Transportation Authority) into Boston on Saturday afternoon, go to a movie and sit in the balcony by myself, with a box of popcorn." On one level, that matched my Saturday excursions into Pawtucket to browse alone through the stores, pick up a trinket here and there and feel satisfied. Sometimes, though, I shopped with friends and didn't label myself a *loner*.

By April of 1969, a routine had established itself. I cleaned the house on Saturday morning and the afternoon often found me alone, as I had been before I met Dean, at the South Shore Shopping Center in Braintree, a city near Quincy. He either returned to his job to catch up on something he hadn't finished or visited a counselor at Foxboro State Hospital or an alcoholic who wanted to talk. I'm not sure what I expected but it wasn't that I would continue to spend Saturdays alone. Actually, it was probably the best arrangement for both of us but I rebelled against the feeling of bending to his way of life and not having it reciprocated.

We usually attended an A.A. meeting together on Saturday night as we did on weekdays, something I didn't do as a faithful wife but because I wanted to be with him and hear the stories that came after, "Hello, my name is John and I'm an alcoholic." Even my social life was tied to his alcoholism. In Canton, I walked down the hall to the Al-Anon meetings, as he had suggested. At times, in North Attleboro, I slipped into the Al-Anon meeting but hurried back to wait for him while he chatted with his friends. A few times in Walpole, another neighboring town, I sat in on the Al-Anon meeting, leaving as soon as possible to join him, to immerse myself in his world.

He accompanied me shopping once, before our wedding, to help me find shoes for the occasion. We searched in several malls that day without success and I learned that he clearly was not a browser. In the first shoe store we found at the South Shore mall, he reached into a display and pulled out a pair. I hesitated. They weren't quite what I wanted but I was getting tired, too. I settled for those shoes but never really liked them. He didn't *shop* – he *bought* which precluded any thoughts of strolling through stores with me.

At the meetings, he talked with his friends and I tried to do the same but they soon drifted away. We had nothing on which to base a conversation. They weren't there to chat idly but to get help. I tried to concentrate on the speakers but gradually my first rush of enthusiasm palled, overshadowed by the mixture of anger, resentment and loneliness that had taken seed, causing me to criticize their words or anything else I saw in the room. The meeting in Norwood had no Al-Anon group. One Saturday night, I stared at the hairdo of the woman in front of us which was pulled forward, leaving a thin patch on her crown. *Why doesn't she comb it back? What did the speaker say? Why is everybody laughing?* The thoughts leaned toward anger. *Will I have to trail after him and wait for his attention for the rest of my life?*

We had a lot in common but I tended to focus on the things we didn't have in common. I loved being near the water, for instance, swimming from time to time and sunning the rest of the time whereas Dean confessed, "I always liked sitting on the beach but only as long as I could drink." One day, after listening to my broad hints, he agreed to go but didn't bring a bathing suit. Instead, he stretched out on a towel, fully clothed, even to his shoes, as though to say, "Well, I'm here." That was the last time I urged him to go with me. He found his recreation at Foxboro Raceway, our local track, where he could watch the harness races and do some betting. Though I liked the graceful gait of the trotters as they moved around the oval track, betting held no appeal for me. He also liked to follow the dog races which held even less appeal for me. "I like the challenge of betting," he said. "It's my outlet." I couldn't argue with him in that regard. As a normally quiet- spoken man, he morphed into a yelling, screaming stranger as the horses or dogs flew down the home stretch.

The simple idea of sharing my feelings didn't occur to me. In our family, though we loved each other, flare-ups had been followed by deep, long silences until the injured or angry person "got over it." We didn't talk it out because the "other person" was expected to "know" what he or she had done to cause the flare-up. My parents handled domestic problems as many people did before communication and airing grievances became a better option. Unfortunately, stifling my feelings in what I had anticipated to be a glorious marriage caused my abdominal muscles to tighten, bringing on an occasional sick feeling in my stomach. *I'm 43. Am I pregnant?*

The nausea turned out not to be unfortunate after all. Its part in the solution arrived in a short conversation on the night we walked into a meeting of Dean's home group in Wrentham. After pouring myself a cup of coffee, I spotted a woman I'd seen at the North Attleboro Al-Anon meeting and made a beeline for her. The minute she asked, "How are you?" the dam burst.

I poured out my anguish and ended with, "I feel sick to my stomach and it's tied in knots." I laughed nervously. "I wonder if I'm pregnant."

She touched my hand and asked gently, "Have you thought of Al-Anon?"

"He isn't drinking!"

"He's an alcoholic." Her simple words set me free. Why had I believed he had to be drinking? The meeting began. I thanked her and took a seat next to Dean, clapping as people spoke but not hearing the words, as my decision to join the Canton group solidified. Although it lay the farthest away from Foxboro, I knew the members' names and felt comfortable with them. Dean, when he heard it, applauded my decision with his comment, "Good. I think you'll enjoy it."

The following Friday, the Canton group welcomed me and during the next few weeks, allowed me to vent my unhappiness. No one tried to change my mind or give me advice or rebuke me but they all just listened as I dumped my pile of garbage. With that discarded, I could hear their words telling me Al-Anon would show me the way to help myself just as A.A. helped the alcoholics. I had a place to go! I belonged there! I immersed myself in the positive way of thinking and the philosophy of helping without interfering and allowing others to take responsibility for themselves.

Being in the toddler stage in this *live-and-let-live* way of thinking held my attention, leaving little time to worry or wonder about Darcy until she called to ask a favor. "I have a summer job at Cranberry Cove, in the restaurant. It's a resort area on Cape Cod. Can you go there to make sure I still have it?" In late May, on a blue-domed afternoon in 1969 we went in search of Cranberry Cove only to find it had not yet opened for the season. Immediately, worry took over.

"What will I tell her? If it's closed, how can we check on her job?"

Dean quietly replied, "It's a beautiful day. We're here on the Cape. You can't do anything until we get home so why not just stop worrying and enjoy the day?" His simple lesson in living *one day at a time* did the trick. We were together and were taking care of our daughter. Wasn't that what I wanted? All turned out well. We didn't have to go back to check on the job. We told her it hadn't opened yet for the summer and would let her know when it had opened. She called and had the job. Once she settled in at Cranberry Cove, she asked whether she could borrow my car. We agreed since we used Dean's most of the time. That summer we had several chances to visit her and meet a few of the new friends she'd made.

In September, my almost-a-teenager niece, Ann, went along on the trip back to Oberlin. This time we stayed overnight, giving us a chance to have our evening meal together and show Ann a little of Oberlin. Darcy appeared to have adapted to her fork in the road, but that didn't dispel my uneasy feeling of having abandoned her. It would take many years to accept the fact that I wasn't the only parent who felt that way and to learn that I *had done the best I could with what I had at the time*. On the other hand, I felt a certain relief that I no longer had full responsibility for her. I had taught her as much as I could, based on the wisdom handed down from my parents and would have to hope it would prove to be adequate.

She flew home for Christmas break but that story has already been told.

GETTING TO KNOW YOU

BUILT IN 1889, THE Massachusetts Hospital for Dipsomaniacs and Inebriates in Foxboro, had what was considered state-of-the-art treatment facilities for alcoholics during its early years. It gradually began admitting psychiatric patients and was renamed the Foxboro State Hospital in 1910, accepting mostly psychiatric patients, but still admitting alcoholics who were accompanied by a police officer or another person. At the time Dean and I met, Foxboro State Hospital had two *Institution Meetings,* which are different from the standard-type conducted by a group. They're held in a building such as a hospital or a prison, for instance. One person is responsible for making the coffee and contacting General Service (the A.A. State Office) to be sure an outside group comes to "put on the meeting" which means each person shares his or her story with those in attendance.

At the time I met Dean, alcoholism had been recognized as a *disease,** defining the drinker as a person who had an addiction to the drug of alcohol and not as a drunken sot or a weak sinner. A.A. accepted that explanation. It was helping Dean stay sober and lead a productive life so I accepted it, also, and still do.

Dean's story, which I heard innumerable times, went something like this, "I was working as a second cook in a restaurant in Abington, Massachusetts, in 1964 and it was New Year's Eve. I left my shift and began drinking *viciously*. On New Year's Day, I was too drunk to make

---

* The American Medical Association officially named it an *illness* or *disease* in 1956. They call it a "biological chemical disposition" which is inherited and explain that alcohol "breaks down differently in the stomach and has a different affect on the brain of the alcoholic and the non-alcoholic". Environment, they say, makes no difference.

it to work so decided to check myself into a hospital. I called the local police and they said I'd have to go to Foxboro because Abington was in that geographic location."

"At Foxboro, I was considered a hopeless case and was put in a "back ward" and given something to knock me out and I lost three days of my life. I have no recollection of those three days. When I woke up, I felt good enough to get up and walk around so I began helping the attendants with the other patients. They were amazed that I was able to do that. They liked me and told me about the A.A. meetings. When they said I could get cigarettes and coffee, I decided to try it."

He goes on to say, "I owned nothing but the clothes on my back which had been given to me by the hospital. My wife had divorced me and moved to New Hampshire with our two sons. I knew that I was all I had left at that time. I had no money, no car and no place to live. What have I got to lose, I decided, so I began listening at the meetings. I consider February 14, 1965, as my official anniversary date."

The man in charge of the meetings, and his wife, noticed Dean and offered to take him to outside meetings. Dean kids about that. "He was of French-Canadian descent and spoke French, as did his wife. Two other people in the car also spoke French. Sitting in the back seat between the other two, listening to them all speaking French, I felt happier and more peaceful than I had in my whole life. I had no possessions and nothing to worry about and I felt free. I was sober for the first time in twenty-two years. I had finally figured out what had been causing all my trouble, my illnesses, my loss of jobs and I was at peace, one day at a time".

He talked the hospital into letting him stay for a while, helping with the patients and getting his bearings. When he felt ready, he walked to the nearby Foxboro Company and into the Personnel Department to apply for a job. "The man I talked with," he recalled, "was also named Dean. He told me that they had never hired anyone from the hospital. It took me six weeks of showing up in the Personnel Office to convince him but he finally hired me to work in the factory, calibrating the precision instruments made by Foxboro".

He also liked to add, "I didn't keep my alcoholism a secret because I wanted to help others. Some people avoided talking with me because they were afraid they'd also be labeled alcoholics, but many others were curious and I was able to pass on what I was learning. They kidded me and called me the *town drunk* but that gave me more publicity."

His potential didn't go unnoticed. Six months after he began working in the factory, he was offered a job in the Plant Accounting (or Cost) Department, which calculated the cost of making each instrument. That allowed him to wear a white shirt and tie to work and be well respected by his fellow workers.

Those who met him at St. Mark's during that period told me he walked from the hospital to church every Sunday morning. The minister and several of the parishioners invited him to dinner and helped him in other ways. I asked him about the day I saw him on the sidewalk and wanted to speak but he had totally ignored me. "I was concentrating very hard at that time on staying sober," he told me, "And possibly didn't even see you." I forgave him.

I also asked about the woman I'd seen him with the day I invited him to the Parents Without Partners meeting. He said, "I met her in A.A. but my friends kept urging me to break up with her because she had trouble staying sober and they were afraid I'd start drinking again out of frustration. I thought I was in love with her and was trying to help her. I broke up with her before you and I began dating." In the same vein, I immediately left Parents Without Partners when he asked me to marry him.

It wasn't hard for me, when I considered the differences in our backgrounds, to understand the reasons we had difficulties in adjusting, but we also had in common a wish to be kind to people and to be loved and to love in return and to share it with others. We wanted to work as a team and not struggle against each other.

A counseling session as a couple and individually with Walter at St. Mark's Church helped immensely. I have no idea and never asked, of course, what he and Dean discussed but a few weeks later, he followed up with a letter to each of us. In mine, he made clear I had unreal expectations of what marriage would bring and I couldn't argue with that. We didn't need to consult him again so I can only assume we were doing something right.

I thanked God many times that I hadn't been allowed to marry any of the other men who'd been in my life. None would have claimed my heart the way Dean did, or been as interesting or intelligent. *It will be all right* and it was.

THE GOLDEN YEARS

THE YEARS THAT FOLLOWED, with the help of Al-Anon and Dean's love, saw me stretching and growing and leaving negative thinking in the dust. I loved my new life. Being a wife and no longer a single parent - the anomaly I'd been in the *mother-father-children* atmosphere of the 50's – helped tremendously. A picture of me coming into my sister's house one Christmas, a big smile on my face and presents in my arms, tells it all.

Our families continued to celebrate Thanksgiving separately. Ruth and Tom shared it with Tom's relatives. Jack joined us – my mother, Darcy, Dean and me– bringing our group to five, but Christmas belonged to the whole family. We gathered around the table at either Ruth and Tom's house or ours. After dinner, we opened our presents one by one so everyone could see them. Loving thoughts and good will surrounded us as we exchanged news at the table or in front of the tree or exclaimed over the gifts. Each family birthday became an occasion, also. The menu, once the presents had been opened, always consisted of cake, ice cream and ginger ale. Even today, Darcy and I laughingly mark our birthdays with cake, ice cream and what we call the *ceremonial* ginger ale.

I've always thought of those as "The Golden Years" because that slice of family history, before my nieces and Darcy moved permanently into their own lives, seemed to embody all of my fondest dreams. Happiness had caught up with me and I luxuriated in it, fire-walling any thoughts that it might not last forever.

I called occasionally to talk with Darcy at college and she called for permission to go on trips or for other reasons. I also drove her back to

Oberlin every fall, hoping she wouldn't get hurt in any out-of control anti-war protests. Oberlin is a free-thinking college but remained relatively peaceful during that era. In 1970 she told us, "I'm moving into a co-ed dorm," and I approved of that and life continued on its pleasant journey.

As though that weren't enough, Dean and I found another third-floor but much larger apartment just around the corner from Maple Avenue on Cocasset Street, one of the main spokes in the five streets branching off the Common. Though I couldn't see The Foxboro Company from my kitchen window, I could still walk to work and we had a front and back porch and two bedrooms, besides a garage and a small stand of trees to give the back yard privacy. To make it even better, Snagglepuss accepted it, possibly because it wasn't far from Maple Avenue and he could visit there whenever he pleased. My old life disappeared into the mist and I gave myself completely to the new one, with no backward glances or regrets. I had stepped through the door into a room filled with light and love and dreams come true.

Part of the magic lay in my new way of life. Early in 1972, after a few years with the Canton Al-Anon group, I made the move to the Walpole meeting, secretly dreaming of forming a group in Foxboro. My dream came true in a totally unexpected call I received from the Al-Anon state office in Braintree. "Foxboro State Hospital called us to ask about the possibility of having an Al-Anon group at that location. Would you be interested in starting one?" The coincidence told me that my Higher Power was in control, taking care of me.

I talked with Judy, a friend I met in Walpole and contacted the Al-Anon state office for guidance. The Foxboro State Hospital assured me, "We have space you can use." Earlier, the A.A. meetings had relocated to a room in an unused building on the campus of the hospital. In that same building, we were offered a snug 12' x 15' room which held a soft-drink machine and was known as *the coke room,* a name that brought numerous, tongue-in-cheek comments. Somehow we made the tiny room work. Dean bought a coffee maker for us and in November of

1972, we held our initial meeting, joined by Elsie from Foxboro and a few visitors who dropped in while their spouses attended the A.A. meeting. Al-Anon had come to Foxboro.

I wish I could say the same thing was happening with Darcy. She came home in the summer of 1971, obtained a summer job and returned to Oberlin, but at the Christmas break, she announced, as soon as I picked her up at Logan Airport, "I want to quit college." I didn't protest as I had a myriad of other things taking up room in my brain. I also knew that Dean and I had been asked to pay a much larger share of her tuition since I was no longer a single parent. To my everlasting regret, I didn't ask why she wanted to leave but just accepted her decision, even though she was scheduled to graduate in the spring of 1972. If I had asked at that particular time, we might not have lost many years searching for each other.

She did return to Oberlin after the Christmas break but moved off-campus to live with a few friends for a month. Finally, I contacted her to say we were driving out to pick her up. She came home to Foxboro, her belongings in our trunk and overflowing into the back seat along with an empty spool she had acquired from the telephone or electric company and had been using as a coffee table. It stayed in our dining room for some time but the years have erased the memory of what eventually happened to it. With our nieces still in the vicinity, we returned to the Golden Age and I settled back into my life.

Our Al-Anon group slowly expanded. We laughed together and helped each other in our cozy space and before we realized it, a year had passed. For our first and what would turn out to be our last anniversary celebration at the hospital, the staff found us a larger room. A few months later, we were evicted from our little coke room and assigned to an unused corridor. The era of institutionalization had run its course.*

The A.A. group at the hospital disbanded but found a new home at St. Mark's Episcopal Church – my church. "What could be better?" I mused and approached Russ, our new minister. He was deeply pleased

---

* See the History section at the back of the book.

with the idea of having Al-Anon at the church, and offered a room next to the A.A. meeting – a considerably larger one than our original spot and we didn't have to share it with a soft-drink machine. We notified Foxboro State Hospital, no doubt easing their minds about possibly having to ask us to leave. Our new location helped us to grow and flourish, my contentment and happiness keeping pace. We held a casual contest to find a name for our group. Elsie came up with the winner and from then on we were known as the "Foxboro Seeking Serenity" group.

Dean decided around that time that we suggest to Darcy that she would either have to get a job or move out. I'm not sure why I agreed but my whirlwind schedule made up my mind for me. She didn't protest but turned in a good direction by enrolling in a typewriting class which eventually figured in her finding a job at Foxboro State Hospital which, though working with a smaller crew, was still open. She also moved in with her cousin, Jan, who had rented an apartment in Foxboro. Our nest was suddenly empty and the change I hadn't taken into consideration had sneaked up on us and spilled over in another direction..

Our vacations had consisted of driving from point to point, crossing over and under Chesapeake Bay on the bridge-tunnel, marveling at the gorgeous scenery on the Cabot Trail in Nova Scotia, Canada, exploring the Finger Lakes in upstate New York and Lake Champlain in Vermont and even ending up in St. Louis, Missouri, for a few days.

Dean had lived there for six months, designing bows for shoes and flying home from time to time. We visited his old boss, a man who had invited Dean into his home and into his church in an effort to encourage him to give up drinking. When he saw Dean, sober and happy, he beamed and gave us the key to the company cabin, on the Lake of the Ozarks. "Stay as long as you want," he said. At the cabin, which turned out to be a two-story cottage, Dean tried his hand at manning the speedboat tied up at the dock, treating us both to a wild ride around the lake. That night, after viewing the well-stocked refrigerator with its supply of beer and food, we decided we'd stay the night and start home the next day. We had done what we had come to do and Dean felt uncomfortable with all that beer.

The only complaint I had to our driving trips was we traveled in April and May to take advantage of the cheaper rates and avoid the crowds but the pools were usually closed until the summer months. As we stood beside yet another empty pool at a motel, I asked Dean, "How would you like to take a vacation in the summer so I can sit on the sand and swim and possibly there'd be a race track for you to enjoy?"

"If you can find a place like that," he replied, "I'd be willing to try it."

The *place* revealed itself the following winter in an ad in a magazine, complete with a picture of a red and white lighthouse on a spit of land. *Prince Edward Island, Canada. Visit our sandy beaches, watch the trotters at Charlottetown Driving Park or Summerside Raceway and taste our lobster dinners.* I showed it to Dean and he was sold.

We took a chance on a small cottage in 1975 and drove once more but this time in July to St. John, New Brunswick, to spend the night in a Holiday Inn and continue the next day to Cape Tormentine where we boarded a gargantuan car ferry to take us across Northumberland Strait to Port Borden on Prince Edward Island.

Our first view of it told us we had made a good choice. Fields of vegetables – potatoes, peas, carrots and green beans, to name a few – stretched in all directions along two-lane, country roads bordered by comfortable-looking, white-shingled or weathered, satiny gray shingled houses. Just in case that didn't work, the dories, lobster and fishing boats bobbing at the wharves, as well as the wildflowers along the sides of the roads, finished me off. This was the place we had been seeking.

For a few summers, we sampled locations around the island, ending up eventually in the town of North Rustico. The owner of the cottages and his wife lived in Connecticut in the winter but spent summers in a small house on the grounds of their North Rustico property. Cavendish Beach became my favorite. I loved its white sands, soft dunes and rosy-colored bluff that rose at the far end of the beach, its color coming from clay in the sand. Occasionally, I swam at Brackley Beach where the sand itself held that lovely hue. I discovered that the Gulf of St. Lawrence proved to be warm enough for swimming.

In the evenings, I sat with Dean in the stands at Charlottetown race track or Summerside. We enjoyed a production of "Anne of Green Gables" in the Confederation Centre of Arts in Charlottetown, later visiting the house featured in the book. Lucy Maud Montgomery, the author, had grown up on the island.

We also established a tradition of attending a meeting of the North Rustico A.A. group whose members always greeted us warmly. "It's July so we knew you'd be here soon," they'd say. Each time Dean celebrated his sobriety in his own group, he received a medallion showing the number of years. He saved it to donate to the North Rustico group, in case they wanted to pass it on to a member. It's easy to understand why our days on Prince Edward Island remain a precious memory to me.

THE RELUCTANT
CAREER WOMAN

BEFORE WE DISCOVERED OUR perfect vacation spot and the Al-Anon group was firmly established, we wept, in 1969, through the loss of our beloved Snagglepuss. He came in one night, looking wild-eyed and with flecks of blood on his fur though we couldn't find any open wounds. He may have been in a fight with another cat or been hit by a car. We never learned what caused it. Due to the late hour, we knew the vet's office would be closed. The only option we had was to clean him up and make him as comfortable as possible. Dean took him early the next morning. He came home without him. With sadness showing in his eyes, he said the vet had suggested euthanasia due to the age of Snagglepuss and the inability to determine the cause and extent of his injuries. My old buddy had found a peaceful home and I would miss him terribly but was grateful he hadn't been put through a long period of suffering.

Another opportunity kept my life busy and full. In a conversation one night, Dean mentioned, "Our group has a commitment at Walpole tonight. It's the first time I've been there." "Walpole," meant the maximum security prison in the town next to Foxboro. Now that our Foxboro group was alive and healthy, I wondered aloud whether an Al-Anon group could be formed to visit the prison once a month but I couldn't solve the puzzle of what an Al-Anon group would do in a maximum-security prison. I didn't have long to wait. As usual, my Higher Power took over and I received a phone call from our State office asking whether I knew anyone in our group who would be interested in forming an Al-Anon group at Walpole State Prison! What perfect timing!

Of course, I said, "Yes. I would" and then I learned the history behind the call. An inmate at a correctional facility in the town of East Bridgewater who had attended Al-Anon meetings at that facility had been moved to Walpole. Wanting to continue them, he asked about a meeting at Walpole. I visited the prison and talked with the guard in the outside office who put me in touch with the Superintendent. He, in turn, welcomed the news. My idea was to use the A.A. system. Each month a few men from the groups in the area did what was known as a "commitment' and put on a meeting in the auditorium of the prison to tell their stories. An Institutions Chairman scheduled the commitments for the groups. I became the Institutions Chairman for our District and began rallying the Al-Anon groups to do the same thing but found few volunteers. I was willing to go in myself but wasn't willing to do it alone. In time, I managed to round up a few others and the adventure began.

At the facility, we identified ourselves in the front office and were escorted across the grass space between the outside office and the prison itself. At that point, we walked through a "man trap" where we could look up and see a guard high above us with a rifle, checking us out. We continued on and checked in with another guard who took us along a corridor, past cells where the inmates greeted us with hoots and cheers as we followed the guard. With his guidance, we entered a small room. Those who wished to attend had already gathered and formed a circle of chairs. The man who had asked for the meetings introduced himself and the rest greeted us warmly. The guard left and locked the door from the outside. The men treated us with a great deal of courtesy which calmed our pounding hearts and we answered their questions about Al-Anon and the affect of alcohol on the family. They listened and we relaxed and felt glad we had taken the chance.

After that first experience, though, I found it hard to put together the few volunteers needed but we struggled along for a while until I voiced my doubts at a District meeting. Fortunately, Joan stepped forward. She had a better idea and I gladly gave up the leadership of the group. She cancelled the plan of following the A.A. system and put together a collection of women from various groups who were willing to go in each month. I joined her band of five.. We asked the men if they wanted to name their group. One came up with, "The Hanging in There" group which was officially registered in New York, the national headquarters location at that time.

Each month Joan raffled off a "One Day at a Time" book by totaling the number of men and silently thinking of a number within that total. Next, going from man to man, to find the winner, she asked what number each had chosen. The first man to name her secret number won the book. We laughed with them, listened to their stories and the Hanging in There Group flourished for six years.

In another area, my professional life, change crept in. The process and control instrument business grew in the 60's the same way the technology industry did in later years and The Foxboro Company, in on the ground floor, found themselves competing with Hewlett- Packard, Texas Instruments, Robertshaw-Fulton and Honeywell, to name a few. The Credit Department kept pace in its growth and soon we had Phil to help approve the orders and collect payment on delinquent customers. Most of the problems could be traced back to an equipment glitch or an inexperienced person handling the instruments, but someone had to solve the problem or find a person who could and that fell to the Credit Department. Solving it meant the customer would then pay us, which was the ultimate goal.

By the time Phil joined us with the title of Credit Specialist, the Accounts Receivable Department had moved to a different building.. In that period before Foxboro adopted a computer system, in order to review a customer's account it was necessary to walk to the Accounts Receivable Department and view the card. Cy asked me to train Phil since I was familiar with the system and also hired another woman to be my assistant. I trained her. When Dean and I married in 1968, that was the make-up of the Credit Department.

The Foxboro Company continued to grow and Cy felt we needed another "man" which prompted me to comment to Dean, "Cy says we need another man. I think I'll ask him why it can't be me." Dean smiled his agreement. Cy haltingly agreed but my title wouldn't be "Credit Specialist," but a convoluted combination of words saying I was an assistant to Phil but not a full-fledged Credit Specialist, with the unspoken proviso that I wouldn't be making the same salary. At least I was no longer on hourly pay. Later Fred retired, Cy moved to the Corporate office and Phil took his position. When he left to take a more lucrative job nearer to his home, Harry became our Credit Manager. As soon as possible, he informed me I would thenceforth be known as a Credit Specialist but unfortunately would still not receive the same salary as the two men who had also joined us. In time, when Harry moved to the Corporate Office and Kevin took over, we all became Credit Administrators and my salary increased. I never asked and never learned whether it was in keeping with the other two. I felt better not knowing.

Kevin felt it would be beneficial for us to meet the branch office personnel and also the customer employees we usually contacted and he received approval for business trips. Each of us traveled at least once a year, to visit our branch offices and drop in on customers along the way. Not only was I a salaried employee, I had a briefcase with my name on it to take on business trips and I had business cards. How had all of that happened? The job requirement application now included a Bachelor's Degree which, of course, I didn't have but I was "grandfathered in" since I had been there when the application was updated. I had never yearned to have a professional life yet here I was, in the middle of one, doing a job that required a college education. I enjoyed the challenge even though I still considered myself a reluctant career woman.

Feeling fulfilled in my job and in my personal life, I didn't waste any thoughts on how long my bubble would last, but tried to live a day at a time, hoping Darcy would find the same joy in her life. If change was "blowing in the wind", as the song of that period suggested, I had no inkling and saw no signs.

TIME WAITS FOR NO ONE

THREE YEARS AFTER WE lost Snagglepuss, my friend, Judy, knocked on our door one night. When I opened it, I saw she had a cat in her arms. "I know you lost your cat several years ago," she said, "and I thought this might help." She had brought us a beautiful brown cat with blue eyes that I immediately recognized as a Siamese. "This is Kim,' she said. "My sister breeds Siamese cats but if you look at the stripes on his haunches, they'll tell you he isn't a pure-bred."

Somehow, one of the females had wandered away and become pregnant and Kim was the result. He became our little prince. He stepped daintily through the plants on the windowsill without upsetting any of them. His distinct "meow" sounded every time he saw me coming through the stand of trees in back of the house and he hurried down the stairs to greet me. It was difficult not to love him.

He brought joy into our household, something we needed a year after Kim arrived. Sometimes change edges into your life as that had done but at other times, it barges in when you're not at all prepared to receive it. Ruth and Tom and Dean and I were on separate weekend trips in October of 1976 when my mother, always robust, with an occasional ache and pain but never in jeopardy of having to spend long periods of time in hospitals or in bed, suffered a heart attack. She called Carol, a friend of Ruth's and a retired nurse, who handled the emergency but was unable to contact us. We all arrived home on Sunday afternoon to messages from Carol, "Your mother's in Norwood Hospital. She had a heart attack". We hurried to Norwood to find my mother recovering in the Intensive Care Unit, talking with anyone within earshot, having the time of her life with all the attention she was receiving and apparently not feeling the effects.

She stayed for several days until the doctor declared her to be out of danger. I picked her up, amazed at her energy. "I'll need groceries," she said. "Will you go for me? I'll give you a list." Of course, I said I would. When I brought them to her apartment, she said she'd be able to put them away so I left for home since she seemed to be her old self again but the next day, an ambulance rushed her back to Norwood. She'd had a massive heart attack.

That night, Dean and I found her with a respirator tube in her throat, unable to speak. I kissed her and told her I loved her which I had seldom done in the past. It wasn't part of our family routine. The doctor said we could visit again in a few days. When we did, we were relieved to see her lying comfortably in bed, without the respirator. The minute we walked into the room, kissed her and stood by her bed, she introduced us to a nearby nurse, "See," she said in her English way, "This is my daughter and son-in-law."

"Would you like to sit up, Mrs. Grayson?" the nurse asked. My mother nodded and was hoisted to a sitting position with two pillows plopped behind her back but before she could speak she coughed and turned pale. "Please leave the room," the nurse ordered.

Very shortly after that, the doctor came into the waiting room, "I'm sorry. We did everything we could, but fluid rose in her lungs when she sat up and she literally drowned." I felt disoriented, not comprehending immediately what had happened.

"May we see her?" "Yes."

I kissed her once again, grateful that I'd had the chance to tell her I loved her, still unable to believe she was gone. Before we left the hospital, I called Ruthie and could tell she had the same feeling of disbelief and confusion. Our mother had been a major figure all our lives. She couldn't be gone.

On the way home, an overwhelming flow of warmth and peace filled the car. I smiled and turned to Dean. "My mother's happy". When

I shared the experience with Ruthie, she smiled, too, and said she had "seen" our mother that same night, tucking her into bed. "It didn't scare me," she explained, "but I felt her peace and her love." We both agreed she was in good hands.

Since then, she's been in the same grave with my father in Moshassuck Cemetery in Central Falls, Rhode Island, under a shared stone with the name, "Grayson," etched into it. It's the same cemetery where several other Grayson names may be found.

Apparently, it takes about a year for me to absorb a grief. One day in 1977, as I drove along Union Street in Foxboro, an ambulance wailed out of the driveway of the senior citizens' complex where my mother had lived. The deep sorrow that rose inside me forced me to pull to the side of the road where I broke down into torrents of tears. "My mother's gone," I repeated and repeated until I had exhausted my grief and could release her to her new home.

Prior to all the changes rearranging our lives, a large number of the staff of Foxboro State Hospital, including Darcy, transferred to Taunton State Hospital, where she rented an old dormitory room in one of the buildings, bought a bed and bureau and lived there for several years, saving her money to complete her education. By then, Jan was sewing costumes for productions at Stage West in central Massachusetts. Ann, who had won a scholarship to a Scotland university where she would learn the art of backstage theater work, was preparing to travel there. Marilyn had begun studying for a degree in Art History at Framingham State College in Framingham, Massachusetts.

Toward the end of the 70's, Darcy announced, "I've enrolled at the University of Massachusetts in Amherst. I'll be majoring in Environmental Architecture. That means I'll be able to design public parks or recreational areas, for one thing. I've rented an off-campus room in a house. Will you help me move into it?" She had earned and set aside a sufficient amount to be able to attend college full-time. I felt proud of her that she had taken the challenge and had handled it well.

Situated in the lovely Connecticut River Valley in the county of Hampshire, Amherst lies east of the Berkshires in central Massachusetts. I loved it and the UMass campus at first sight and knew she'd made the right choice. When she said, "I should have gone here in the first place," I had to agree with her, doing my best not to let the guilt feelings take over.

Dean and I and, at other times, Ruthie and I visited her in Amherst to take her to lunch and tour the campus and the surrounding area and its spectacular scenery.

Unbelievably, with April of 1977 arriving I realized I had been with the Foxboro Company for 25 years. Once more I was asked to be an officer, this time in the 25-year Club which was similar to the 10-Year Club. Amazingly, I was elected and spent several years enjoying that.

Though it wasn't a college course, I was also studying, having enrolled in January of 1978 in a correspondence course with the Institute of Children's Literature in Redding, Connecticut. Several months earlier, a pamphlet in a rack in a local supermarket caught my attention with its question, "Would you like to write children's stories?" "Who knows?" I thought and reached for one, kept it for a while and finally decided to do it. A proctor showed me the correct way to set up a manuscript and critiqued the ones I submitted. I heard about Writers Market, the book that lists 3,000 or more magazines that accept freelance stories and also lists their guidelines for acceptance, along with a mound of other useful information. I enjoyed the course but with no definite plans in mind I set my new knowledge aside after I received my diploma in January of 1979.

That year held another sorrow. Kim, our little prince, who had brought us joy for seven years, brought us sadness the night he went out the back window and never came back. Dean had just walked in the back door and I was on my way to shut the back window that was Kim's route in and out of the house, but he beat me to it and I saw him disappearing through it, unaware I'd never see him again. Unfortunately, it was Hallowe'en night in 1979. Dean told me he had seen a strange car in our back yard, near the garages, with the trunk open. Kim may have climbed into the trunk and been shut in there. We never found out, though we posted notices, asked all our friends to watch for him and searched and grieved for a long, long time, praying that he hadn't suffered and was safe somewhere..

A few years earlier, Dean, also feeling the urge to complete his education, enrolled in evening classes at Bryant College in Smithfield, Rhode Island. "I know it won't advance me at all at work," he explained, "but I just want to do it." Ruthie and I were there on Commencement day in December of 1979 to proudly watch him receive a Bachelor of Sciences degree in Business Administration.

I stayed involved in the Seeking Serenity and the Hanging in There groups. Since Walpole required the inmates who wanted to attend Al-Anon to also go to the A.A. meetings, I saved Dean's copies of the *Grapevine*, the A.A. magazine, plus my copies of the *Forum*, the Al-Anon newsletter, to take to the meetings. We all cheered when one member told us his wife had begun attending Al-Anon meetings and it was helping her. Several said they realized they were children of alcoholics. We didn't try to hold a discussion group as the atmosphere didn't encourage talking about yourself but we answered questions and the members shared as much as they felt comfortable doing and the meeting prospered. Often the Security Officer had to tell us, "Time's up."

Despite that, the members of the original group slowly dropped out but we didn't ask questions, even while we noticed that new members weren't taking their places. After six years of keeping the meetings going each month, one night only one man showed up and he seemed more interested in seeing women than in hearing about Al-Anon. Before we left, the Social Worker asked us to stop at the prison Counselor's office. "When you first formed this group," the Counselor told us, "The men respected you as they respected anybody who came in from the outside, and they didn't want to do anything that would discourage you from coming. For that reason, we knew you'd be safe with them and so we allowed the meeting to exist." He paused, "The prison population has changed. We get men now who committed drug-related crimes. They have a different perspective. We can't predict what they'll do and frankly, we can no longer guarantee your safety." Disappointed but grateful for what we'd been able to accomplish in the six years we'd been at Walpole, we discontinued the Hanging in There Group and requested that its name be deleted from the national and state listings.

DARCY

ON THE THRESHOLD OF the new decade of the 80's, Darcy called to tell us, "I'll be getting my diploma in May. I'll have a degree in Environmental Architecture. Also I'll be graduating Summa Cum Laude". Despite having to work to put herself through college, she had managed to do it spectacularly and I couldn't have been prouder. We drove to Amherst for the commencement and clapped as we watched her walk across the stage to receive her diploma.

"We want to take you out to celebrate," we told her when we located her in the crowd, but she had already made plans to be at a party with her friends. I suspected then that she had begun the transition into adulthood, entering the life that would be hers from then on. I felt somewhat let down on the ride home but knew I'd have to accept it. After all, wasn't that what I wanted – for her to take responsibility for her own life? Be careful what you wish for – it was coming true.

She found a fulltime job in Amherst and it appeared she might make it her permanent home, but in 1981 she gave us some news which staggered me.

"I've been in touch with Stephanie," she said, mentioning a school friend from Foxboro, who had moved to California. "She's been telling me I ought to go to California. I can live with her in Berkeley until I find a job and an apartment. She's probably right," she reasoned. "They have lots of parks and open space so I might be able to find a job with a landscape company."

Her decision had been made, but even as I agreed that she could leave some of her furniture in our section of the basement, I kept telling myself it couldn't be true and she'd change her mind. On the day of her departure, I helped her fill every nook and corner of her little V W, including the front seat, which left her just enough room to drive and see out the windows. I hugged her and she climbed into the driver's seat and was off. I waved as she drove out of our yard and into her own life. Surely it was a bad dream and I'd wake up soon.

Somehow I walked to work. As I entered a corridor filled with other employees hurrying to their work spaces, I thought my legs would give way. A woman asked, "Are you all right?" I couldn't hold back the tears.

"My daughter just left for California," The woman looked properly sorry. "Excuse me," I said. I had to find the nearest ladies room to allow myself to take a few deep breaths and conquer the tears. I made it through the day but waited anxiously for her calls.

Whenever and wherever possible, she veered off on side trips to see as much of the country as she could and still be able to make it to the motels where she had reservations. I wonder now at the courage it took to drive alone for 3,000 miles in a tiny car loaded to the limit. I breathed a sigh of relief when at last I heard, "I'm in California." I also made a mental note that I'd have to check the time before I contacted her. My daughter, my little girl, had made it across the country and I still hadn't processed the fact that she was three time zones away.

A new little family addition in 1982 brought pleasure but didn't fill the hole she had left. My niece, Jan, who was living in Connecticut by then and planning to marry a man named Kurt, called one night. "Would you like a cat?" she asked. Kim See had been gone for three years and I had to think about it. I said I'd call her. A few days later, I decided it might be a good idea. "Kurt has Monroe, Modigliano and Harold," she said. I liked the name "Modigliano." She promised to deliver him the next time she visited her parents. Dean proposed that we call him "Digger," which was fine with me.

He proved to be quite different from our little prince. For one thing, he was a big tabby, possibly with Coon Cat genes in him. Where Kim had stepped daintily through my plants, he knocked one on the floor the first time he tried it. He also wasn't as outgoing as Kim. Every time company arrived, he disappeared into a closet. In fact, when he came to our house, he spent several days under our bed. I sighed and missed Kim but did my best to be kind to Digger.

I took care of him and was kind but didn't warm up to him until Dean showed me pictures he had taken and I laughed and he became my cat. They showed big Digger reaching for a pen we kept next to the phone and playing with it on the floor. In another one, he was looking under the refrigerator for a toy, his large hindquarters comically thrust into the air. Dean's pictures did the trick. I fell in love with a cat again.

One more welcome and unexpected change, a year after Darcy left, helped me to focus on my life in Foxboro. Each Sunday, driving to church, we passed a white house with a large lawn. One day, a *For Sale* sign appeared on that lawn, planting a tiny seed in my brain. I nurtured it for some time before sharing it with Dean. "Do you think we could buy a house?"

"Let me think about it," he replied. He looked over our finances and a few days later, said, "Yes." By the time we began looking, in the spring of 1983, the house with the sign had been sold, but we found ours on Neponset Heights Avenue, within walking distance of the Foxboro Company and up the street from Neponset Reservoir where I had taken Darcy to swim as a child. One portion of the street swung off to the right, dead-ending at a grove of trees. The other portion ran in a straight line, ending at the water's edge and giving access to a tiny wharf near the Foxboro Fish and Game Club whose members proved to be wonderful neighbors.

Dean didn't admit his fears to me until after we bought our house and moved in. "It was overwhelming. I never dreamed this could happen to me. When I drank, I was always borrowing money to pay the rent or even buy the groceries and explaining why I couldn't pay it back right away and drinking down any excess we may have had. It seems unbelievable that we're living in our own home." Coincidentally, the date we bought the house – 8/29/83 – happened to be Darcy's birthday.

With life settling down, I wanted to visit her. She had been hired by the Oakland Office of the City Counsel and worked in the Oakland

City Hall, learning about law. She had also rented a room in a house where several other tenants lived, but wanted her own place eventually. It was wonderful to see her. We toured Sonoma and Napa, where we visited a winery and I admired the gorgeous surroundings. I liked northern California, being pleasantly surprised to see the older houses and not many palm trees. I mentioned it to Darcy, "It's very different from southern California." I boarded my plane back to Massachusetts, satisfied, even though I missed her, that she had made a wise decision.

That didn't mean I enjoyed having her that far away, though. One night in 1984, I ached to see her and poured out my feelings to her answering machine. I knew she had to have her own life, but I missed her dreadfully.

Several months later, to my surprise and delight, she called to say she was moving back to New England. She wanted to be back in Foxboro, she said, and see her old school friends and New England in general. I didn't learn the real reason for quite a few years.

Ruth and Tom and Dean and I all met her at Logan Airport to hug her and tell her how glad we were to have her back. In Foxboro, she renewed her acquaintance with the town, called her friends and seemed happy in her old surroundings. She eventually found work as a legal secretary in the office of a probate lawyer and moved into an apartment in Arlington, near Boston, and acquired a cat named Lorraine. I relaxed, happy to have my old life back, unaware of a huge change waiting to rearrange it once more.

The Foxboro Company, in the fall of 1985, announced it was *downsizing* and offered a retirement plan for all employees over fifty-five years of age who had been with the company ten years or more. I didn't have to think twice about that. On December 27, 1985, at the age of sixty, after thirty-three years and eight months of employment, I walked out of the Foxboro Company for the last time. The reluctant career woman had the job she coveted – that of wife and mother, with my daughter close enough to visit. What could be better than that?

I found in January of 1986 what <u>could</u> be better when I pulled Darcy's portable typewriter out of the attic, bought a metal typewriter table, a supply of bond and carbon paper, an eraser and a Writer's Market. I set everything up in the room we used as an office. To anyone who asked, I explained, "Now that I'm retired, I plan to write children's stories." All I had to do was step onto the path that stretched ahead of me into a shining future.

THE WORST IS YET TO BE

ON MONDAY MORNING IN the second week of January, 1986, I sat staring at the blank sheet of bond paper in my typewriter. *Where and how do I begin?* At least, I knew one thing. I'd treat my new career as a part time job. As soon as Dean left for work, I made the bed, fed Digger, and washed the dishes. *I'll write until lunchtime, five days a week.* Even my Writers Market had done its bit by helping me list all the magazines who'd be thrilled to receive my stories. Though I had yet to write the opening sentence of a children's story, titles crowded my mind – "The Mischievous Cloud," "Hooey, the Daylight Owl" and "The Flying Gift," for instance.

An idea caught me by surprise. *Why not write from titles rather than the other way around.* "The Mischievous Cloud" brought to mind one that had disobeyed the orders of the Chief Cloud Dispatcher and rained on a children's picnic which taught him a lesson about obeying.

Also, I could do a series called "The Leafy Green Forest" where characters such as Sabrina Skunk, Sammy Squirrel, Wendy Wren and Phil Fox shared adventures.

Taking a deep breath, I typed, "The Mischievous Cloud." After several dismal starts, I felt satisfied with my opening sentence and my fingers flew along the keys. On the log that I had been taught to keep, I noted that my first story went out on February 7th to *Lollypops, Lady Bugs and Lucky Stars*. My second, "The Flying Gift," left on February 20th. "Cloud" came back on March 7th and "Gift" arrived back on March 9th. Undeterred, I sent them to other magazines and continued pumping out children's fiction.

Unfortunately, *Cricket, Highlights for Children, Wee Wisdom, Jack and Jill* and several other magazines were polite but didn't share my belief that my stories were good enough to be published. I persevered but by the end of March dejection set in. One day in April, as I rolled yet another fresh sheet of paper into my typewriter, I smiled. *Why not write about Snagglepuss and his flight back to our old house on Vernal Avenue.* The story almost typed itself. Along with a picture of him, I sent it on April 24th to *Cat Fancy.*

Thirty-eight days later, I slit open an envelope from the editor and shrieked, sending Digger under the cedar chest. "We have read and evaluated your manuscript," it said, "and would like to publish it in a future issue. Our rate of payment for this type of article is $40." I grabbed the nearest pen, signed the acceptance letter, added the date – 6/9/86 – and called Dean and Ruthie who celebrated with me. If the editor had offered to pay me nothing, I would have done the same thing.

By the time it appeared in October of 1986[*], I was awaiting publication of "Spinning Your Wheels," in the December issue of *Byline Magazine.* I dumped sixteen children's stories into a folder and dropped the folder at the back of a file drawer where it still sits. Who knows?

During that year and the next, some personal experience stories caught an editor's eye and some didn't but I knew I'd found my niche. Ideas filled my head. Carrying four articles with the title, "I Remember..." in my briefcase, I approached Jack, the editor of our local paper, *The Foxboro Reporter.* "These describe Foxboro the way I remember it before 1-95 ran along the edge of town," I told him. He liked them, published them in June of 1988 and accepted four more for fall publication. In the years that followed, in spite of some big bumps in my life, I sold twenty-one stories to various national magazines, plus an anecdote to *Reader's Digest.* That brought me $150 and a bumper sticker, "I found money, fame and glory. Reader's Digest bought my story."

---

[*] See MY WRITING CREDITS at the back of the book.

At Christmas in 1986, Dean really surprised me with an electric typewriter. I had been admiring them at a stationery store in North Attleboro and thinking I'd upgrade some day. The only problem with Dean's gift was its age. The Foxboro Company held an annual auction of used office furniture. Dean bid $25 for a 1966 IBM typewriter that had a greenish-gray metal exterior, a long carriage designed for large office forms and a lot of mileage. He had it reconditioned and set it under the Christmas tree, along with his love and encouragement.

My ecstasy with my new typewriter lasted until the day I ended the first sentence of a story and hit the carriage return key. As the carriage flew to the right, the metal stand that had easily held the much-smaller portable, rattled ominously and the monstrous typewriter inched precariously close to the back edge of the stand, forcing me to return it to its original position. I overcame that problem by treating myself, on a trip to the stationery store, to a new and sturdy wooden stand and a foam rubber mat, both purchases exceeding the cost of the typewriter.

Other drawbacks gradually revealed themselves. A few months of use brought on the jamming of the shift key which set off a grinding sound in the belly of the typewriter. Though I became familiar with the noise, I had no time to shut off the power before several capital letters marred my manuscript and had to be erased.

My biggest challenge turned out to be replacing the ribbon. The myriad of office supply stores where I searched didn't carry ribbons which prompted me to check with IBM itself. I learned the awful truth that the model was obsolete. The spools that fit my typewriter could no longer be bought.

With no options left, I became inventive. I bought a ribbon, stripped the old one off the spools and wound the new ones on. My solution worked but left me with smudges everywhere and a new problem. I had to monitor the ribbon each time it reached its end because the warning bell no longer worked.

The devotion that had prompted Dean to buy it showed in his voice each time he bragged about my writing which kept me from telling him the truth. I came very close, though, the day he sheepishly admitted that the $25 typewriter had cost $182 to be reconditioned!

With my writing career established, I readily agreed when Ruthie reminded me, "We've talked about going to England. Now that you've retired, why don't we do it?" We studied Fodor's "Travels in England" and wrote to cousin Marjorie who invited us to stop at her house in Newcastle-upon-Tyne. Her mother, Bessie, and I had exchanged letters during World War 11 but Bessie passed away before we could meet. Ruthie and I bought our tickets, planning to leave on the 8th of June in 1987 and return on the 22nd.

Our trip together didn't happen. My sister loved Girl Scouting. The Plymouth Girl Scout Council gave her their Director's Award for being an outstanding Girl Scout volunteer and leader. She had been recognized by the Foxboro District Council of Girl Scouts of America for her thirty years of involvement. She reveled in being outdoors but the sun had betrayed her. My happy life crash-landed the day she told me, "The biopsy came back on those two lumps on my head that I showed to you. The doctor says they're skin cancer and they may be melanoma." As I had when Darcy left for California, I told myself it wasn't true. It couldn't be true.

"We can still go to England," she continued, "I feel okay and I want to do it." However, a month before the departure date, she confessed, "I don't think I should be that far away from the doctor. Maybe we can get the ticket transferred to Darcy. We have the same last name." Though I wanted very much to have Ruthie with me, I agreed, still in a state of denial about her diagnosis. The transfer worked and Darcy and I set out for England.

Tears of wonder filled my eyes as the plane touched down at Gatwick and I had my first glimpse of the green of England, the land of my roots. I had come to find a world seen only through the eyes of my parents – windswept moors, lofty cathedrals, quaint cottages in cozy villages. I was actually here. Darcy and I picked up our luggage and found transportation to Victoria Station in London where we rented a car. With Darcy doing the driving, we set out for Salisbury to see the Cathedral and Stonehenge. I offered to drive but she said, "No, it's hard enough for me to remember to stay on the left without you having to go through that, too."

The majestic cathedral and the haunting aura of Stonehenge delighted us. We drove on to Bath to tour the Roman ruins. There we had the good luck to be in an outdoor shopping area when Darcy yelled, "Look, the Kerry Dancers are here." My heart filled with joy as I recalled my mother's numerous stories about them. Once more, I felt tremendous gratitude that we had come - that my dear sister had made it possible.

After staying the night at a bed and breakfast in Bath, we traveled to the Cotswolds and marveled at the picture-perfect, thatched-roof cottages set beside meandering streams. We sat by the Avon River and toured Shakespeare's house before stopping for a walk-through of Warwick Castle, exclaiming at the peacocks strolling the grounds. Later, we found Marjorie's house and enjoyed a home-cooked meal and her company. "When you get to Edinburgh, you can stay a few days in my condo," she told us, much to our delight. On the way back to our bed-and-breakfast, we noticed a certain glow in the fields. I stared, unbelieving. "It's the gloaming," I said. Robert Burns spoke of the "gloaming" in his poetry and I was seeing it – a glow at twilight unlike anything I had ever seen before and wouldn't see again. We were driving at just the right time.

The next day, we headed for Wales to travel through the Wye Valley and tour the ruins of Tintern Abbey. Back in England, before we reached Scotland, we walked along a piece of Hadrian's Wall, fascinated by the thought that Roman soldiers had been quartered there. In Edinburgh, we located Marjorie's condo and she joined us for one night. Nearing the end of our trip, we decided to turn in the car in Glasgow and take the train back to London and Gatwick. We landed in America on June 22nd, as scheduled. As soon as I could, I called Ruthie. "I'll have the pictures developed and bring them so I can tell you all about the trip."

Two weeks later, that promise was snatched away. The cancer had spread through her body, reaching her brain. Tom called, "Ruthie's in the hospital. She had a seizure". I rushed to see her. We clung together. I could no longer push away the nightmare. With the help of Hospice, Tom had a hospital bed set up in the den. My three nieces and Katy, Ruthie's two -year-old granddaughter, took turns visiting, as did other relatives and friends. We all relieved Tom as much as we could, feeding Ruthie and doing our best to keep up her spirits as well as our own. True to her personality, she tried not to be a bad patient. She could no longer eat solid food but subsisted on Ensure.

On July 15th, in a bittersweet celebration, we wished her a happy 64th birthday. That night, torn between our plans and her obvious decline, Dean and I told her, "We'll cancel our trip to Prince Edward Island," but she wouldn't hear of it. At her insistence, we reluctantly agreed to go. "Here's Howard's number," we said to Tom. "He owns The St. Lawrence Motel where we'll be staying." Needless to say, for the short time we were there, I felt miserable and wanted to be back with her.

A few days into our vacation, Howard knocked on our cabin door to give us the news that my sister had passed away. We packed that night. I forgot to bring an alarm clock. Worried that we might not make the 6:30 A.M. ferry, I breathed a little prayer, "Please, God, wake us up in time." It worked. That gave me the faith to go through the next few days and the ones that followed. I lost my sister on July 28, 1987, thirteen days after her birthday. She lies now in Rockhill Cemetery in Foxboro.

My big sister was, in my opinion, the best one in the world. We had our differences but rallied when either of us needed help. Until we were adults with children of our own, I didn't know she had resented me at times. Often, she confessed, our mother called her back as she set out with friends, "Take your sister." Hiding her feelings, she let me tag along. I always felt her protection. On my first day of school as we stood in line at Garvin Memorial, a girl asked my name but I kept my head down. I heard Ruthie say softly, "She's shy." The year after her graduation from high school, it seemed strange to be walking alone to school where I could no longer depend on her presence. A few years later, when I became a single parent, she invited me and Darcy to live with her and Tom until I could find a job and a place of my own. I have missed her ever since, but life is seldom without its bright spots..

In that year of sadness and loss, they revealed themselves in my new career and the joy of seeing England, but one event stood out above the others, memorable in its display of love. In the spring, before we knew of the tragedy that would mark that year, Dean surprised and thrilled me with his decision. "I want to adopt Darcy," he said. "She's alone. I want to make her my daughter so she'll have legal rights and won't get left out." On July 9, 1987, a month before her 37th birthday, Dean officially became her father.

DEAN'S LAST BET

THE FOXBORO COMPANY DOWNSIZED once more in 1987, giving Dean the opportunity to follow me into retirement in December of that year. Early in 1988, eleven months short of his sixtieth birthday and not yet ready for full retirement, he found a part-time accountant's job in the city of Brockton. His boss, a young man in a hurry to make his business grow and prosper, welcomed Dean's experience and acumen.

The job lasted through June. Having overreached himself, Dean's boss declared bankruptcy, as Dean had feared he might. Though I felt sorry for both of them, it coincided with our plans for our yearly trip to Prince Edward Island.

In our packed car, we started off on July 12th, approximately a year after Ruthie's death. That sad thought caught up with me in the dining room of the Holiday Inn in Saint John, New Brunswick, *My sister's gone.* I quickly excused myself to find a place where I could weep uncontrollably in private. When I returned to the table, Dean didn't ask any questions.

The next day, as soon as we checked in at our cabin on Prince Edward Island, Howard and his wife, Edna, expressed their sympathy. At the A.A. meeting, members of the North Rustico group, on hearing the news, did the same. The sun shone, I sat on the beach and swam in the Gulf of St. Lawrence and went to the races with Dean but something seemed missing. I knew it would take time but at least I had let down my defenses and acknowledged the dreadful loss.

Going back to Massachusetts, I did most of the driving because Dean complained of pains in his back. At home, I rubbed liniment on the area and suggested he see our doctor. He put that off until September. The doctor lost no time in setting up an appointment for an MRI at Norwood Hospital and the attending doctor just as quickly gave us the results. "You must be a smoker. You have a growth in your lungs which has begun to invade your windpipe. We're admitting you today for more tests." He turned to me, "This will take awhile." It reminded me that he had talked with a doctor several years earlier and the doctor advised him to quit smoking. He tried but admitted it was harder than learning to live without alcohol and had abandoned the attempt.

Through the window of the waiting room, I could see a McDonald's across the street. *I probably should eat something.* In McDonald's I ran into a friend from St. Mark's and smiled and spoke and did my best to share a few words but avoided a long conversation. I couldn't manage it right at that moment. As I re-entered the waiting room, the doctor on duty, filling in during vacation time, hurried through the room. I asked about Dean. Without breaking his stride, he said, "Oh, it's cancer. It's terminal." Bam! I wanted to grab his arm, to pound on him, to scream that it wasn't true.

A nearby nurse, sensing my dismay, spoke in a kinder, gentler tone, "You can see your husband now."

In the Intensive Care Unit, not wanting to upset Dean with the news, I kissed him and attempted to smile, thanking God when another doctor strode into the room, "I've taken over your care." His manner told me that Dean was in good hands, a fact borne out when he added, "I'm Chief Oncologist at Southwood Hospital," naming a satellite of Norwood Hospital located in Norfolk, a town next to Foxboro. I drove home alone, not daring to think about what lay ahead of us.

Two weeks into his stay, after many tests and losing his patience, Dean told Dr. P., "I want to go home." We still had no clear idea of what we faced except that he probably would need chemotherapy, if he chose to go that route. For now, he was free to leave.

With my mind striving alternately to comprehend Dean's situation and yet deny it, I couldn't at first grasp Darcy's announcement. "I'm moving back to California in October". It was important yet my mind still reeled from Dean's diagnosis. I agreed to drive her to Amherst in my V W. There she rented a UHaul to transport to Foxboro the furniture that had been stored in a friend's attic. After loading the van, we opted for a swim in a local pond, swinging out on a rope to drop into the water. *Just like the naked boys at the New River in Cumberland.* The thought made me smile.

"May I borrow the V W?" Darcy asked, "I'd like to visit some friends while I'm here." That meant I'd be driving the UHaul back to Foxboro. The picture is still vivid in my mind. As I approached our house and swung the big UHaul into the driveway, I could see Dean on the front steps. Although the trip back along the Massachusetts Turnpike and Rte. 495 had been a big challenge, I hopped out of the truck and said, "Piece of cake."

Dean laughed, kissed me and said, "I made some lunch for you." Ray, a California friend, arrived a day later, to help on the drive to the West coast. At last I knew the reason Darcy had returned to Foxboro. "After she heard your message," he told me, "she thought you needed her." The knowledge that she loved me enough to do that helped ease my pain as I hugged and kissed her and waved goodbye. I knew this would be her final move but she had left something precious behind - Lorraine. She couldn't immediately take her to California and asked whether she could stay with us. We had Digger and I wasn't sure how well they'd get along but said, "Yes," anyway.

Poor Lorraine had to stay in our basement for the first week. I felt sorry for her and allowed her to come upstairs but Digger had trouble with that. He hid in corners and drooped but at least they didn't fight. One day, by accident, Lorraine slipped through the door and I panicked. I ran out in time to see her disappearing under a bush, with only her tail showing. I grabbed her tail and she yowled but I hung on, managing to drag her out and pick her up. From then on, for the two months we had her, I kept a close watch on her and was very glad when Darcy called to say I could send her. I took her into Logan Airport and watched until the plane carrying her was off the ground. Digger sniffed around for several days after that until he convinced himself that she had left and he relaxed and stopped creeping around.

The bad news, meanwhile, had not yet run its course. A month after Darcy left, the husband of my dearest friend from childhood called from Wisconsin. "Louise passed away on November 28th," he told me, adding that she had died of a brain tumor. Memories of World War 11 and dancing with the servicemen at the Pawtucket YMCA Canteen flooded my mind. "They met at the canteen," I whispered to myself, swallowing hard so I could thank him for calling.

Dean, who had grown thinner, still seemed to be his old self. He puttered around the house, raked the leaves, cleared the driveway when the snow arrived and we made it through Thanksgiving and Christmas. On a crisp and clear day in January, he said, "I think I'll go play a few races." He returned about an hour later, shivering uncontrollably. I wrapped him in a blanket but the shivering continued, "A tire blew on the car before I left Foxboro," he explained. "I tried to change it but finally had to call A A A." He rubbed the upper area of his right leg. "It hurts like hell. You'd better call 911."

When the EMT's arrived, one handed him a paper bag. "Breathe into this," he said. That stopped the shivering which had been caused by anxiety and not cold. At Southwood Hospital, we found he had pulled a muscle. Dr. P authorized his admittance and told us, "He needs chemotherapy."

While Dean was in the hospital, I climbed the stairs each night to our bedroom, hoping I could fall asleep quickly and not lie there and think. Usually I was tired enough, so tired that I seldom dreamed but I did have one that troubled me. In it, I was sitting in the Norwood Elks hall again, listening to dance music, watching the dancers and feeling desolate and alone. I almost sighed in relief when I woke up. Fortunately, I slept again that night and the dream didn't return but I had trouble erasing it from my mind.

I also remember the hoot of an owl, something I had never heard before in that area. I tried to dismiss it as I had the dream, but it didn't add to my peace of mind.

Dean managed to take the sickness from the chemotherapy shots in stride. One day I found him in the patient's social room where he had pushed his IV pole to have a smoke. It seemed futile at that point to chastise him, even though his smoking had caused the cancer. A month later, the tumor had shrunk and he no longer had pain in his leg and was allowed to return home. Jubilantly, I wrote to the Wrentham A.A. Group to tell them. On the 14th of February, five of his A A friends trooped into our house to help him celebrate his 24th year of sobriety.

Desperate hope kept me going. I refused to believe he wouldn't get better even when Dr. P. gently told me, "The tumor will grow again. He needs radiation." I resolutely made sure he received each treatment and was still in denial when Dr. P. said, "He needs Hospice care. With your permission, I'll order a hospital bed to be set up in your living room along with an oxygen supply. A Hospice nurse and Visiting Nurse will each come once a week. They'll show you the basic things you'll need to know to take care of him." I set sheets and pillows on the couch for myself. I would no longer be sleeping upstairs.

The Hospice nurse, who had an upbeat, positive manner, asked Dean on her first visit, "Did you plant the tulips out front?" He nodded and she replied, "I'll bring a wheelchair so you can see them." After she left, Dean grumbled about not being interested in seeing the tulips or sitting in a wheelchair.

Soon after that I called Dr. P.for an update. In the kindest of voices, he asked, "You know it's terminal, don't you?"

With the truth banging me over the head, I could no longer deny it. "How long?"

"Could be 13 weeks," he answered, which I eventually found was the standard reply. He added, 'I'm very sorry."

I climbed the stairs to our room. I wanted to scream and rant but couldn't because Dean would wonder what was happening. I felt numb and just wanted to fade away and not have to face the truth. It made sense to my muddled mind to tell myself, "Okay, I'll take care of him and when he dies, I'll die, too." I didn't intend to commit suicide but somehow it seemed reasonable to think that way since I knew I couldn't live without Dean. Gathering all the calmness I could muster, I clumped back down the stairs, sat next to him, took his hand and gave him the news. He didn't seem surprised but just held my hand as we sat quietly together. The tears stayed inside me. Somehow it didn't seem the right time to go to pieces.

The next afternoon, Dean announced, "I want to sit up." I didn't ask why but helped him edge to the side of the bed where he sat for a few minutes before saying, "I want to get dressed and get into the wheelchair." I kept a straight face as, without disturbing his catheter, I inched on his pants, got him into one of his favorite flannel shirts, put on his socks and shoes, told him he'd have to go without underwear and settled him in the wheelchair. Assuming he wanted to see the tulips, I rolled him to the window. He stared at them, commented that they were growing well and said, "I'd like to go to the track."

I blinked but knew he wasn't kidding. "Okay," I said, doing my best to stay calm as I pushed the wheelchair to the top of the two steps down to the dining room. "Hang on," I told him while I bumped his wheelchair to the bottom and continued out to the patio. "Let me lock up and get my bag," I said. From the patio, I maneuvered him and an oxygen tank into the car, hooked up the oxygen and off we went to Raynham Dog Track.

Knowing he couldn't go inside, I explained to the ticket taker and picked up a program. Dean chose his dog and gave me the money to place his bet. Inside, I waited until the race had been run. His dog didn't win. Back in the car, I gave him the news. Repeating that process for four more races, I teased him, "You know, I could tell you the dog had lost and keep the money." We laughed and his old bantering style returned. We enjoyed ourselves until he admitted he was tired and wanted to leave.

I couldn't pull the wheelchair up the two steps at home but could push him from behind while he clung to the railing. I hauled up the wheelchair to get him to the bed, breathing a huge sigh of relief once he was in it and hooked up to his permanent oxygen supply.

He made the trip three more times, once with an A.A. friend who had volunteered. I took him on the fourth try, but he couldn't climb the two steps when we arrived at home. I summoned a young neighbor to pull him up in the wheelchair. He had placed his last bet.

Possibly that prompted him to say, quietly, a few days later, "Let's plan my funeral." We had agreed to be cremated. "Bury my ashes in the Memorial Garden," he instructed, naming an area taking shape behind St. Mark's Church. He listed his favorite hymns and asked me to contact Roberts Funeral Home, our Foxboro mainstay. He did it all with a matter-of-fact attitude and without complaining or bewailing his fate. An A.A. friend came to sit with him while I visited Bruce at Roberts Funeral Home to make the arrangements. He also smoked up until the very last minute. It seemed ridiculous to deny him that. My only prerequisite was that the oxygen be turned off until the cigarette had been discarded. We talked and laughed and tried not to dwell on the future.

Late on the evening of May 25th, he developed a cough. Not sure what to do, I found some cough syrup to soothe his throat. He took the spoonful and lay back. As I was making myself comfortable on the couch, I heard him say, softly and distinctly, "Mama." That puzzled me since he had never called me "Mama." I checked on him but his eyes were closed and I went back to the couch. I flopped down on it and immediately dropped off to sleep myself. Around 2:00 A.M., I awoke to a deep stillness in the house. Pulling myself up and off the couch, I saw that he was lying on his back, one arm across his chest, seemingly peacefully asleep. I leaned over him and knew he wasn't sleeping and also realized he had been speaking to his deceased mother..

As I had been instructed to do, I called Hospice and Roberts Funeral Home before calling my brother-in-law. He arrived first and coaxed me outside for a while. The cool night air felt good. Through the window, I could see Dean, still appearing to be asleep. For some reason, that gave me peace. It was Friday, May 26, 1989, Memorial Day weekend. He had not reached his sixty-first birthday. In the front of the house, the tulips bobbed in full color, unaware of the dreadful loss and I was glad I had never told him the truth about the green typewriter.

Darcy, Foxboro
High Graduation,
June, 1968

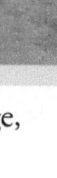

Darcy at Oberlin College,
September, 1968

Violet and Dean, November, 1968

Kim See, 1979 (above) and Digger, 1982 (below)

Dean at Prince Edward Island, Canada, late 70's

Dean at Ft. William Henry, Lake George, NY, late 70's

Darcy at Stone Henge, 1987

Darcy and Violet,
Golden Gate Park, 1983

Violet and Darcy,
Marin Headlands, 1983

Neponset Heights Avenue, 1987

Peter and Dean working on the wall, August, 1987

Violet and Darcy, Neponset Heights Avenue, 1989

Violet and Darcy in California, 1990

THE REMAINDER OF THE YEAR

I DIDN'T DIE. WHEN DEAN'S life slipped away that night, my common sense – was it a blessing or a curse? – declared that someone had to take charge of the debris scattered in the wake of his passing. Ethel, the Hospice representative, arrived to fill out the death certificate, followed by Bruce and Margaret from Roberts Funeral Home. Bruce asked, when the moment came to move Dean, "Do you want some time alone with your husband?" Yes, I did. I stood beside his bed, stroked his arm, whispered through the lump that choked my throat that I loved him and always would, thanked him for a wonderful life together, kissed him and turned to Bruce.

"Thank you," I said, my voice breaking, "I'm ready." He and Margaret carried Dean out. It all happened very quickly, everyone left and quiet settled on the house. I didn't want to see the empty bed or think any more. I climbed the stairs to our bedroom undressed and fell into bed, emotionally exhausted, and was soon asleep.

The next morning, I broke the news to Darcy, Peter and Mark, as well as Dean's brothers. All expressed their sympathy and asked how I was doing. I really didn't know but automatically said I was bearing up. "I haven't decided on the day for the funeral but I'll let you know," I added. Our new minister, Bill, offered to come, but I assured him it wasn't necessary. Later in the day, two men from Hospice removed the bed and the oxygen machine. I visited Bruce to discuss the funeral. We set it for the following Thursday with visiting hours on Wednesday afternoon and evening.

Coming out of the funeral home, I did a double-take. Was that Dean's car outside the police station? Why was it there and why did it have new plates? I rushed into the police station to report it. They promised to call if they found anything. I hurried back outside. The car had disappeared. Seeing it without its familiar plates infuriated me.

I'd been slapped in the face. Nobody should be driving his car so soon after his death. I sped home to make a phone call.

The garage owner who had taken care of our maintenance had offered, a few weeks earlier, to park it in his driveway on Main Street to help find a buyer. Hearing the anger in my voice, he instantly apologized. "I sold it to a friend," he explained, "and he promised to go to your house and pay you and give you the old plates. I'll call him right now." Half an hour later a young man arrived, flustered, with the old plates and the money. He admitted he had used plates from his car and was driving illegally, a fact that didn't improve my attitude. I thanked him but couldn't smile and assure him it was all right because it wasn't. He was driving on Dean's insurance, in Dean's car. I thanked God he hadn't been involved in any accidents On the other hand, I can't say that I wish it hadn't happened. It forced me to release some emotions and proved that I could still function.

That didn't help on Monday, though - Memorial Day. Families gathered in neighboring yards, sending their laughter and chatter to my empty, except for me, back yard where I lay in my chaise lounge, vainly trying to rest for the week to come.

I returned the plates to the DMV on Tuesday, notified the police that I had solved the mystery of the car being outside the station without telling them the whole truth and breathed a sigh of relief., Darcy, Peter, Mark, Tom and Jack all stood with me at the funeral home on Wednesday as people arrived to pay their respects. I still cherish one particular memory. Ruth, the old friend from Rhode Island, who knew what loss was like, having lost her parents, her brother and her husband, took my hand to say, "You don't believe it now, but you will be happy again." Those simple words helped at that moment and often echoed in my mind during the months and years to come.

Dean's casket, on Thursday, rested very near the spot where we had stood together on November 30, 1968, to be married. Darcy and Peter walked to the pulpit to say a few words about him. Mark declined and I couldn't do it. Before we left the church, I reached out to touch his casket and collapsed into weeping at the realization that he was in it. Peter and Mark supported me as we left the church.

By the time friends began arriving at the house, I had recovered enough to greet them and accept their words of sympathy and make it through that day. Darcy stayed on with me for several days. Together, we established a rock garden on a slope facing the lake. To assuage our nostalgia, we toured areas in Rhode Island and Massachusetts that we both remembered. I showed her an old mill on the banks of the Blackstone River in Cumberland that had been converted to Senior Citizen Apartments. "Who knows where I'll be some day," I commented. We laughed over familiar family jokes and I missed her deeply when she returned to California.

I missed Dean beyond describing. *Where is he?* Though I knew the answer, in a classic case of denial I wandered through the house and into the yard in a futile search for him. I even drove to Raynham Dog Track one night and sat near the betting window, hoping to see him in line. Melancholy thoughts claimed me. "It reminds me of an interrupted conversation," I thought. "I don't know what he wanted to say and never will". He couldn't be gone. We had so much life left to experience together – our 25th anniversary, for instance, that we'd never celebrate.

Tears often filled my eyes when memories caught me off-guard. Strenuous physical work helped keep my grief at bay during those first months. Without wondering whether I could do it, I pulled up the carpeting in all three of the downstairs rooms to reveal well-maintained hardwood floors. Through a local want ad magazine, I sold the carpeting. I found a large piece of slate in the garage that someone had given us. Stoop-shouldered from the weight, I lugged it to the end of the sidewalk to the back yard. I dug strenuously, on my hand and knees, into the ground to set it in place. The shrubbery in front of the house badly needed pruning. I tackled that and cleaned out the growth under the trees near the rock garden.

In the midst of my projects, Alan, a friend from A.A., called to see how I was doing. "I long to hear Dean's voice," I told him. "It sounds silly but I'm afraid I'll forget what he looked like. If I could hear his voice, I could picture him." A few days later, Alan showed up with a tape of an A.A. anniversary, one in which Dean told his story and introduced the speakers. Thrilled, I played it over and over, smiling and crying simultaneously.

Alan called again to ask, "Would you mind if we buried Dean's ashes at the campground in Plymouth where we go every summer?" Gratitude flowed through me. The Memorial Garden had not yet been completed. I didn't want to think about Dean's ashes lying in a box at the funeral home but couldn't face bringing them home and having to stare at that box. Five of us drove together to Plymouth to say a few prayers and lay Dean's ashes to rest, if only temporarily.

Mark surprised and pleased me one night by calling just to chat. Somehow we fell into a loving review of Dean's faults. That call helped more than if he'd been somber and sympathetic.

Eventually, I ran out of physical chores. That led me into the daily habit of walking. The sidewalk bordered the campus of the old Foxboro State Hospital. Just beyond the hospital, I turned right onto a side street and followed the sidewalk to its end. One day, I murmured, "*Where The Sidewalk Ends*. That would make a good title". My mind opened to let titles flow in as it had when I thought I'd be a children's story author. Each day I added a few more to a list I was keeping. Along with my wish not to write about personal experience and stir up memories, the titles pushed me into attempting fiction. I sent out my first one, "My Real Mother," on August 30, 1989. It came back, rejected, but I continued writing fiction. Though my initial attempts didn't find publishers, I enjoyed it. Dean had given me "The Fifth Season," which I listed.

The year wouldn't let me go without one last surprise and one last jolt. The surprise arrived on my birthday, October 11th. Darcy sent the perfect gift for a committed baseball fan – a ticket to the Red Sox – Oakland A's playoff game at Fenway Park. I checked transportation and heard of a train for fans that I could board in Attleboro. I sat among a horde of hopeful fans all headed for Yawkey Station, right outside of Fenway. At the game, I cheered, along with the mostly young fans surrounding me, each time the Red Sox brought in a run. They lost and didn't make it to the World Series but the memory is still a warm one for me.

The jolt came soon after that.. On October 17, 1989, a 6.9 earthquake, the *Loma Prieta*, hit the California Bay Area. Named for a peak in the Santa Cruz Mountains on the San Andreas Fault, it caused sixty-three deaths. The Nimitz Freeway in Oakland collapsed on itself, trapping motorists in a lethal sandwich. It shook Candlestick Park where sixty-two thousand fans sat waiting to watch the third game in the World Series between the Oakland A's and San Francisco Giants. The A's won again, as they had in Boston. One section of the Bay Bridge, a main artery from the East Bay to San Francisco, dangled just above the waters of San Francisco Bay, with a bus poised at its edge. Darcy worked in the city and rode a bus home to Berkeley. Anxious for news, I tried to call but couldn't get through. All I could do was hope and pray that she was all right.

At 10:00 P.M., Eastern time, to my relief, Ray called. "I just heard from Darcy," he told me, "She's at my cousin Lester's house in San Francisco. The power's out in the city and everybody had to walk down from the twenty-fourth floor in her building. She thought she'd have to walk thirty blocks to Lester's house, but a man and woman stopped to pick her up so she's okay." At last I could relax.

That Christmas, we had a welcome reunion in California. Darcy took me on a tour to see the collapsed freeway and some of the other damage while I thanked God she had survived a dreadful disaster.

A surprise awaited me back in Foxboro. I found phone messages from two of my nieces. "How's my father doing? Was the operation a success?" Completely baffled, I returned the first one to learn that Tom, while I was away, had suffered a heart attack which led to a quadruple bypass. I checked with the hospital and was able to tell both of them that his condition was "stable." They arrived soon after that to stay for a few days. My other niece flew up from Florida for a quick visit with her father and returned to Florida that night. We all found him in good spirits at the hospital and recuperating quickly.

It felt good to say goodbye to 1989 and to hear the good news that Tom had been released from the hospital and was staying with a friend before returning home.

THE SPACE BETWEEN

EIGHT MONTHS AFTER DEAN'S death, the trauma of the past three years had ebbed somewhat. Tom recovered well and 1990 seemed off to a good start but that didn't speed up my adjustment. As far as the world was concerned, all was well with me. Though I had stopped looking for Dean and wearying myself with heavy projects, my mind had no anchor. Drifting and wondering, faithfully attending church, I sat alone in the pew near the front of the church that we had favored. The role of the poor pathetic widow didn't appeal to me, but I had no desire to sit with another person. A good friend of mine who was also a member of the church lost her husband just after Dean died, but she cried easily in public and showed her emotions which brought her a lot of comforting hugs. I envied her that ability but couldn't handle the intimacy of so much attention. I rejoined the choir - not as conspicuous a move as changing pews. Also, Neponset Choral Society began rehearsals for a spring concert and I was still a member and had remained a member through Dean's illness and death. At a rehearsal, a fellow-member urged me to join a group of widows who met for lunch occasionally and attended shows and I agreed to do that. May 26th came and went. A year had passed. I let out the breath I had been holding.

One morning in July, I sat on the edge of my bed to put on my slippers. Digger jumped up to greet me. I petted him and told him, "I'm glad you're still around." I picked him up to set him on the floor to allow me to stand up but stopped in alarm when I felt several lumps in his stomach and made sure I wasn't imagining things. Immediately after breakfast, we visited the local veterinarian. He felt the lumps and frowned, "I'll do a biopsy." Okay. Digger was in good hands but then he added, "If they're cancerous, I'll have remove them, unless the cancer has spread and we're too late."

I thanked him, wrestled Digger back into his carrier and tore home. I released him in the kitchen and escaped back to my car, desperate to put space between me and the possibility that Digger might be next. All thoughts of having recovered flew out of my mind, the peace along with them.

Out on Route 95, I hit the speed limit and held the accelerator down, not caring where I went but just driving. The off-ramp for Rte. 295 South came into view. I swerved onto it and headed toward whatever lay along its route. It crosses the deep and fast-running Blackstone River in Cumberland. Just before I reached the bridge, a strong urge grabbed at me. *I'll just drive off. What's the use of going through any more grief? I can be with Dean and be peaceful.* A shred of faith deep inside me kept me, at the last minute, from obeying the urge, but I couldn't hold back a longing glance down when I crossed the bridge. As I neared Woonsocket, Rhode Island, I left 295 and, minutes later, turned into the parking lot of the first coffee shop I saw. I thanked God it was almost empty. I ordered my coffee, grabbed a seat and let my despair take over. In all of my life, I couldn't recall ever having felt this deep in misery and so lost in a huge pit of sorrow. *Oh, God, I wish I had driven off. I wish I could sink through the floor and fall into oblivion. Let me disappear into that deep, dark pit and dissolve somehow.* I dropped my head into my hands and let the tears roll down my cheeks. *Please help me.*

My prayer got through. Possibly Dean sent a message because words I'd heard often at A.A. meetings pierced my gloom. "When you hit bottom, there's no place to go but up." Slowly, achingly slowly, the meaning of those simple words seeped into my brain. No wild weeping claimed me as it had a year after my mother and, later, my sister, died but I knew something had shifted inside me. I dragged myself back to the car and started home.

Crossing the river on the way back, I had no urge to drive off. At home, Digger looked up when I walked in and rubbed against my legs. I thanked God I hadn't done it. "Who would have found you or fed you?" I stroked him and smiled and let out my breath once more.

As though to confirm my faith, the veterinarian called the next day to tell me the lumps were benign. On July 9th, he removed them and Digger recovered and I did, too.

On a night shortly after that, I had a dream which still holds its clarity. I just have to shut my eyes and it comes to me. Dean and I were standing together at the edge of a small and shallow pond in the woods. Through the trees, a shaft of sunlight showed fish swimming in the pond and a lily pad on its other side. Dean reached across to pluck a white flower from the lily pad to give to me. I felt wrapped in a serene sense of peace and love. When I woke up, I wanted to go back. I thought of that dream each time I felt lonely and it comforted me.

August drifted by, St. Mark's church held the annual parish picnic in September at a member's home on the edge of the Wading River. The Senior Warden* of our church strolled over to where I had plunked down on a rock near the river. We talked a while before he commented that Bill, our minister, had received a letter from Dan, the Director of New Beginnings Singles Ministries, a group formed by the United Church of Christ in Norwell, Massachusetts. Dan inquired whether St. Mark's would be interested in starting a weekly group. "How would you feel about doing that?" he asked. I hesitated and he continued, "It's ecumenical and would be sponsored by our church and we'd pay the leader." Though I had no interest in singles groups, the challenge of setting it up appealed to me. I agreed, telling myself I'd do that and then back out of it.

A few months and many phone calls later, we held our first New Beginnings meeting and, fortunately, had enough people that night to

---

* In the Episcopal Church, a governing body known as "The Vestry", comprised of volunteers from the congregation and headed by the "Senior Warden", makes the decisions, along with the minister, on financial and other problems.

choose a Secretary and a Social Events Chairman. The leader, John, hired by the church, explained the format. "We'll have a speaker and then we'll separate into small discussion groups. If you have a problem you'd like to discuss, bring it up in your group."

We prospered and began enjoying outside events. One new member offered his back yard for a barbeque and a game of croquet. One night, we danced on the deck of the USS Massachusetts which was permanently docked in Fall River. We had fun on the evening we dined out before driving to McCoy Stadium in Rhode Island to watch the Pawtucket Red Sox, a Boston Red Sox farm team, win a game.

Christmas came and I had the urge to set up a tree, but no presents arrived to go under it except a wreath from my niece, Marilyn. I told myself they had probably been sent to Mark and Mary Ellen's since I had been invited there for Christmas day. I tried to keep my thoughts positive on the drive to their house in Worcester, noticing, when I arrived, all the presents piled under their tree. We had dinner before finally gathering in the living room. Mark reached for an envelope resting on a tree branch and handed it to me. I didn't ask any questions but opened it.

I found a check for $300 and a card signed by all seven of my relatives – Darcy, Jan, Marilyn, Ann, Peter, Mark and Tom, along with a note from Darcy. "This is to help you buy a word processor." She had mentioned that I ought to think about buying one to replace my typewriter but I had put the suggestion aside. I stared at the note and the check, speechless and overcome, trying to take in Mark's explanation.

"Darcy planned it for months," he said, "and sent a card around the country so everyone could make their contribution and sign the card." Nothing, absolutely nothing, could have pleased or touched me more.

THREE STRIKES AND YOU'RE OUT

AS SOON AS I could, after Christmas I found a store in Brockton where I browsed through word processors for the first time and settled on a Brother. Fortunately, with the explicit instructions and a few phone calls to Darcy, I was able to teach myself to use it and fall in love with it. Unable to carry the green typewriter down the stairs into the basement, I bumped it down, a stair at a time and set it on an old desk and covered it. The word processor fit nicely on my typewriter table and with no carriage to throw, it didn't wobble. I no longer had to erase and hope it didn't leave a smudge but could delete and re-write a word and save it all on a disk, taking my first step into the world of technology. For sentimental reasons, I saved the carbon paper.

Though I had promised myself I'd leave New Beginnings once it was up and running, the shred of stability it provided changed my mind and knowing that I had made it possible imbued me with a small sense of importance and a modicum of pride in my accomplishment..

That spilled over to my house and the improvements I'd made in the two years Dean had been gone. A stockade fence now enclosed the side and back yards. A local handyman and a good friend, Rob, set a door in the garage to allow easy access to the back yard. He also began where Dean's sickness had forced him to leave off on rebuilding a low stone wall that bordered the front lawn. A new front light showed off a new front walk and the completed stone wall.

The happy news that Peter and his love, Nancy, would be married in September of 1991 added to my sense of life moving on. Mark and Mary Ellen invited me to ride with them and we all stayed at the house

Peter and Nancy owned in Waterford, Maine. The other guests - Edith, (Peter and Mark's mother), Nancy's mother and Nancy's sister - made it a joyful and merry weekend. At the First Congregational Church in Andover, Maine, as Dean's wife, I was led to a seat on the groom's side of the altar. The whole experience of having been so completely included warmed my heart on the return trip to Foxboro.

That Thanksgiving, to thank the neighbors for not complaining when they held their annual summer picnic and filled our little area with cars, music and people, the members of the Fish and Game Club passed out frozen turkeys. I mentioned it at a New Beginnings meeting and someone suggested a potluck dinner. "I'll roast the turkey," I yelled. On Thanksgiving Day, six members arrived at my house bearing food to share. Six more showed up later in the day with dessert. We chatted and laughed together, making the day truly one of thanks.

In spite of all that, a sense of impermanence, of being untethered, hung over me – a feeling of drifting with the current, not knowing or even caring where I might come ashore. Past memories ebbed and flowed through my mind, especially the one of my cousin, Barbara, taking off for California in 1948 and wanting me to tag along. My engagement to Don and our impending marriage made the decision for me, but our divorce in 1952 often had me questioning that decision. The answer to myself always told me that if I had gone with Barbara, I wouldn't have had Darcy and she made it all worthwhile.

During Darcy's growing-up years, several times Barbara said, "If you want to try your luck in California, I'll take care of Darcy while you work," but something kept me in New England. In my trip to southern California in 1967, I loved what I found but when Dean came into my life, all thoughts of moving to California disappeared, but now they were resurfacing.

One thing I absolutely knew for sure was that I would never, ever love another man. Dean had been the love of my life and I wanted no others. I couldn't even imagine myself with anyone else. Period.

The Christmas of 1991 found me flying west again, ruminating on the strange quirk of fate that now had Darcy in California, a co-owner, with Ray, of a house in Berkeley. During my short stay, I meandered around the neighborhood, admiring the numerous little cottages. *If I could buy one of them, which one would it be?* Wandering along, I mulled over something that had happened on this trip. Just after I arrived at San Francisco Airport, I glanced out at the hills as I walked along a corridor and a wave of familiarity washed over me - a strong and warm sense of having come home to a place where I belonged. I asked Darcy how she'd feel if I moved to California. "I'd be glad," she said, "but it's a big move and I might decide I want to live somewhere else."

It was such a small seed of an idea that I didn't mention it to anyone back in Massachusetts except my friend, Gail, who said, "Remember that psychic I told you about? Let's go see her." That was fine with me.

During the visit, the psychic, a gentle, older lady, asked for a personal possession to hold in her hand. I gave her my wedding ring which I still wore. She sat silent for a while before surprising me with, "You're thinking of moving to another state." I nodded but her next comment made no sense to me. "Who's George?" I named all of the Georges I knew but she kept shaking her head and finally said," Let's move on."

Gail whispered, "Tell her about the dream."

I described it as I remembered it. She smiled, "Your husband took you to where he is now to show you what it's like and that he's happy. White flowers mean love. He wanted you to know he loves you." She didn't see any other significance in it but that was enough for me. She added that a baby girl would be born and there would be three children. That proved to be true in later years when Peter and Nancy had two daughters who were step-sisters to his son from his first marriage.

From then on, it seemed as though I couldn't turn around without bumping into California. A visitor to New Beginnings had recently moved back to Rhode Island from Walnut Creek in California. I attended an A.A. anniversary in Wrentham to see my old friends and sat next to a woman who was visiting from California. At a Chinese restaurant with friends, my fortune cookie read, "You are heading to a land of sunshine." Even the game I had attended between the Boston Red Sox and the Oakland A's had an off-hand connection.

To top it off, our minister, Bill, had grown up in southern California, prompting me to talk with him. "I can't tell you whether or not to go," he said, "but I can give you an exercise that might help. Put two identical chairs next to each other. Label one *Massachusetts* and the other *California*. Sit in each one and go over the things you like about that state."

I took his good advice. In the *California* chair, I thought, among other things, "Darcy, Marilyn, Barbara and Bill are there as well as four of Barbara's brother's five children." In the *Massachusetts* chair, I thought, "I have my house, my old friends, my church, my heritage and my memories- and the graves of all my family." It helped but I still had some narrowing down to do.

One thing I knew for sure - living alone in a seven-room house with a 90x100-foot yard had become a chore and, without Dean, it no longer felt like home. "Even though I can't make up my mind about California," I reasoned, early in 1993, "I can sell the house and move into an apartment in Foxboro." With that in mind, I attacked the attic first, purging it of anything I deemed unnecessary and, over the next few months, moved on to the garage, followed by the shed out back and the basement where the green typewriter still sat on the old desk.

New England basements or cellars have a "bulkhead" or short set of cement steps to the back yard, protected outside by a pair of diagonally placed metal or wooden doors set on low cement walls. On junk collection day, I yanked up the bulkhead doors and situated the wheelbarrow nearby. One step at a time, resting the typewriter on each one, I lugged it up to the wheelbarrow and with one last mighty effort, plunked it in and wheeled it around to the front yard to be set at the curb. Inside the house, I waited for the dump truck. When it arrived, I hid in a back room, not wanting, out of pure sentimentality, to watch the typewriter being taken away.

A redeeming thought struck me. If Dean hadn't bought it and I had been using a perfectly-working electric one, Darcy would probably not have sponsored the idea of a word processor for me.

While I prepared my house for its sale, changes in my personal life became part of the journey. Neponset Choral Society's new leader, in her belief that women's voices lowered as they grew older, plucked me from the soprano section and put me with the altos. As the organist and choir director at St. Mark's church, she did the same thing. I rebelled against what I felt to be an erroneous assumption and resigned in 1992 from both the Neponset Choral Society and the choir. Longing to sing, I joined the Chaminade Opera Group, a light-opera company. Its members had begun rehearsals for "The Mikado" whose score I knew fairly well since I had sung in the chorus in high school. I reveled in the familiar numbers and loved the dances, but after the performance, didn't remain with the group. Gradually, too, I drifted away from Al-Anon. Its message and philosophy stayed with me, though, making me extremely thankful for my twenty-one years of active membership. To this day, I continue to subscribe to "The Forum," the Al-Anon publication.

By May of 1993, with a yard sale behind me, I put an ad in the local paper to announce the sale of the house. One couple showed up, looked at it, asked a few questions but never contacted me again. June and July came and went, along with twenty-three days in August before I gave up and listed it with Mary, a real estate agent with our local Century 21.

The decision came quietly, without warning, during the first week of September, possibly induced by the placement with Mary. No fireworks filled the sky, no trumpets blared, but I knew I belonged in California. "I don't want to be sitting here in my old age," I explained to relatives and friends, "knowing I had struck out on my third time at bat, wondering what it would have been like. I'm going."

It came to me later that unconsciously I had been preparing myself or had been forced to do it by leaving the Neponset Choral Society and the church choir, two strong links to my life in Foxboro. New Beginnings was thriving. My writing would go with me. Nothing was holding me back.

CALIFORNIA, HERE I COME!

A S THOUGH IT HAD been waiting for my decision, everything fell neatly into place. Mary called two weeks later, on September 19th, "I have someone who'd like to see your house." In a reassuring coincidence, it was Lucille, a friend from New Beginnings. Four days after the showing, I heard from Mary again. "Lucille wants to buy your house, but," she cautioned, "don't make any permanent plans until the mortgage has been approved." When I passed that on to Darcy, she had a question.

"What would you like to have?"

Many years before all of this happened, I read Norman Vincent Peale's, "The Power of Positive Thinking" and recalled his suggestion to "form a picture in your mind of what you want and expect to get it." I decided to try my hand at positive thinking and imagined a tiny cottage on a bluff with a large window facing the ocean, framing the view and bringing the sun into the room. A fireplace, rafters and hardwood floors completed the picture. I didn't mention any of that to Darcy, except to say, "Small and cozy would be good and a first floor would be even better," and laughingly added, "It's California. There should be a palm tree in the yard."

She checked out Benecia, El Cerrito, Albany and Martinez, all small cities in the East Bay. A friend suggested looking in Alameda.

Immediately after I gave her the good news that the mortgage had been approved, she did that and reported back. "Betty from Kane & Associates showed me a one-floor duplex on Santa Clara Avenue that just became available," she said, "She also said we're lucky because those particular units don't come open very often. The woman who's moving has been there for ten years." I sent my deposit and promised to sign the rental agreement the minute I set foot in Alameda.

I called MacDonald's, a local agent of United Van Lines and we set November 22, 1993, two days before Thanksgiving, as the date he'd pick up my belongings. The preparations continued in the same smooth way. Since I'd be staying with Darcy for two weeks and she had two cats, Digger would be lodged at the Alladan Kennels in Mansfield temporarily. I made arrangements with a garage in Canton to ship my trusty Honda Civic to Darcy's house in Berkeley. Of course, I had already shared my original decision with Tom, my nieces and my friends, my stepsons and St. Mark's and New Beginnings. On hearing the latest update, they all congratulated me and wished me good luck.

With no idea of when I'd see my home town again, I drove to Cumberland for a last look at our old house on Lilac Street and my childhood haunts. In the Moshassuck Cemetery in Central Falls, I stood at my parent's graves to tell them my plans and whisper, "I love you." I did the same at Ruthie's grave in Rockhill Cemetery in Foxboro. Though thrilled at the prospect of the change, strong emotions often overwhelmed me at the thought of all I'd be leaving behind.

Something else happened during that period. A dream that I can clearly recall came to me on three separate nights. I lay in the arms of a man, deeply in love and wondrously happy. Oddly, his face was blurred but I naturally assumed it to be Dean.

A member of New Beginnings asked which meeting would be my last. On the night of that last meeting, they surprised me with a farewell party, complete with a cake and gifts. One that I cherish, a glass rose, lies on a shelf in my California dining room. At St. Mark's, the Sunday before I left Foxboro, Bill invited me to the front of the church so the whole congregation could bid me a fond farewell. I also shared a goodbye dinner with my friends - Ruth, Marge and Gail – and promised to keep in touch.

Phil, the driver of the MacDonald's van, picked up my furniture on the 22nd of November. As he closed the back door of the mammoth van and locked everything in, he told me, "I'm going home to Portland, Maine, for Thanksgiving but will start out the next day for California." After he left, I cleaned the house to the side door, took a deep breath, swallowed the lump in my throat, stepped out and closed the door behind me for the last time.

My plane reservation was for the 24th and Digger was safe at Alladan Kennels. I headed to North Attleboro and the mobile home Tom had bought. He took me to dinner to give us a chance to talk and reminisce and I bunked at his place that night. The next morning, he followed me to Canton to leave my Honda for its trip west. After lunch, he drove me to Foxfield Plaza to board the Bonanza bus which stopped at that midpoint on its back-and-forth trip between T. F. Green Airport in Rhode Island and Logan Airport in Boston. That afforded me one last look at the little brown house that my mother, Darcy and I had shared during her growing-up years. The bus arrived. I hugged Tom and thanked him, letting the tears fill my eyes. I drank in as much of Foxboro as I could before we reached the on-ramp to I-95 and headed for Boston.

As the plane gained altitude, I watched Boston grow smaller. I had no regrets about my decision but was leaving sixty-eight years' worth of memories, making it difficult to handle the turmoil of mixed emotions. Once I could no longer see the trees of Boston or the blue of the harbor, I pulled in a deep breath and forced myself to look to the future and my new home in Alameda, a city I had only glimpsed from a distance. On one of my past visits, Darcy took me to see where the trains rumble along the middle of the street in Jack London Square in Oakland. We parked facing the Oakland-Alameda Estuary on an open area that existed before the Oakland Embarcadero waterfront had been given over to condos. She pointed across the Estuary. "That's Alameda." I knew the name because Tom, a Navy fighter pilot during World War 11, had been briefly stationed there in 1945.

Six hours after we left Boston, around 11:00 P.M., we began the descent into San Francisco Airport. In the baggage claim area, as I plucked my suitcase from the carousel, the thought struck me. *I have no home, furniture, car or cat. Right now, I'm holding in my hand all that I have in the world. Is this the way a refugee feels?* In spite of that, I knew my boat had stopped drifting and had come ashore at the right place. That night at Darcy's house, Lorraine, the cat whose tail I had grabbed in Foxboro, slept at my feet. Through the window I glimpsed the tiny cottages that had planted the seed. The next day, I'd celebrate my first Thanksgiving as a resident of California.

It's hard to remember all of the emotions and thoughts that darted through my mind on Thanksgiving, except for one - my absolute certainty that I belonged in California. The next day, thanks to Darcy, I had my first up-close glimpse of Alameda. The minute we crossed the Park Street bridge that crosses the Estuary and connects Oakland to Alameda, I liked what I saw, a feeling that increased when I stepped inside the little duplex. I smiled and thanked God and Norman Vincent Peale. My new home had a large window to let in the view and the sun, rafters, a fireplace and hardwood floors. It didn't sit on a bluff above the ocean but the large window faced toward San Francisco Bay, half a mile away – good enough for me. Darcy pointed to a neighbor's yard. "There's your palm tree."

The two weeks I stayed in Berkeley gave me time to deposit my savings in the local Wells Fargo bank, have the gas turned on in my duplex and a phone installed – and to choose my own phone number. My Honda reached Berkeley on Thursday, December 2nd, begrimed from the 3,000 mile journey atop the car carrier. Phil had already called to say he and my furniture would be in Alameda on Friday, December 3rd. Darcy took the day off to help me and to follow me to Alameda to be sure I didn't get lost. Not that night but on Saturday night, I slept in my own bed, at home in Alameda, ready for whatever adventures lay ahead.

Digger arrived in California on the 6th. Ray took me to the airport where I found my cat, bewildered and meowing pitifully inside his carrier, with front-end loaders clanking around him in the huge space of the freight terminal. All the way across the Bay Bridge and into Alameda, he refused to stay quiet until we reached our new home where he flew into the nearest closet. He ate, slept and used his box inside the closet for four days. On the fifth, he warily crept out to prowl the house. Once he had sniffed everything and was satisfied that no danger lurked in the corners, he jumped on the bed and settled down.

ALAMEDA

THE BIG, UNOPENED PACKAGE that was Alameda lay in front of me, making me impatient to find out what it contained, but that would have to wait until I at least had some basic information – where to buy food, for instance.

Darcy offered, on the Saturday after the move, to show me the way to the Safeway Supermarket. "No problem," I thought, making mental notes of the street names as we rode down Park Street to South Shore Center. "The avenues run one way and the streets cross them. If I found my way around the New England cowpaths, this should be a cinch."

On my later solo trip to South Shore Center, I had no trouble finding Safeway but after I had done my shopping I exited onto Shoreline Drive to park for a short time in order to soak in the exquisite view of San Francisco across the Bay and the peninsular below it. A glance at my watch sent me heading for home.

Inadvertently, in my search for Park Street I passed the entrance to South Shore Center and continued to where Shoreline Drive curves to the left and becomes Broadway. Momentary panic melted into laughter a short while later when I saw the Estuary lying ahead of me with no Park Street Bridge in sight. "You can't stay lost for long in Alameda," I chuckled to myself. "If you reach the Estuary on one side or San Francisco Bay on the other, you simply retrace your steps because Alameda is an island and you won't wander forever in a maze of city streets."

On the way back up Broadway, I found the Santa Clara Avenue sign I had missed on the way down. A short drive later, at the Chestnut Street stop sign, Darcy's good advice came back to me. "Use the Presbyterian

Church as a landmark. It's big and it's white and you know you're at the corner of Chestnut Street. Lafayette Street and the driveway are just past it on the left." That saved me many times until finding the driveway became second nature. The map she bought for me helped a great deal, too.

Slowly, the piles of boxes in my living room and along the wall in my bedroom dwindled. The garage that came with the unit helped tremendously, especially with the "where-shall-I-put this?" items. Luckily, with good planning and careful maneuvering, I was able to squeeze my car in, too.

Digger wasn't a wandering cat but had enjoyed a large yard and nearby woods in Foxboro. The day I felt he was ready, after his many hours and weeks of standing near the front door and meowing, I let him out. Following closely behind, I watched him sniff around the yard. As he inched toward Santa Clara Avenue, I ran to head him off but a big bus rattling by sent him scurrying back to the house. He decided it was off-limits and stayed, from then on, for the most part, within the bounds of the almost six-foot fence surrounding the yard.

At times he sat, watching curiously, as I tried to shoe-horn one more item into the garage. I always called out and waited for his answering "meow" to be sure he wasn't in the garage or under the car before closing and locking the door. Once that method failed me. I called him for his supper but he didn't show up. I checked Santa Clara Avenue and peeked over the fence into the neighbors' yards, calling and calling until it grew dark. In between, I ate a quick meal, praying he'd show up, but at 1:00 A.M., weariness took over and I fell asleep on the couch, fully clothed. The minute my eyes opened the next morning, I snatched up my garage keys to check once more. This time I heard it the minute I pulled up the garage door – a faint meow coming from the back of the garage. I had no idea how he had become lodged in a tiny space between a tall plastic bin and the rear wall of the garage but it left him no room to back up and spring onto the top of the bin. We were equally glad to see each other and we both slept well that night.

Apparently, he needed one more escapade. Curiosity lured him over or around the fence on the day he came home without his collar and the new California tag I'd just recently attached to it. The mystery deepened when, shortly after that, the collar and tag showed up in my mail slot along with a note from a neighbor, "I found this in my yard today." Fortunately, the writer had included his phone number.

"I live a block over from you, near the corner of Lafayette and Central Avenue," he told me when I called to thank him and assure him my cat had made it back home. Digger didn't enlighten me but also never left the yard again.

Able, at last, to peek into the Alameda package, I began with Christ Episcopal Church which stands at the corner of Grand Street, a two-block walk from my new home. I told Zelma, the lady who greeted me, that I was a newcomer. She introduced me to her friend, Alberta, who invited me to sit with her. After church, they asked me to join them and five or six other women for lunch at a local restaurant and – just like that - I became part of the group that had lunch every Sunday after church. The following Sunday, I told Dan, the Rector, that I'd like to become a member. "Welcome, Violet," he said, "it'll be a pleasure to have you with us." At the midnight service on Christmas Eve, I thanked the guiding Power that had brought me to Alameda and Christ Church. Though I don't remember all the details of Christmas day, I recall that Darcy and Ray joined me for dinner and I can still smile about the novel experience of hearing a lawn mower that morning.

The whirlwind pace of my adjustment continued into 1994. In Foxboro, I had been diagnosed with high blood pressure and advised to walk every day. Alameda made that easy. First, I tried the path along Robert W. Crown Beach, continuing on to Crab Cove where I watched the curlews and egrets search for food. In time, I ventured to Memorial Park in the Bay Farm Island section of Alameda, discovering to my delight that I could walk as far as the San Francisco ferry dock, the newest one of two in Alameda. A young lady I talked with in Safeway suggested I check out the bayside trail beyond where Harbor

Bay Parkway borders the Oakland Airport and where sea lavender brightens the side of the trail and you have an unobstructed view of San Francisco Bay. Getting braver, I drove to the tip of Ballena Boulevard at the western end of the island to walk the path that meanders above the rocks and affords a view of the ships moored at one end of what was then Alameda Naval Air Station. On another drive, I found the area on Main Street where I could park and watch the ships – big and little –cruise up and down the Estuary, including the original Alameda-to-San Francisco ferry whose landing dock sits just below where I parked. Walking in Marina Village showed me another section of the Estuary and I found the old, abandoned outdoor theater.

On those walks and drives, I reveled in the beauty of Alameda, smiling at the number of trees sheltering the streets and adding their grace to the scores of handsome Victorian houses. Driving down Grand Street, I caught my breath at the sight of the bay seemingly spread out in front of me. Going back in the other direction, I could see the cutters moored at Coast Guard Island, poignantly reminding me of our connection to the sea.

Every so often, after my walk at Crown Beach and especially on windy days, I sat on a bench to watch the windsurfers. I also walked on the hard sand at low tide and noted the shallowness of the water, but soon learned that, due to the slope of the beach, it deepens by several feet at high tide. "I'll find a tide table," I promised myself, looking forward to the pleasant prospect of swimming, "and I'll come in the summer, at high tide."

All of this prodded me into visiting the Alameda Museum where I was finally able to delve into Alameda's past.* The detailed history given to me by the docents told of the discovery of six shell mounds at the eastern end of the peninsular that would become Alameda. Skeletal remains buried beneath other shell mounds scattered in various places around San Francisco Bay told archeologists that the area had been inhabited about 3500 years ago. The accepted belief is that the mounds

---

* See the History section at the back of the book.

belonged to members of the Miwok tribe. Alameda's aptly name *Mound Street* now runs through that area. Much more information lay in the pages that I took home with me but it would have to wait until I could slow down and read it.

Meanwhile, proof that I had truly found a new home came the day that I spotted Peggy, one of the ladies from church and – at last - a familiar face in the Safeway supermarket. Her broad smile almost matched mine.

BEYOND ALAMEDA

EIGHTEEN YEARS AFTER THAT January day in 1986 when I pulled Darcy's college portable out of the attic to find out whether an editor would not only publish my writing but also pay me, to my delight it had happened and was still happening. Shortly before I left Foxboro, in my pre-computer days, I wrote to Sandra, the Editor of *Writers' Open Forum*, to give her my new address and confess my excitement that her November-December 1993 edition would include "Your Cookies or Mine?" the first fiction ever to appear under my byline. In a thrilling coincidence, as though to welcome me to California, the original batch of mail forwarded from Foxboro included a copy of that edition of the magazine.

Earlier in the year, the editor of *Gotta Write Network Magazine*, a woman I had come to know through my submissions, phoned to ask whether I'd be interested in doing an article on senior markets.

I lunged at the chance and did the legwork. "Focusing on Senior Markets," was featured in the Winter 1993 issue. Somehow, my writing – a lifeline in the midst of havoc – had held fast through the tragic loss of three people I loved deeply and the cross-country move of my beloved daughter and my own move. To keep that lifeline intact, I needed to find a writers group.

My search revealed that a Romance Writer's conference would be held in a hotel in Emeryville, a city near the busy entrance to Bay Bridge, the span to San Francisco. "Why not?" I thought, though I was definitely not a romance writer and was still a novice on 880, the freeway connecting the cities along the East Bay, as this area is called. I followed the big green and white signs and reached the maze at the bridge, misread the directions and panicked when I realized I was heading to San Francisco. The toll taker saved me. "Go off at Yerba Buena Island," she instructed, naming a halfway point, "and you can come back on, heading in the right direction." Outside of seriously spooking a few other motorists, I made it safely to Powell Street and the conference. Though I enjoyed meeting the other writers, it convinced me that romance writing wasn't my genre.

Fortunately, the Community Activities page in the *Alameda Journal*, a local weekly, listed Writers West of Alameda. At that period in their almost 20-year history, the group met on the second and fourth Tuesdays of every month in a room at the Alameda Hospital. At the first session I attended, January 24, 1994, I became a member. The meeting consisted, for the most part, of the attendees evaluating each other's manuscripts and offering kind and helpful suggestions – a new and valuable experience for me. With that taken care of, I could partake of the buffet of activities offered in the area.

On a sunny, breezy day in March, Darcy and I boarded the ferry to cross under the Bay Bridge on our way to Pier 39, a tourist and shopping center along the San Francisco Embarcadero and near the ferry docks in San Francisco. Passing close to the huge freighters tied up at the Port of Oakland and getting a fish-eye-view of the underbelly of the Bay Bridge added to the thrill of the ride. Another surprise greeted me after we docked. Several years before my visit, sea lions* had begun congregating in the harbor, attracted by the fishing boats and possible meals from toss-outs, competing for space in the limited area. Their presence caused a major headache for the city until an imaginative person suggested making them a tourist attraction. The city built little docks where they could "haul out" and bask in the sun, barking and putting on their own little show for the Pier 39 visitors. I had never been

---

* A new choir friend, Janet, cautioned me not to call them "seals" and named a few differences. "They bark loudly," she said, "use their flippers to walk and have visible ear laps."

that close to sea lions and now I was watching them slip on and off the docks, creating a fond memory.

Another favorite memory came into being when Barbara and Bill called to say they'd be visiting on May 28th. The tour I set up included a drive around Alameda, a visit to Christ Church and of course, a ferry ride to Pier 39 and the sea lions. My cousins loved it and we loved seeing each other. We all agreed it was comforting to be in the same state and be able to be together whenever we felt the need. That trip became the quintessential destination whenever I had visitors.

They were also pleased, due to our mutual singing history, to hear I had joined the Christ Church choir. The organist and choir director, Terry, had no problem with putting me in the soprano section. The Thursday night rehearsals pleased me immensely and gave me an opportunity to meet more of the parishioners. Being in the choir also led to a change in another area of my life. During our summer hiatus, other singers or organists filled in.. One Sunday, a lady named Diane did the honors. During the coffee hour, I complimented her. "Thank you," she replied and went on to ask, "Do you like to dance?"

I laughed. "I love to but my late husband didn't so I haven't been on a dance floor since the day I met him in 1967."

She smiled in understanding. "Well, if you ever feel the urge, come to the Eagles Club on Alameda Avenue at 7:30 on Sunday night. I take the tickets and I sing with the band." I filed the information into a back corner of my brain, possibly for future use at some unspecified date.

The fast and furious pace continued. That fall, I joined St. Margaret's Guild, a group that met once a week to discuss a variety of subjects or projects we might like to adopt. I met Rosemary and Ann, two other newcomers to Alameda. They said they met every Friday at *The Vines,* a coffee shop located upstairs in a charming old Victorian which shared its location with *Thomsen's Nursery* and invited me to join them. They introduced me to John, the owner of the coffee shop, and his wife, Iris, who ran the nursery. Chloe, Rosemary's friend from the local photography club, was already part of the group. In one of our conversations, I commented that I knew nothing of the area outside of the East Bay. Ann spoke up. "I'm out of work right now. I'll show you around if you'll do the driving." That sounded perfect because driving had always been a pleasure for me. I loved the freedom of it and looked forward to the chance to explore new areas.

Our first trip took us to Jamestown in gold rush country. I struggled to keep my attention on the road, wanting to gape at the spectacular scenery as we headed through the mountains and into the open country. Wandering the streets of Jamestown, I marveled at being in a real gold country town. After lunch, we visited a Native American gift shop run by a friend of Ann's. I found a pair of ear rings, hand- made out of small stones. When people admire them, I relish telling that story. On the way back, Ann pointed to a high gate that opened to a vast stretch of land and said, "That's a ranch." On the straight road, I could admire it without endangering us.

On other trips, we ate in a local restaurant in Half Moon Bay, on the peninsular below San Francisco, and stopped in a nursery in La Honda where I bought a cement cat sculpture for my front steps. Another day we walked on the pier at Santa Cruz and stepped inside Santa Cruz Mission. In its quiet and serene atmosphere, I reviewed all of the blessings of the past few months. Ann's days and my days became full after that and the trips ended but I had one more to take on my own.

In October, I rode a Greyhound bus up over the Donner Pass into Reno to visit Judy, my friend who had helped me establish the Al-Anon meeting in Foxboro. Now divorced, she had relocated to Reno to be near her sister. I was free in the bus to enjoy the splendor of the Pass and marvel that I was 7,056 feet up in the Sierra Nevada mountains, with my thoughts often turning to the Donner party and their dreadful fate. I didn't do any gambling in the "Biggest, Little City" but ate a few meals with Judy and her sister, Louise, in the glittery and glitzy casinos. Judy and Louise also took me to Virginia City where Mark Twain had worked for a newspaper and where the Comstock Lode silver mine is open for tours. I walked on the sand at Lake Tahoe and smiled at its grandeur. Those moments and being with Judy again stayed with me all the way back to Alameda.

My friend, Ruth, had been absolutely right when she said, "You don't believe it but you will be happy again." Darcy, Ray and Stephanie joined me for Thanksgiving dinner. With a fire in the fireplace and my home smelling of turkey, stuffing and pumpkin pie, I knew what she meant.

WHO'S GEORGE?

MEMORIES OF THE EVENTS of 1994 danced through my mind as I watched the televised scene of the ball drop in Times Square and heard the New York crowd chanting the seconds left until 1995 appeared. My writing, for one, had continued on a positive path. The *Alameda Journal,* one of our two weekly newspapers, ran a contest in September, "Why I Love Alameda." Though I didn't win, my entry was one of five chosen to be published along with the winning entry. My byline appeared on another short story, "It's the Thought That Counts," in the November issue of *Writers International Open Forum.* The Winter 1994 edition of *Gotta Write Network Magazine* carried my article,

"Capturing the Essence of Flow." I could legitimately call myself a free-lance writer.

The new year lost no time in throwing opportunities my way. Lola, our faithful Writers West Secretary, announced that she wanted to step down. The challenge appealed to me. It meant, among other things, that I'd be the writer, editor and publisher of our monthly newsletter.

With the help of Office Depot in San Leandro (Office Max had not yet come to Alameda) and Lola's input, I mastered the easiest way to print and assemble the pages.

I sensed, as I had in the past, a shift coming in my life but had no inkling of its direction and decided to go with the flow. February found me taking a mammoth step, surprising myself and Diane by following her suggestion to check out the dance in the Eagles Hall. She smiled when I appeared at the ticket desk and I thanked her for telling me about it. Empty chairs were at a premium inside the hall. I spotted one but it meant I'd have to cross the room. I had barely sat down when someone leaned over to say, "I'm sorry but that's being saved." Back in the doorway, my thoughts turned hostile. *If nobody asks me by eight o'clock, I'm outta here* Luckily, that wasn't in the plan.

A lady sitting near the doorway beckoned to me. "My friend, Ben, is dancing," she said. "I can't dance tonight so would you like to sit in his seat?" I accepted her kind offer and introduced myself. She said, "I'm Mary." When Ben returned, she explained, "Violet is new. Would you mind dancing with her?" As soon as I stood up, the beat caught me and it all came back. Ben, affable and pleasant, danced well. When the music ended, Mary introduced me to two women from Alameda – Laura and Ann – and they found room for me. I had stumbled across my Sunday night activity.

Each week, I was assured of at least one dance with Ben. Slowly, my circle widened to include Dick and Hal and a few others, plus Dwight who also invited me to have coffee with him after the dance. Feeling high and happy, I agreed to meet him at Lyon's, a restaurant near South Shore Center. "I come up from Fresno to check on some property I own in Pacifica," he told me, naming a city on the coast, below San Francisco. "I'm a widower so I try to take in the dance, too." In spite of my pledge never to become interested in another man, the fact that I missed their company had just raised its undeniable head.

He walked me back to my car but when I put out my hand he grabbed me and kissed me. "Thank you," he murmured. "I'll keep in touch." Even in the midst of my shock, I enjoyed it.

The following Sunday, we danced together again and later had coffee and another quick kiss. Even though I enjoyed Dwight's company, I still fought the idea of letting another man into my life. It had been six years since I lost Dean and I still considered him to be the love of my life. I wanted no others. Again, as had happened so often in my life, somebody had other ideas. During the week, I was walking home from a nearby store and glanced idly at the message on the board in front of the First Congregational church, "Never place a period where

God has placed a comma. God is still speaking." I stopped and stared at it for several minutes. Wow! The timeliness of it stunned me. I had to do some thinking.

Dwight showed up a few more times and talked about seeing me outside of the dance, but we didn't name any specific date. Meanwhile, to everyone's surprise, the band, Nob Hill, announced its plan to move to a dance hall in Piedmont, a city just beyond Oakland. I wasn't willing to drive that far yet, especially after Laura and Anne told me that Nob Hill also played on Friday nights in Oakland at the Veteran's Hall. By late June, I had become a part of the Friday night group, still dancing regularly with Dick, Hal and now, Marty. Dwight showed up once or twice but, though I missed him and our chats over coffee, I still hesitated to make definite plans with him. Deep down inside, I wondered, in spite of his property, why he drove so far just to dance. Weren't there any closer to his home? Was he really a widower?

On the 4th of July, I found a spot on Park Street to watch the Alameda parade. It brought back fond memories of past times in Rhode Island when the whole family piled into the car to see the parade in Pawtucket. I also found room among the cars jamming the area around the ferry landing to view the fireworks across the estuary in Jack London Square. The old-fashioned ritual helped me to feel even more at home in Alameda.

The shift I had sensed had not been my imagination. Two Fridays after that 4th in 1995, George asked me to dance. It was easy to see, with his perfect beat and obvious love of dancing, that he *felt* the music. I loved swinging and swaying to the 40's and 50's tunes. Since it was the last dance of the night, we talked briefly. He gave me directions to Piedmont. I had no plans to go but listened and nodded politely. We didn't exchange last names but I assumed I'd see him again in Oakland.

On Monday night, my phone rang. "Hello, Violet. This is George. Where were you last night? I went to Piedmont and looked for you." I apologized, scrambling for a plausible excuse, wondering how he had found my number until he explained. "I'm a member of a San

Leandro Kiwanis group," he explained, "And I told your friend, Anne, when I asked for your number, that I planned to sell you a ticket to our Crab Feed." I chuckled when he added, "The crab feed isn't until next January." He asked me to go to dinner with him that night but I had already eaten. We talked a while and I hung up, still smiling at his exuberance.

He called again on Tuesday night. This time, I agreed to join him for coffee since, again, I had already eaten. Listening to his stories of growing up in Brooklyn, I told him I hadn't laughed that much in a long time. "My wife, Miriam, and I took a bus across the country to California in 1935 to be near her sister and her family because they had moved out here," he said. He said he still lived in the house they bought in Oakland, adding, "She passed away in 1991." One thing especially struck me. He seemed open and transparent, someone who spoke the truth and expected it in return.

Just as I was leaving for my daily walk on Wednesday, he called. "I'll go with you," he offered and I agreed. While we were walking, he suggested picking me up for the Piedmont dance. I quickly thanked him but said I'd drive there by myself. The message on the church board had given me permission but my life was moving too fast and I hadn't completely taken the period off it. He also mentioned a monthly dance sponsored by a group called Soiree Singles and held in Bay Fairway Hall on Bay Farm Island in Alameda. "Would you like to go to the next one?" I said I'd have to think about it and let him know.

During August, Dwight showed up in Oakland and again in Piedmont. It was confusing. I liked Dwight and felt more attracted to him but wasn't entirely sure he wasn't hiding something. I enjoyed and trusted George but he was overwhelming me and it had all happened so quickly.

On the day of the dance at Bay Fairway, tired and uncertain, I stretched out on my sofa. "In about two months I'll be seventy years old," I thought. "I should be old enough to know what I want, but I don't. Please help me."

I had barely finished my plea when my phone rang. "Hi, this is George. Will you be there tonight?"

I took the period off my life, replaced it with a comma and said, "Yes."

That night, sitting next to him in Bay Fairway Hall, I felt ready to step through the door into an unknown future. Dwight didn't come to any of the dances again. Possibly his only role was to break down my barriers.

Several days later, I was standing in front of my sink in my new kitchen and froze in place. The words of the psychic from Rehoboth had come back to me, "Who's George?" He had been in my life even before I left Massachusetts.

Interring Dean's ashes at St. Mark's Memorial
Garden, Foxboro, June, 1996

Mark and Mary Ellen
in Mass., 1996

Violet holding Maggie,
June, 1996

Maggie, Nancy, Peter in June, 1996

Violet at the
Ronald Reagan Library,
piece of Berlin Wall, 1996

Katy at 15 in
Santa Y nez,
California, 2000

Violet at Waikiki Beach,
1998

Violet and George on the MS Statendam, 1998

Violet's 75th birthday, Panama Canal cruise, 2000

Violet and George,
dance party, 2002

George, Barbara and Bill,
Long Beach,
California, 2003

George and Violet dancing, 2005

George and Violet at Christmas Party, 2004

INTO THE WHIRLWIND

THE QUIET LIFE I had envisioned for myself in California fell by the wayside when George took my hand and pulled me into his whirlwind life of music, dancing and laughter. He claimed to be eighty-five to my seventy but had an energy and vigor that made it hard to believe. Besides living alone and taking care of his house, he danced as often as possible and worked out once a week at a gym in downtown Oakland.

He explained both the dancing and the work-out schedule. "When Miriam died, we'd been married fifty-nine years. I was lost and sat at home until Cliff – that's my son - told me to go back to dancing and I've been doing it ever since - in Oakland, Piedmont, on cruises or anywhere there's a band and a dance floor." His obvious delight in the music and the movements attracted numerous dance partners as it had attracted me.

The working-out routine was established when he played baseball in Brooklyn, his home town. "When I was sixteen, I went to Ebbets Field a lot but I didn't have money for a ticket so the guys at the entrance let me help take tickets and I got to know the players and the coaches," he said. "Of course, that was 1926 and things were a lot different. The players traveled in buses and stayed at flea-bag hotels and weren't looked-up to the way they are today and they didn't get the same kind of money." The coach and the managers came to know him and began letting him shag fly balls during practice. They liked the way he threw the ball and tried him at hitting which he did well. "They took me with them on one of the away games," he continued, "And let me play, but I pulled a muscle in my arm somehow. Back in Brooklyn, the scout for the team said they'd send me to a farm team where I could have my arm massaged and learn more about playing baseball. I guess they thought I had potential."

He paused and smiled a little. "I went home and told my mother and she said I wasn't going anywhere but to school until I graduated. That was the end of that." I laughed – not at his disappointment but at the picture in my mind of his mother sending him back to school even while his story drew me to him. He played softball, though, whenever and wherever he could, until he was seventy-five, he told me, and established a habit of working out at gyms which he was still doing when we met.

The new tempo also reached into my personal life. For my upcoming seventieth birthday in October, for instance, Darcy and my family presented me with a September weekend in Yosemite National Park. Just before I climbed the steps of the Greyhound bus, George, who had driven me to Oakland, kissed me goodbye and said, "I'll be here to pick you up." Making myself comfortable, I watched the California landscape slip by, thrilled when we passed through the entrance and I read the sign, "Yosemite National Park". In a small cabin near Yosemite Lodge, I set down my suitcase, awestruck by the view of Yosemite Falls. My mind arced back to Rhode Island and the numerous times my mother, my sister and I assembled a jigsaw puzzle with the title, "Yosemite Falls in the beautiful Sierra Nevada." In all of my dreams, I had never imagined I'd see the real place, much less be close to it. Emotions welled up at the thought of the precious gift my family had given me.

At dinner in Ahwahnee Lodge, a group of women invited me to join them for the tram tour the next day. We walked along the banks of the Merced River and wandered through the Mariposa Grove where I stood next to the tallest tree I had ever seen in my life. The majestic beauty of Yosemite Valley overwhelmed all of us at Glacier Point. We took pictures of El Capitan, Bridalveil Fall and Half Dome and aimed our cameras again when we emerged from Wawona Tunnel and saw them all spread out before us.

That night, George listened to my gushing recap of the day. "I miss you but I'm glad you're having a wonderful time," he said. Another ride on Sunday showed us the tourist accommodations for those not wanting to stay at the Ahwahnee Lodge or Yosemite Lodge and anything else we hadn't covered yet. That afternoon we were entertained as we sat in the Amphitheater outside the Yosemite Lodge. After our evening meal, chattering and content, we boarded the bus. The sight of George waiting in Oakland brought a safe and comfortable feeling, one I'd always have with him.

To add to my happiness, later that month, my short story, "Where the Sidewalk Ends," was published in *Show and Tell*. I grabbed the phone to tell George but found he wasn't feeling well. "I called Cliff," he said. A few hours later, I heard from Cliff.

"My father has the flu so I thought he'd be better off in the hospital." He gave me directions in case I decided to pay a visit. I did and George beamed in surprise when I walked into the hospital room. "Thanks for coming," he said. "I'm doing well and can go home tomorrow."

I was surprised in return to hear from Cliff once more. "Would you be willing to let my father stay with you?" he asked. "He's at home and doing well but my wife and I have had a trip to Hawaii planned for some time and don't want to leave him alone." I agreed, grateful that I could do something for him. I managed to locate his house from the directions Cliff gave me and found him lying on his living room couch. He packed a little bag and I took him home with me for several days.

He told me about his business as a sub-contractor. "I furnished accessories for new and old buildings," he explained. That meant flagpoles, stair banisters and skylights, to name a few. In the 70's, with his business doing well, he and Miriam decided they could afford to go on cruises. "Miriam loved to dance," he said, "but I didn't know how so one day she told me she had signed us up for dance lessons and that's when it all started."

It didn't take long for him, when he recovered, to involve me in his love of cruising. "The MS Oosterdam is in San Francisco," he told me. "How would you like to tour it?" Naturally, I agreed and we took the ferry into San Francisco. With no idea when, or even if, I'd ever be on a cruise, I joined the small group following the Tour Guide around the ship. George, however, loved to stop and chat with everyone and anyone. Trying not to lose sight of either him or the Tour Guide became part of our relationship from then on but it didn't take away from my pleasure at seeing, for the first time, a ship's cabin, a dance floor called "The Crow's Nest," or a dining room with a view of the ocean through all of its windows. The ship's arrival during Fleet week allowed us to watch delightedly from the fantail as the Blue Angels performed their aerobatics..

In spite of all that was happening in my life, it amazed and pleased me that I was able to keep writing and being published. In fact, that November, *Good Old Days Specials* published "I Remember the Mittens."

Also in November, Cliff and his wife, Hilary, invited me to their house for Thanksgiving and included Darcy. I thanked him but Darcy had already made plans to cook and had company coming. George and I compromised by eating dinner at Darcy's house and dessert at Cliff 's. There I met Hilary and George's grandsons, Stephen and Jason. Their house in Orinda, in the East Bay hills, overlooked a valley – a fascinating experience for me.

Christmas rolled around and once more, Cliff and Hilary invited me and even had a small present for me. Again, George and I split the day between both houses. The hospitality of his family and their kindness added to the joy of my new life.

On New Year's Eve we mingled with a crowd of friends at the Colombo Club, an Italian fellowship hall in Oakland, for a dinner and dance. At midnight, I looked back on 1995, not believing the pace I was keeping.

The only slowdown came in January at Writers West. We decided to meet on the fourth Tuesday of every month instead of having two meetings a month, but a week later we changed it to the second Tuesday, where it has remained. With my new hectic lifestyle, serving as Secretary, getting out the newsletter besides doing justice to my social life, became difficult. I asked for a year off. Lola took over again, but we discontinued the newsletter.

One thing I vowed to do before the new year slipped away from me was visit my nieces, Marilyn and Ann. They lived in Simi Valley in southern California where Marilyn had a position as the Registrar for the Reagan Library, also in Simi Valley. Ann was the Lighting Director for several television programs, such as General Hospital and Wheel of Fortune. In February, I flew down for a weekend. Marilyn gave me a private tour of the Library which sits on a hill at the top of a winding driveway and has a spectacular view. I admired President Reagan's collection of saddles, viewed unique presents from other world leaders and had my picture taken next to a chunk of the Berlin Wall, besides seeing his private office. Later, in a television studio, sitting next to Ann, high above a television show, I watched in fascination as she directed the lighting.

I told them about George. "We'll come down together some time," I added. We had become a *couple*. Any invitations either of us received always noted that the other was included but there were some things we agreed should be done separately. Word came in June, for instance, that the Memorial Garden behind St. Mark's Church in Foxboro had been established. George understood when I said, "I'm going back for two weeks to settle Dean's ashes," and didn't invite him to accompany me. I felt it to be my personal business and intended to stay with relatives and friends for most of my visit. "I'll give you their phone numbers" I promised.

COMPANIONS

WE SAID OUR GOODBYES at Oakland Airport on June 15th. With my emotions see-sawing between not wanting to be away from him for two weeks but being anxious to see my old home and friends, I stashed him in a corner of my mind as you would a lovely expectation. In Massachusetts, driving the dear, familiar streets of Foxboro, nostalgia took over, especially as I headed down South Street toward St. Mark's. There I found my brother-in-law, Tom, and Marge, Gail and Ruth, three longtime friends, plus Frank, Dottie, Dino and Walter from Dean's A.A. group; waiting to greet me. Their loving presence and that of the current minister and several close friends from St. Mark's helped me through the emotions of interring Dean's ashes and being in "our" church again. After the brief service and before gathering with the others in the Common Room of the church, I stole a quick moment to meander around the garden and to linger near the place where Dean's ashes lay. "I'll be back some day to be with you forever," I whispered. At last, I felt ready to sit, have coffee and chat for a while.

That night at Gail's condo, we laughed and reminisced. While she was at work the next day, I strolled along the country road that passed her house, reveling in the trees and broad fields. The following morning, I thanked her, hugged her and headed to Cumberland.

Our old house on Lilac Street had flourished under its new owners. The oak tree still held its place in the front yard but new bushes also graced the area, giving it a cozy, lived-in appearance. For a moment, I considered knocking on the door, curious and eager to see the inside again, but didn't feel up to the emotions it might evoke. Instead, I drove past slowly, filling my mind with its look of contentment.

At Marge's house in Pawtucket that evening, her phone rang. She answered, grinned at me and said, "Yes, she's here." George missed me, he said, and wanted to make sure all was going well. I smiled, overjoyed to hear his voice and his words and to know he'd be waiting.

Marge delighted me with a trip to Newport the next day and the day after that, I raved about it to Ruth and my cousin, Betty, who had joined us for lunch. "We walked along the pier and strolled through the shopping area and just had a wonderful time." All of us had kept in touch but being with them and sharing my news in person brought more satisfaction.

On the road again, I turned toward Medway, Massachusetts, to be with another Ruth, a friend I'd met in 1989 in an athletic club swimming pool after we both lost our husbands. That night, with her agreement, I squeezed in a trip to see Rue, a singing buddy from St. Mark's choir.

Ruth's plan for my visit also delighted me. We toured Boston aboard a "duck", an amphibious vehicle that left the road to give us a ride on the Charles River, a unique experience where passengers were invited to sit in the driver's seat for a few minutes. With Ruth's encouragement, I did it. Of course, you actually just drifted with the current and didn't have to steer, but it added to my fun. Back on solid ground, we walked through the Public Garden, checked out Faneuil Hall and poked around in Quincy Market, the shopping mall established in old waterfront buildings when the Central Artery through Boston had been demolished.

Time raced by and soon I was on my way to Worcester for a quick, full-of-love, two-day visit with Mark and Mary Ellen. It pleased me to be with them and to be able to tell them that Dean's ashes now rested safely in St. Mark's Memorial Garden. I bid them goodbye and headed to Waterford, Maine, to find Peter and Nancy's house. Peter took me to a market and invited me to pick out my lobster for dinner. To add to that, I had my picture taken sitting on their porch, smiling broadly in my bliss, holding Maggie, my new step-granddaughter,

I spent my final two nights in North Attleboro, Massachusetts, at Tom's house, telling him all my news and hearing his. Unbelievably, the time had come to fly home. Early on Friday, the 28th of June. I hugged him goodbye at Foxfield Plaza as I had in 1993 and boarded the Bonanza bus for Logan Airport. Once more, climbing into the sky, I cried as I looked down on the green trees. However, in Los Angeles, my last stop before San Francisco, I called George and when he asked, "Are you home?" I said I was because I suddenly knew it to be true.

I also knew I was happy with him. He spent weekends at my place and sometimes picked me up after Thursday night choir rehearsal at Christ Church, raising the question, "How shall I introduce you?" We decided we were *companions.* He drew some boundaries, though, telling me not to expect him to sit in church with me. Since I'm an Episcopalian and, therefore, a Christian, and George was Jewish, that had never entered my mind. We respected each other's beliefs, often having conversations in which he referred to Jesus as his "countryman" which tickled me.

In turn, I expressed my admiration for his race. "People have discriminated against you, driven you out of countries or tried to eradicate you for a few thousand years," I noted, "but you're still here. You have strength and faith." Religion never became an issue.

The whirlwind schedule prepared me for his next question, not long after I had unpacked and picked up my mail. "Now that you've seen a cruise ship, where would you like to go?" Taken by surprise, I blurted out the first place that came to mind. "Alaska." That was fine with him. At least he gave me time to go through the accumulated mail where I found a copy of the July issue of *Mature Living* which gave my story, "A Silver-Gray Box," four pages in the middle of the magazine and added an eye-catching picture of vari-colored mailboxes lined up on a wooden ledge, giving my writing ego a huge boost. The article covered the history of Rural Free Delivery.

That completed a happy but short home-coming. "We'll be leaving August 20th", George announced. "We'll fly to Seattle and board the MS Noordam for a ten-day cruise through the Inside Passage." I had approximately seven weeks to make arrangements to board Digger and decide what to pack for a whole new experience..

On the plane ride to Seattle, I let out my breath and relaxed somewhat before we plunged into our walk around the city and our ride to the Space Needle on the Metro. True to a promise he made of finding a place for us to dance no matter where we were, George found a Senior Citizens' dance near the Space Needle. I shook my head in amazement and humor at his uncanny ability. The next day, a photographer waited at the top of the gangway of the ship to take a picture of each group of passengers. Standing next to George and smiling, I couldn't believe I was actually on a cruise.

Ketchikan became the first place where I set foot in our 49th state. Having read the brochure in our cabin, I knew about Dolly, the prostitute madam. Her cottage, Dolly's House, stood on Creek Street above the banks of Ketchikan Creek, among a row of others that also had housed prostitutes. All had been evicted in 1979. With that in mind, I wise-cracked to George, "This is where I made all my money." He smiled but, shortly after that, grinning hugely, he beckoned to me and pointed to a poster he had been reading. As soon as I saw it, I burst out laughing. Prominently displayed beneath a picture of "Violet," a prostitute in a long coat and fur collar, was the message, "Goodbye, Vi." Fortunately, George had a great sense of humor.

At our stop in Juneau, we viewed a collection of totem poles and saw the State House. Later in Sitka, we watched a Russian dance group and admired the icons in a Russian church. By then I had fallen in love with cruising and wanted to keep going. When we disembarked in Sewell and boarded a bus, I felt we were leaving an old friend behind but the views of the Alaska countryside made up for it. The tour guide pointed out the top of Mt McKinley before we reached Anchorage and our waiting luggage at the airport. On the plane home, the images still filled my mind - glaciers, bears, sea lions, a whale and a flock of puffins plus the Ocean Bar where we'd had a glorious time dancing, making my first cruise an outstanding success.

At seventy-one, I was having the time of my life but I wasn't alone. Together with two resident cats, Annabelle and Julius, Digger spent many happy hours lying on the strip of grass that ran up the middle of our driveway. Actually he loved stretching out in the sun wherever he could find a spot. Once in a while, if I had a quick errand to do, I left him outside. A neighbor commented on it. "He reminds me of a dog. He waits on the steps for you and when you drive in, he walks up to the garage to greet you and to walk back with you." I laughed at the truth of it. We were never quite sure of his age but he appeared to be having the time of his life, too.

BITTERSWEET DAYS

IN THE PILE OF mail that greeted me after the cruise, I found the September 1996 issue of *Good Old Days*, with my "No Privacy" story inside. My exuberance lasted through Christmas and our New Year's celebration and into January of 1997 when I agreed to take the Writers West Secretary spot once more. I stored the metal case that contained our history and old data in my garage, along with a carton full of photographs and press clippings. We had discontinued our monthly newsletter so the job was made easier.

My attention went off in another direction when I heard that the Alameda Naval Air Station would be closing on April 25. George was unable to go with me so I went alone, joining several hundred other people with the same idea. It felt great to drive past the guard station at the Main Street entrance and peek into areas formerly off- limits to civilians. I gawked at the military buildings and cavernous hangars, trying to visualize it as a working base. In order to hear the official closing ceremony, I found the area where it would take place and picked up a free t-shirt that commemorated the event. The crowd grew quiet as the Commanding Officer approached the microphone. In somber silence, we listened to his speech and watched the flag being lowered for the last time. Even while I rejoiced that we had no further use for the base, nostalgia washed over me. I drove home feeling a little sad and bereft. It represented a large chunk of Alameda's history.* I'm very glad I made the effort to be there and be part of the ongoing story of what would later be named "Alameda Point."

---

* See History at the back of the book.

My writing continued to do well. The May/June 1997 issue of *I Love Cats* ran my story, "A Cat of a Different Color," which explained the way I fell in love with my new cat, Digger, after our Kim See disappeared. A month later, on June 4th, in a heartbreaking coincidence, I lost my beloved Digger. He had suffered for some time from an incurable urinary tract problem which dried out his skin causing him, many times, to lick himself to relieve the itching. At regular intervals, I took him to the veterinarian for a shot that lubricated his body and gave him relief. Unfortunately, he was losing weight and much of his vitality. As he lounged in his favorite spot on the back of the sofa, he let his legs hang down, giving him a rag- doll appearance. I took him and my aching heart to the veterinarian who had already warned me Digger wouldn't get better. He and his assistant sympathized with my pain at having to make the awful decision to have him euthanized. The vet's assistant walked out to the car with me later while I carried my Digger and fought back tears.

At home, I wrapped him in an old t-shirt of mine and used a shoebox for a casket. I buried him under the hydrangea bush near the back door where he often sat, waiting to be let in. My neighbor, Bill, in a kind and touching gesture, gave a donation in Digger's name to the veterinary hospital. Another neighbor, Claudia, sent a sympathy card and told me about Annabelle, her cat. "She walks down and sits staring at your front door," Claudia said, "waiting for Digger. Sometimes she goes around to the back door. I feel so sorry for her." I did, too, and was glad to hear that she finally gave up her vigil and apparently accepted that he wasn't coming back.

Sadly, I heard of one more death at that time. Mary, the lovely woman who befriended me on my first night at the Eagles Hall, had also died.

In a happier vein, George suggested in August that we visit my nieces in Simi Valley since he had never met them. That sounded like a good idea. Both of them, Marilyn and Ann, immediately liked him as did their boyfriends, Lee and Dave. On Saturday night, Lee and Marilyn invited us to a country dance, making the weekend a completely happy one.

My emotions did a tail-spin, though, when George announced he'd be taking an 18-day cruise around South America aboard the MS Rotterdam, leaving on September 12th. It would be a sentimental last cruise for that ship and the same cruise he had taken with Miriam. He sweetened it a little by saying, "We'll be leaving from Vancouver and will stop overnight in San Francisco. Why don't you meet me at Pier 39 and we'll have a few hours together." That turned out to be as romantic as it sounded. We walked to a courtyard near Pier 39 where a small band was playing and enjoyed ice cream while we sat and listened and were even able to dance a little. When the time came to say goodbye, George stood with me at the ferry landing, waiting to be sure I was safely aboard.

With him away, I had time to examine my emotions. Though we definitely belonged together, our relationship had not moved forward in the area of a spoken commitment. On the one hand, it relieved me that I didn't have to thwart any steps toward marriage but on the other, it rankled my pride that he made no overt effort to announce to the world that we were a couple and now he was taking a cruise by himself. After pursuing and winning me over, he seemed to have, figuratively speaking, settled on the couch.

As my ire rose, I fought to squelch it, telling myself, "You're in your seventies and you're happy with him. He takes you to dinner and dances and pays all the bills. You've met his family and been invited for holidays. He has made no secret of his desire to be with you and nobody else. He's loving and kind to you. What more do you want?" I told myself this might be his final goodbye to his lonely life and a farewell to his life with Miriam. I also knew that he and Miriam met when they were both eighteen and married at twenty-two. Neither of them ever had anyone else in their lives, except for a short relationship George had with a woman soon after Miriam's death. The woman had a terminal illness which was in remission when they met and she didn't tell George. It returned and she didn't survive. Possibly, he wanted to get all that straightened out in his mind. Viewing the pros and cons, I decided to be patient. Our friends raised their eyebrows and made comments about the fact that I *allowed* him to go off without me but I considered it to be *our* business.

Besides all that, he was wise enough to bring gifts from his cruise - a gold bracelet and a pendant and ear-ring set.

It helped my spirits also to receive notification from *Mature Living* that they had given permission to *The Lutheran Digest* to re-print "A Silver-Gray Box" in their Fall 1997 issue and I would be receiving a copy. With that happy news, before I knew it, Christmas and New Year's came and went and we were into 1998.

I have to admit I didn't mind telling George, in May of 1998, about the invitation that I alone had received,, "I'm going to Marilyn and Lee's wedding. It'll be on the patio at the Reagan Library," I said.

The weekend turned into a delightful family reunion. Barbara and Bill drove up from Downey and she and I reminisced for all of them – Ann, her new husband, Dave, Marilyn, Lee and Jan. They loved our stories of growing up in Cumberland, especially the anecdotes about their mother, my beloved sister, Ruth. Fate had given me a chance to do something nice for myself.

It always bolstered my spirits to have something published. The May/June 1998 edition of *Dogwood Tales* carried my short story about a cat, "Toby or Not Toby," and the June issue of *Good Old Days* contained my personal experience story, "Skunked." What proved to be my last magazine article appeared in the October 1998 *Mature Outlook* under the title, "A Repotted Life," which recalled my move to California from Massachusetts.

Mature Outlook wanted to use it for their end piece, saying they'd need a photograph. They would also pay me $500. I gasped and signed the contract. Their Art Director contacted Franklin Avery Shoots in Steve Rahn's Studio on Clara Street in San Francisco. George drove me to the appointment. The photographer took a thousand shots, it seemed, with me posing and feeling like a white-haired supermodel. I relived the thrill when I viewed the finished product in the October 1998 issue. I felt I'd been sent out in a blaze of glory.

LET GEORGE BE GEORGE

TAKING A HIATUS FROM articles would allow me to write a book, "In the Village of Lonsdale," that was begging for my attention. Often, during our growing-up years, my sister and I listened to my mother's stories of her experiences in 1912 as a newly-arrived transplant from England and a new bride, living on a farm in Cumberland, Rhode Island, with six of her in-laws. The stories, both humorous and tragic, provided the bedrock for my book. Though I couldn't wait to begin, the delightful alternative was to take another cruise with George. "Where would you like to go?" he asked.

We'd been to Alaska so it seemed natural to say, "Hawaii." That November of 1998, in Los Angeles, the MS Statendam became our home for the next sixteen days, with our first stop, to my surprise, being Ensenada. Even though we didn't go ashore, it thrilled me to see Mexico for the first time, but made me wonder why it was on our itinerary. In time I learned of the Merchant Marine Act of 1920 which bans port to port travel in the United States by ships of foreign registry, such as our ship which is registered in Holland. In doing so, it discourages coastwise trade between the ports.

Crossing the Pacific, seasickness struck me a few times but with the help of Dramamine pills, I was able to enjoy the well-prepared meals, swim in the pool, dance at night and exalt in just being there. In La Haina, on Maui, I walked on Hawaiian soil for the first time. Eventually, we moored at Kona, Oahu and Kauai before swinging back to Oahu for a bus tour ending at Waikiki Beach. George sat at a table, under an umbrella, while I swam and drifted in the blue water. Diamondhead rose in the distance. I had to keep reminding myself it was all real. Other thrills included gazing into a volcanic crater on Maui and standing on the rim of the Waimea Canyon on Kauai. Needless to say, I reveled in the whole experience.

The memory of one particular incident still makes me smile. Our assigned dinner companions, three pleasant, friendly couples, shared their reasons for taking the trip. Two were celebrating fiftieth wedding anniversaries which led one of the ladies to turn to us and ask, "And how long have you two been married?"

I hesitated, considered telling a lie but quickly reverted to the truth, "We're not," I said.

"Oh," she blurted "but you're not in the same cabin!"

This time I didn't hesitate. I put my arm around George and said, clearly and distinctly, "Yes, we are. I'm seventy-three. What am I saving it for?" Everyone, including George, laughed and the moment passed. Later, when she and I met in a corridor, she hugged me and thanked me for my honesty, making me glad of my decision to accept my life as it was and acknowledge it.

Cruising to Alaska and Hawaii helped me feel more and more at home on the west coast. That gave me the confidence to take on other challenges such as agreeing, in January of 1999, to be President of Writers West. Henry, a new member, assumed the Secretary's position and a new year lay ahead.

It included Kiwanis bus trips with George to Reno and Monterey, one of the places on my wish list and as beautiful as I had been expecting it to be. In October, we flew to southern California to help celebrate Barbara and Bill's fiftieth wedding anniversary. I had the pleasure of re-meeting their now-adult children, Gary and Suzan. I hadn't seen them since 1967. They introduced us to Carol and Bruce, children of Barbara's brother, Sam, my Rhode Island cousin. The music lured us to the dance floor. Being seniors in an overall young crowd brought us several compliments on our dancing, sending me further into my happiness. When they learned of George's stint with the Brooklyn Dodgers, several of them crowded around to hear more about it.

We had no warning of the cloud that appeared on our horizon in December when I passed out at my dining room table with George sitting next to me. As soon as I came to, he took me to the Emergency Room at Alameda Hospital. "Dehydration," the doctor said after several tests ruled out anything more serious. I didn't know that the medication I was taking was drying me out.

I had been diagnosed in Foxboro with high blood pressure which spurred me to immediately seek a family doctor once I moved to Alameda. I trusted the one I found, took the medication she prescribed and followed her advice to walk every day, but I guess I didn't ask enough questions.

One day, a short time after passing out, as I was walking, tremendous pressure in my chest sent me back to my car, alarmed and determined to make an immediate appointment.

"Both of my parents died of heart attacks," I told the doctor during the visit.

"Would you like to have a stress test?" she asked. Of course, I said I would.

At Alameda Hospital, Dr. R., the Cardiologist in charge of the test, stopped it soon after it began. "Your blood pressure is dangerously high. It's 250," he said. "I need to examine you but your doctor has to authorize the visit." The doctor agreed but didn't follow up, prompting me to take over. In a quick decision to switch doctors, I located Dr. T. and made an appointment. He lost no time in sending me back to the Cardiologist who, in turn, cancelled the medication I was taking and put me on his regimen. Dr. T. agreed to allow him to monitor me for a while. Dr. R.'s first instruction was to, "Drink eight glasses of water a day." I filled my new prescription list and made an appointment with Dr. R. for two weeks later. The next time I saw both Dr. T. and Dr. R., I thanked them because I felt they had saved my life.

Long before we knew my health needed attention, George had made plans to again go on a cruise alone in February of 2000, this time on the new MS Rotterdam. The trip would take him from Buenos Aires to Mombasa, Kenya. He made absolutely sure I was all right before he decided to go ahead with it but that didn't assuage my resentment.

The memory is still strong. I was standing in front of the sink, as I had been when the memory of the psychic asking, "Who's George?" came into my mind. This time I was washing dishes and muttering to myself once more and even considering breaking up with him when it happened. I perceived a presence, but not a scary one. I froze and waited and soon had the sensation of someone stroking the back of my neck, in a loving gesture. I didn't really <u>hear</u> the words but knew they had been spoken. "Let George be George." The presence disappeared.

I couldn't move for a few seconds but relaxed when the thought shot through my mind. "It's Miriam. She likes me and wants me to stick around." She had been with him for fifty-nine years and certainly knew him well. Her words bolstered me and helped hasten the time along until George came home, once more bearing gifts - a beautiful shawl from India and a carved jewelry box, along with a silk parka to wear with an evening skirt. I silently commented to Miriam that I'd wait and see. After all, I had nothing to lose.

Dr R. said, on my next visit, "I've ordered an angiogram. If we discover blockage, we'll do an angioplasty." They did and I became the proud owner, in April of 2000, of a stent in my left anterior descending artery (LAD in medical terms).

Another procedure, a *carotid endarectomy* (translation – my carotid artery had to be rotor-rooted) followed in July, with George by my side, encouraging me and helping when he could. As soon as I recovered, I enrolled, per instructions from Dr. R., in the Cardiofit program at Alameda Hospital, a full-fledged cardio patient.

The pressure in my chest which had started the whole series of changing doctors, tests, procedures and office visits brought yet another picture into my mind - the day I took up the carpeting in all the downstairs rooms of our house in Foxboro. I remembered my beet-red face and my pounding heart and the pressure in my chest as I pulled and tugged at the carpet, trying to get it out from under the couch, cursing when, in the midst of my struggle, my phone rang. I tried to ignore it but felt a strong urge to answer.

"Hello, I just called to check on you." It was Dottie, a friend of Dean's who had become a friend of mine. Her call forced me to sit for a while. My face slowly paled back to normal and my heartbeat slowed and the interruption probably saved my life. In a flash of understanding, I knew someone was watching over me.

BEYOND YOUR
WILDEST DREAMS

D RINKING EIGHT GLASSES OF water a day isn't as easy as it sounds, but passing out in church, in the middle of a service, convinced me, in September of 2000, that it had to be done. I had time in the Emergency Room at Alameda Hospital to weigh that against some plans I had been considering for my upcoming seventy-fifth birthday. "I'll make it a priority to always carry a bottle of water with me," I promised myself, "but I'm not canceling the trip."

My dream of going through the Panama Canal, inspired by the reading of "A Path Between the Seas," had become a reality, thanks to George's encouragement and a listing in the numerous cruise catalogs he received. Though some friends jokingly accused me of getting even, it was simply that I had decided to give a present to myself for my birthday. George understood and had already been through the Canal, anyway. Sammie, a woman from our dance crowd, asked, "Do you want company?" I agreed and on October 5th, she and I boarded the MS Veendam in San Diego. By then, I had sewn together a small bag to carry my water bottle and felt lost if I couldn't feel it hanging on my arm.

From our assigned dining room table, we could clearly see the wake of the ship in the blue-green sea and the wildlife, enjoying ourselves even before we reached Puerto Vallarta in Mexico. At that port, we boarded a bus for a mountain trip, a walk through a private family's home and gardens and a view of the lush valley. On our descent into that valley, we sipped cool drinks at an outdoor café near the Mascota River while a mariachi band entertained us. That evening we danced and chatted with the three male hosts on the ship, Tony, Marlen and Marvin, and were assured of dance partners for the remainder of the voyage.

The night of my birthday lived up to every expectation. We had visited San Juan Huatulco, a lovely Mexican city with hilly terrain and secluded sandy beaches and were at sea on October 11th, cruising toward Nicaragua, relaxing and chatting with the other diners at our table. At Sammie's request, immediately after we finished our meal, the waiter set a cake in front of me. Surprised and pleased, I blew out the candles, the cue for everyone at the table, including the waiter, to sing, "Happy birthday." To my absolute delight, I glanced out just in time to see a school of fish, maybe even dolphins, leaping across our wake. Nothing, except maybe having George there to share it, could have topped that.

Masaya Center, a unique, outdoor collection of shops inside the high stone walls of a former prison in Nicaragua, proved fascinating, as did Costa Rica whose rugged beauty and mountainous terrain reminded me of California. I can understand the reason it has become a home-away-from-home for a large number of Americans.

Just past Costa Rica, with the Bridge of the Americas coming into view, the captain announced, "We'll be entering the Panama Canal at 5:00 A.M. tomorrow morning." Despite the early hour, Sammie and I made it up on deck in time to take in the view and also snap a few pictures. Each day, during that most important segment of our trip, we spent as much time on deck as we could, watching the water rise and the gates open to allow our huge ship to pass through the locks. It amazed me that those locks, built in 1914, could still be operable. I admired the luxurious green land on either side of the Canal even as I marveled at the immensity of the job of digging it, especially in the ever-present humidity. It became obvious, though, that it had been engineered with smaller ships in mind. The side of the canal could be plainly seen, slipping by just outside the porthole in our cabin.

Once we had inched through the eastern locks at the other end of the canal, the Caribbean Sea spread out ahead of us, looking huge and endless. In the next few days, we walked on the dazzlingly white, sandy beaches of Aruba and delighted in the colorful houses along the waterfront in Curacao.

Fifteen days after embarking in San Diego, we cruised past the landmark El Morro Fort tower and into the port of San Juan. As soon as we disembarked, we hailed a taxi to take us to San Juan airport for our flight back to Oakland, where I knew George would be waiting. Though he had taken the same trip, he wanted to hear about it through my eyes, even showing a noticeable touch of jealousy when I mentioned the hosts and the dancing.

The whole adventure reminded me of an image that Aann, a good friend who's also a psychic, had once described to me. "I can see you dancing and singing, flinging your arms into the air, happy beyond your wildest dreams." That joy had already captured me and just as I thought it couldn't get any better, my Massachusetts stepson, Mark, and his wife, Mary Ellen, called to say they'd be with us for Thanksgiving.

I gladly accepted Darcy's offer to cook dinner for the four of us, plus four of her friends who were happy to meet our company. George opted to eat with his family but the day after Thanksgiving, he joined us for the ferry ride from Alameda to San Francisco. That and watching the sea lions at Pier 39, shopping and eating in San Francisco, as well as riding a cable car and viewing the Golden Gate Bridge, fulfilled Mark and Mary Ellen's desire for a California experience. Though it had been a short trip, I felt deeply thankful they'd been with us, unaware I'd be seeing them sooner than I expected.

At Writers West, Henry's news that he had cancer and would be giving up the Writers West meetings saddened all of us. We told him we'd miss him very much and thanked him for his willingness to be of help to the group. Another member, Jonnie, took over the President's position when I opted to become the Secretary again.

Soon after that, Dr. R. informed me that I needed another stent in my LAD artery. "I've made a 7:30 A.M. appointment for you at Stanford Hospital," he said. That put me, with George driving, on the 880 Freeway at 5:30 A.M., which, we learned, can be amazingly busy at that hour. The procedure went as planned and the drive back to Alameda wasn't quite as nerve-wracking.

Darcy, knowing that baseball is my favorite sport, suggested going by ferry to the new Giants' ball park on the San Francisco waterfront. Frankly, I can't recall whether they won or lost, but I do remember the ferry ride, McCovey Cove where fans sit in boats to catch the home run balls and seeing the giant Coca-Cola bottle Superslide in the Fan Lot. It's an impressive ball park. Just sitting in the stands is fun in itself.

On another day, George and I used my Christmas present from Darcy - two tickets to the San Francisco Symphony, a first for me and another dimension added to my life, especially with Michael Tilson Thomas conducting

Last, but far from least, I knew Aann had called it right when George presented his news. "My niece, Stephanie, has invited us to her daughter's wedding. It's in Woodstock, Vermont. I told her we'd be there." Dancing and singing came into my mind as I hugged him and held him.

We left Oakland Airport on September 6, 2001, bound for the Manchester, New Hampshire, airport. At the car rental in Manchester, George said, "You drive. You're in home territory." Bliss bubbled up inside me on the way to Woodstock. In the darkness, though I couldn't see their green slopes, I could make out the silhouettes of the surrounding mountains. The warm welcome I received from Stephanie and her husband, Bill, set my cup to overflowing.

With the wedding scheduled for Saturday afternoon, we spent the morning meandering along the main street of Woodstock, stopping to look down from the bridge over the Ottauquechee River which runs through that quaint and lovely town. Eventually, George found a bench and suggested that I browse the shops while he waited. I was happy to oblige. Three-quarters of an hour later, I came back to find him talking with three women, with all of them enjoying themselves. Everyone, including me, laughed when he remarked, as we left, "Don't forget — same place, a year from now. I'll be here."

The pretty bride and good-looking groom and their perfect wedding that afternoon, along with the reception where we danced and celebrated, topped off a gem of a day and gave me the opportunity to become better acquainted with Stephanie and Bill.

To keep to our tight schedule, we left early Sunday morning to make it to a pre-arranged luncheon in Manchester with Mark, Mary Ellen, Peter, Mark's brother, and his wife, Nancy, Maggie and Sophie, my step-granddaughters and Edith, Peter and Mark's mother. We took pictures, cramming everything into the short time we had with them before our trip south on I-95 for a rendezvous in Foxboro the next day with my friends, Gail, Ruth and Marge.

On Monday, as I knew he would, George charmed them all. We reminisced and shared stories for him over lunch, but said goodbye once more, hugging and promising to keep in touch. We took a minute in our room to review our schedule. "Tomorrow, we do Foxboro and on Wednesday, you get to see Rhode Island," I told him. "We'll be at T.F. Green Airport on Thursday to turn in the car and catch our flight back to California."

WHERE WERE YOU ON SEPTEMBER 11TH?

THE NEXT MORNING, TUESDAY, September 11th, we walked into the motel coffee shop just in time to hear the television announcer say, "A second plane has hit the World Trade Center."

Without taking our gaze off the horrific scene of smoke and flames belching out of the World Trade Center, we reached for the nearest chairs, slightly breaking the deep silence that had settled on the room. More details trickled in, seeping into our consciousness, convincing us this was not a movie but a real life happening.

George, recovering faster than I did, spoke quietly, while I was still dumbstruck and staring, "Let's not change our plans. We can still go to the airport on Thursday, book a room nearby and turn in the car. We'll be close to the airport and can check in at the ticket counter." His calm, reassuring tone halted my swirling thoughts. He was right. Panicking would lead us nowhere. I forced my mind to focus on the day in front of us.

"Okay. I'll call Darcy right after breakfast and tell her we're all right."

It seemed somewhat anti-climatic to begin our tour of Foxboro but playing the tour guide kept my mind busy. I pointed out the little bungalow my mother and I had owned on Vernal Avenue before I headed up Central Street to the Common, the hub of Foxboro. I circled the Common and turned down South Street for a visit to the Memorial Garden behind St. Mark's Church where Dean's ashes rested and where mine would also be interred. George admired the church and the Garden in back and let me have a moment by myself in the Memorial Garden.

Back at the Common, I half-circled it onto Cocasset Street, slowed a little in front of an old apartment house and pointed, "Dean and I lived on the third floor." Of course, he had to see the Foxboro Company offices and factory on Neponset Avenue. That led to Neponset Heights Avenue and our house, with Neponset Lake and the Fish and Game Club just down the street. The familiar sights tugged at my emotions and I wanted to go to a neutral place. "You have to see Friendly's. That's where all the locals go," I said, not explaining until I found a parking spot at the ice cream store on Central Street. To prove me right, we found two of my St. Mark's friends inside, a delightful surprise, and they asked us to join them.. The normalcy of laughing and talking and having ice cream in Friendly's somewhat offset the dreadful news, offering a bright spot in a confusing day.

Continuing our schedule, on Wednesday I took him to Cumberland and past my first school, Garvin Memorial, on Diamond Hill Road. A short time later, we paused in front of my grandmother's house on Lilac Street. "That's where I was born and brought up," I told him, nostalgia choking my throat as it did again on Broad Street at Cumberland High and again in Lincoln when we drove past Christ Episcopal Church, our last stop. All the emotions of the day had caught up with me by that time, making me grateful when we returned to the motel in Foxboro for our final night.

Thursday, before returning the car, we booked a room at a motel near T. F. Green Airport. Its third-floor window gave us a clear view of the field and the United Parcel gate where brown planes sat motionless. No droning sounds of any planes taking off or coming in broke the silent air, giving it an eerie and unworldly feeling. Again, George brought me back to reality. "Let's turn in the car and take the shuttle to the airport."

The clerk at the ticket counter confirmed our fears. "All planes have been grounded. I can't give you any promises right now." In spite of that, we found an amazing and impressive calm among the people standing in the lines, hungry for information, learning, as we did, that they couldn't leave.

We walked back to the hotel area to aimlessly search for a place to eat, finally locating a Burger-King on the other side of busy Post Road. Somehow, we managed to sprint across during a lull in traffic. During our meal, I reminisced on the history of the airport. "It was called *Hillsgrove* and was just a local airport with a chain-link fence around it," I told George. "My father liked to take rides on Sunday. Sometimes we came to watch the planes land and take off," laughing with him at the thought. He understood even before I added, "We didn't have television in the 30's and that seemed exciting," and we laughed again.

Friday morning I walked to our window as soon as I woke up and that brought a welcome surprise. "The planes at the UPS gate are moving!" I shouted to George who was still in bed. We showered and dressed and hopped the shuttle to the airport, sighing in relief when the ticket agent said, "I can put you on a United Airlines plane next Tuesday, but check daily to be sure it hasn't been cancelled for some reason." On our stroll back to the motel, a sudden thought interrupted my joy. "I only have enough medication to last until Saturday. I'd better call Dr. R."

He directed me to "go to any pharmacy, tell them your story and they'll fill them." The desk clerk suggested Walgreen's at Apponaug Circle, a familiar name that stirred up fond memories of visits to my cousin, Violet. She and her husband, Henry, once lived in the town of Apponaug which is on Narragansett Bay. We called a taxi and the driver found it easily. The pharmacy clerks made a wonderful audience, listening, wide-eyed, to our story of being stranded by the terrorist act. That made us feel special.

In our room once more, I switched on television to hear the familiar words of the Episcopal funeral service at the National Washington Cathedral, warmed by the thought of millions of Americans joining in prayer. I sat on the foot of the bed through much of the service until George asked if I'd like to go down to the lobby. We found a cluster of people talking and watching newscasts and we joined them. Once more the apparent acceptance of the situation impressed me, bringing tears of pride to my eyes.

George suggested on Saturday morning that we take a bus ride into Providence and do some sightseeing as long as we had the time. First, though, we headed to the airport for a leisurely breakfast, swapping stories with other stranded passengers, dallying a while before ambling to the ticket counter. The clerk's words snapped us to attention.

"I'm sorry. Your plane can't make it on Tuesday. United found it can't cover all the flights. It may be another few days."

Speaking together, we pleaded, "Can you just get us into California? Once we're at least in the state, we can take a bus or plane home."

She checked a few schedules. "If you can be ready by 5:00 today, I can put you on a Delta to San Francisco, through Indianapolis. You should arrive at SFO around 11:30 tonight." We raced to the hotel, threw everything into our suitcases and I called Darcy. She said she'd pick us up and we made it back to the terminal with time to spare.

Just as we settled into our seats, I nudged George. "Look." A fire truck, siren screaming, raced across the tarmac. At that moment, the loudspeaker blared, "Please remain seated. Do not leave the terminal." Once more, our fellow travelers displayed their trust in our system, visibly relaxing when we all heard, "You may resume your business." We never learned what caused the emergency, but were glad it was over. A short time later, our plane arrived, right on time. We all crowded to the boarding area.

At last, we lifted off from Green Airport and headed west. I peered through the window for a last look at my home state and something caught my attention in the otherwise clear air. I leaned in for a better look. "I can see a huge plume of smoke or dust down to our left," I commented to George. "That would be Manhattan, but it's been four days!" The enormity of the horrifying event slammed into us. We stayed quiet and rested for most of the trip.

Six and half hours later, right on schedule, we began our descent into San Francisco Airport, landing without incident and happy to see Darcy. Her first words, as she hugged us, were, "You're lucky. A man took a boat three hundred feet into the bay to see whether anyone could do any damage to the airport from that distance. Security thought he was planning to bomb it so they shut the airport down. It opened about half an hour ago."

Even though our experience had been minuscule compared to others, I can't count the number of times we repeated it to anyone who wanted to hear it, As more details emerged and we learned the true depth and chilling facts, we realized our good fortune that ours had been such a small inconvenience.

POTPOURI

W E HADN'T THOUGHT ABOUT being afraid to fly. We just wanted to get home. It's hard to know whether it was our preoccupation with that or disbelief that kept us from seeing the enormity of the dreadful tragedy in New York. Either way, following the developing news at home, seeing the graphic pictures and hearing the personal stories had a deep impact. The whole unbelievable truth that it hadn't been a random strike but a well-planned terrorist attack sank into our consciousness. We grieved for the families of those lost and felt pride in the heroism of the rescuers. We also absorbed the fact that, along with the rest of the world, our country was a target and vulnerable to terrorism. We would have to live with that going into the future.

Even as we realized and accepted that truth, life continued on around us, with the year ending, at least for us personally, on a happy note. In November, the good news arrived in a phone call. "Hello, Grandma Vi, this is Shane. My friend and I are at Pier 39 in San Francisco. We're back-packing through the Sierra." Excitedly, I told him to stay near the ferry landing and we'd be there as soon as possible.

"I haven't seen him for twelve years," I enthused to George on the trip across San Francisco Bay. "That was in 1989 at Dean's funeral and he was only eight."

My worries about not recognizing him disappeared as soon as we stepped off the ferry. Dean's grandson, now twenty, had grown into a tall, blonde and handsome young man who had a pretty young lady by his side. We spent several very pleasant hours with them, treating them to lunch and showing them a little of San Francisco.

"We were in Woodstock in September," I also mentioned, going on to tell the story, once more, of our delay in Rhode Island, answering questions about it before taking the subject back to Vermont and the wedding. Shane smiled and asked whether we had seen a particular restaurant and we both nodded.

"I was working there that day," he said. We laughed, marveling at the fact that we'd been that close to him yet he had to travel 3,000 miles to see us.

January of 2002 started out with me passing out in church again, a not-so-subtle reminder that I had to keep to my regimen of eight glasses of water a day. By then, I knew the drill – stay overnight in the Emergency room, have all kinds of tests and drink plenty of water. "When you dehydrate," I was told, "your blood pressure drops and so do you." I silently chided myself, vowing to be more vigilant in the future, unaware of the role dehydration would play in my life.

My thoughts veered sharply in another direction when Darcy commented, "I think it's time you bought a computer," echoing an idea that had also poked at me lately. We visited Alameda Business Machines and on January 25th, carried home my first computer. The previous Christmas, in anticipation, Darcy had presented me with a three-hour class at Gateway Center in Berkeley. I added a twelve-day course, "An Introduction to Computers," that was being offered at our Adult Learning Center in Alameda. My beloved word processor found a new home at Berkeley Typewriter, where, I was told, it would be rented out to University of California/Berkeley students. That pleased me.

While I was doing my best to learn the mysteries of my new computer, another surprise hit me. Aann's prediction, *beyond your wildest dreams*, did a re-run through my mind the day George asked, "Would you like to go to New Orleans? Kiwanis is having its national convention there in June." Was he kidding?

My good friend, Carol, whose husband, Phil, was also attending, suggested we find fun things to do while our mates sat in the Convention Center. A ride on the Mississippi on a paddle-wheel boat appealed to both of us. We discovered *The Cajun Queen,* tied up at a dock and climbed aboard for a memorable experience. Another boat trip, this time on Lake Pontchartrain, gave us a glimpse of a well- known old alligator - not close-up, thank goodness. We toured the swamp which proved more interesting than I had expected. Later, at Café Du Monde, we ate *beignets* and learned, when we took some back for George and Phil, that they taste better when they're eaten immediately. On another day, we toured one of the quaint old houses.

With George and Phil finally available, all four of us walked along Bourbon Street, listened to a jazz band in Storyville and danced to Cajun music. Phil and Carol had a few plans of their own so George and I toured the above-ground graves, viewed a bayou and peeked into the St. Louis Cathedral in Jackson Square. I loved New Orleans – its easy-going pace, its colorful history and its music. The gathering of various cultures had provided a good-tasting combination of food. My favorite was the fried shrimp but not with the heads still attached – thank you. I love shrimp but prefer it headless.

In the Convention Hall, Jay Leno put on a show just before our fun-packed trip came to an end. We left with a supply of Mardi Gras beads given out at the Convention Center, but our biggest consolation came when we could brag about having seen New Orleans before Katrina changed it. Unlike our 9/11 experience, the timing had been just right.

Life settled down for a while, allowing me to take a deep breath and begin my first book, "In the Village of Lonsdale." The excitement of being part of the technical age opened my mind to other possibilities. In October, 2002, I read about "Two Cents," a San Francisco Chronicle column known as *citizen journalism.* It asked its members, all volunteers, to answer, in one hundred words or less, questions sent by email from the Two Cents staff. If they felt your reply was worth publishing, you'd see it in the paper, along with your picture.

Officially becoming a contributor meant going to the Chronicle office in San Francisco. I walked in, feeling important, and announced to the young woman sitting behind the desk that I had an appointment with Heidi S., the editor of the column, to which she calmly replied, "Please take a seat. The photographer will be here shortly." I had expected to be ushered into Heidi's office but my ego had yet another blow to endure. After fifteen or more people had also taken seats in the small area, the photographer appeared, set up a backdrop, called us one by one, told us where to stand, snapped the picture and yelled, "Next," taking care of my self-importance.

On the other hand, seventeen of my answers appeared in the column, prompting some friends at Cardiofit to suggest, teasingly, that I had a relative on the Chronicle staff. The questions ranged from solemn and serious to light and humorous. *Is the U.S. winning the peace in Iraq?* for instance, or *What do you recall about the 1964 British invasion*, speaking of the Beatles, of course. Another made me smile. *Giants vs. the A's — who's the hunkiest?* while the first question I received in 2003 caused me to think deeply, *What worries you most — war or the economy?*

All of this boosted my self-confidence which I needed when George announced in March of 2003, 'I'm going on a forty-six-day cruise to Australia, the southern Pacific and Midway." I felt grateful that Miriam's message to "let George be George" kept me silent which allowed him to add, "The ship will be docking in Long Beach. Why don't you make reservations for us and fly down? We can rent a car and stay for a few days." He also promised to send emails, though he had never used a computer. "I'll get the guy in the Computer Room to help me." he said. To lighten the mood, as I kissed him goodbye, I nicknamed him, "My wandering Jew."

His first email arrived on March 12th, "All is well. Sailing up the coast of Australia. Trip so far is a 4. Hope you are well. Say hello to everyone. I'll write you in detail. Love, your WJ." I replied and signed it "Your flower," the name he occasionally called me, which prompted him to write, "Hi Flower. Only nine days since leaving but it seems longer. Rating as of now a 5. Gaining a little weight. Will keep you posted. Papau tomorrow. Love, gbs/wj." His last one read, "Hi love.

Sorry for the delay. The days are slower. En route to Hong Kong. Getting closer to dancing with my flower. Love. GBS."

On April 22nd, in the Courtyard Motel lobby in Long Beach, I watched a taxi pull up. George emerged, paid the driver, walked into the lobby, took me in his arms and whispered, "I'll never go away without you again" and he never did. George had been George and had done it his way.

GOD'S COMMA

I N OUR ROOM, GEORGE gave me the gifts from his trip – a lovely silk shawl from Thailand, a gold watch and a gold and black mandarin dress. His added comment, "Let's walk around Long Beach tomorrow then rent a car so we can take the ferry to Catalina," brought another dimension to my happiness.

Catalina. The name alone stirred up romantic images of sunny beaches and couples in love. I couldn't wait, willing to stand at the railing for the crossing, but the cool weather sent us inside where George described his cruise. "I wandered along the decks and corridors and listened to the dance music and I was lonely. The old friends I expected to see didn't take that cruise." He reached for my hand and said. "I wondered why I was all by myself when I had a lovely girl at home. I couldn't see the forest for the trees. I was searching for happiness and it was right in front of me," but he added quickly, "I wasn't looking for another woman. I don't know what I wanted. You were very patient with me."

On Catalina, we toured the ballroom in Avalon where a sweet nostalgia for the era it represented swept over me. I felt ghostly vibes of the big band music and could imagine, though I'd never been part of them, those long-ago dances.

We walked the streets of Catalina and took pictures while George filled me in on the history of the island. "The Wrigley family of Chicago bought a controlling interest in Catalina in 1919 and built a mansion up there," he said, pointing toward a hilltop. "They brought the White Sox out for spring training." He paused at the foot of a street. "Carol and her husband had a cottage here, too," he explained, mentioning a couple from his younger days who lived in Piedmont, California, but summered on Catalina. "Miriam and I always stayed with them." He considered climbing the hill to see whether she was on the island but instead we found a sandwich shop whose proprietor knew Carol and could reminisce about her with George. "She isn't here right now," he told us.

Though I wanted more than one day to get my fill of Catalina, we had plans to meet Barbara and Bill for dinner in Long Beach, a truly satisfying finish to a spectacular day. "We're going to Palm Springs tomorrow," George told them, as we caught up on the happenings in our lives.

He showed me, the next day in Palm Springs, a cottage where he and Miriam liked to stay. "It has a kitchen," he explained, "so Miriam was able to cook Kosher meals." We stopped for lunch in a coffee shop in one of the hotels. The lady in charge asked whether I'd ever had a date latte. That was a whole new experience. I loved it and the dinner that evening at the same hotel. Before we left the area, we toured Palm Desert where I could visualize the Hollywood stars strolling its sidewalks.

Reluctantly, on the fifth day, we turned the car toward home, but took a side trip for an overnight stay in Santa Ynez and a visit with Marilyn, Lee and Katy. "We hope you'll be back for Katy's graduation," Marilyn said. The little girl whose hand I held at the airport in Rhode Island had grown up. It didn't seem possible. We told them we'd definitely be back.

"Never place a period where God has put a comma; He hasn't finished speaking." The message on the board in front of the Congregational Church often drifted into my mind. Yes, I knew I had made the right move by taking the period off my life and letting George into it.

Before 2003 left us, we visited Judy, my old friend from Foxboro who had relocated to Reno and had married Jack, a very pleasant and likable man. It made a fitting end to a year of being with the people we loved.

2004 brought a reunion in Santa Monica of George's son, nephews and niece. I knew Cliff and had met Ken and Stephanie, but not Don and Roger. I was getting to know George's family and enjoying myself tremendously with them. I also found that Santa Monica is beautiful with its cliff walk that overlooks a far-stretching beach and pier. We strolled along Wilshire Boulevard and browsed through some of the old hotels. I had trouble saying good-bye to that and to the family.

We had hardly settled down in Alameda when we boarded a bus for Yosemite as part of a Kiwanis outing. Though it was my second trip, I fell in love with it again. We toured the valley, had lunch at the Ahwanee Hotel and rode on an old lumber train through the woods.

By far though, the highlight of that year was our twenty-four-day cruise in October to the Mediterranean. It began in Rome and took us up the coast to Venice and down again for a three-day tour of Rome but it almost didn't happen.

In order to be at the San Francisco Airport three hours ahead of the 7:30 A.M. departure time, we stayed in a hotel near the airport, hauled ourselves up to have breakfast at 3:30 A.M. and made the plane. I didn't realize I hadn't paid enough attention to my dehydration problem until I passed out on the way to Newark, New Jersey, where we planned to change planes. Fortunately, a nurse on vacation and on the same plane saw my problem. She sat with me (after I came to) until I drank a liter of water under her watchful care. In the Newark airport, even though I left the plane in a wheelchair, I was able to convince the doctor who met us that I felt well enough to continue to Rome. Secretly, I had sworn to myself that I'd be on that ship in Rome no matter what it took, but I also knew I usually recovered quickly from the dehydration episodes.

I breathed a huge sigh of relief when we set our bags down in the stateroom of the MS Westerdam in Civitaveccia, Italy, the port closest to Rome. At 7:30 P.M. we stood on deck to watch the lines being dropped and feel the ship moving toward open water and our first stop in Livorno, Italy, to see the leaning tower of Pisa which turned out to be a thrill all by itself.

My health continued to improve and two days later, we cruised into the harbor below Monte Carlo and boarded a bus to Nice and the Riviera and the day after that, at sea between Barcelona and Malta, I celebrated my 79th birthday.

Turkey and Greece both stand out in my memory. We met cordial and interesting people in each country but Greece brought an unparalleled surprise. After a visit to the Acropolis where George waited at ground level while I climbed up to view the Parthenon, the Temple of Zeus and the ancient Odean and had an awe-inspiring view of the city, we rode a tour bus around Athens and back to the huge dock. There we found a shopping area. George called me over to a display of rings outside a jewelry shop. "I want to buy you a ring," he said. "Why don't you pick it out." Taking a deep breath to calm myself, I walked inside the shop with him and stared down at the display and pointed to one that caught my eye. I had no idea its Greek design, *Meandrose*, translated, according to the shop owner, into "two meandering rivers came together and flowed as one," a perfect description of our romance. We called it our "commitment ring" since it made our relationship official but it also brought a confession from George. "When I saw you unconscious on the seat and didn't know whether you were all right, I realized how much I love you." At last I could tell him my deepest feelings and let the happiness envelop me and glow inside me for the rest of the cruise and the rest of our lives.

The dream continued. We walked inside the walls of the city of Dubrovnik in Croatia. Venice came next. We had dreamed of gliding along in a gondola while the oarsman sang for us. We did glide along in a gondola but it held four other people and was part of a larger group of gondolas, also carrying many passengers. One oarsman sang for all of us, but just seeing Venice and drifting beneath the Rialto Bridge and down the canals between the age-old brick houses was enough of a thrill. We explored the Jewish ghetto and its synagogue and learned more of the tragic Jewish history. In St. Mark's Square, I bought a painting from one of the local artists who sit in the Square, displaying their talent. It now hangs in my living room, a reminder of that amazing trip.

On the way back to Rome, we toured the Greek islands of Santorini, Rhodes and Crete and wandered through the ruins of Corinth. I stood where St. Paul had preached and tried to picture it as it had been in ancient times. Another thrill and another dream-come- true awaited me when I stepped ashore on the Isle of Capri. At lunch, George had the winning slip of paper under his plate which meant we brought home a poster of the Isle of Capri. I admire it every time I walk into bedroom where it hangs on the wall..

Once more in Rome, we toured the Vatican, viewed the Colosseum and the Forum before staying three nights in an Italian villa with a glorious view of the lake in Castel Gandolfo, the Pope's summer quarters. In addition, I picked up several Italian words before we left for home so I could, somewhat, communicate with the waiters and waitresses.

Yes, taking the period off my life led to sweet, dear and almost unbelievable events. It also solved the mystery of the man in my dreams – the three I had before I left for California. I was lying, blissfully happy, in the arms of a man, but I couldn't see his face. It puzzled me because, for some reason, I didn't have the sense that it was Dean. It came to me on the cruise. It was George, of course.

7,000 MILES FROM HOME

THE FIRST TIME GEORGE said it, we were sitting in a parking area near the Estuary, watching the sailboats drift by and the freighters being loaded. "When we get married," he commented, "we can probably have the ceremony at Cliff's house." What! I didn't reply because I hadn't yet erased the period from my decision not to remarry. I loved George deeply but marriage entailed families and possibly changing my name again, among other things. I made a noncommittal remark and set it aside, thinking we could discuss it when he actually asked me.

Besides, I had my book on my mind. In between cruising and dancing and the excitement of our love, I had managed to complete "In the Village of Lonsdale," but it needed to be edited and prepared for publishing, a whole new experience. Before I could accomplish that, 2005 rang in and George had another cruise on his mind – a long one this time. Labeled the *Asia Pacific Explorer Cruise*, it was scheduled to begin on the 6th of October. He had hoped to make it one hundred and two days but we settled on sixty-two, the most I could handle.

With planning and deciding what to take, the months flew by and I turned around and we were in Seattle aboard the MS Amsterdam. Our first stop in the Aleutians had been cancelled due to fog, sending us to Petropavlovsk on the Kamchatka Peninsula in Russia, a country that has long fascinated me. On the way, we crossed the International Date Line and I lost October 11th, my eightieth birthday! Our new friends on board teased me that I couldn't turn eighty, but we celebrated on the 12th, just in case.

From a hilltop in Petropavlovsk, we looked across the top of a spectacular forest of yellow-leaved birch trees toward the Kuril Islands and the snowy cone of Fussa Volcano. On a drive through the city, an up-close view showed us, in some places, piles of rubble cluttering the sides of the roads from the demolished Communist-era buildings. New buildings stood in other areas, giving it the air of a city in transition. Our Russian guides, with their stylish outfits, perfectly coiffed hair and makeup, were knowledgeable and polite but not really cordial. I have no proof of it but was told that the guides dress that way in the hope of catching the attention of any single men on the cruise. They showed us the Cultural Museum and a Russian Orthodox Church which left me with a strong desire to see more of Russia. I looked back from the deck of the MS Amsterdam, as we cruised out of the harbor, dreaming of visiting again and finding the treasures that lay in its vast expanse.

At Aomori, Japan, our next stop, we moored near a bridge in Mutsu Bay and found a modern, lively city and friendly citizens, which proved to be the general attitude in Japan. We enjoyed a ferry ride on Lake Ashinoko, in Hakone National Park, Yokohama, and I was greeted with a little whiff of my old home. As we were disembarking at the dock, I heard a voice say, "Foxboro." My Foxboro sweatshirt had caught the attention of a couple who were actually from Foxboro! We chatted for a while, all of us amazed and pleased and wished each other a wonderful trip.

The hilltop view from Osaka Castle at our next stop made the climb up and back down worthwhile. We strolled through the grounds of the Shitennoji Temple where an oft-recalled memory still warms me. A tiny, older Japanese woman stepped to the side of the path to allow our group to pass. She and I looked at each other, I smiled and she put out her hand. I grasped it and squeezed it and we both smiled again.

Nagasaki has a museum – the Atomic Bomb Museum - located, interestingly, next to the Peace Memorial Park. I chose not to go inside, preferring to amble around the area and take snapshots. I had seen my share of pictures in 1945 at the time the bomb was dropped. When the group came out, someone asked our Japanese guide whether Japan held any resentment toward America. She replied, "No. You rebuilt our country after the war and helped us recover. We're grateful for that."

Cheju City, South Korea, on an island south of the country, is considered a haven for honeymooners and I can understand that. It has a sandy, clean and inviting shoreline below craggy cliffs, giving it a romantic appeal. George made a comment about finding a good place for a honeymoon and I laughingly said this would be nice. Throughout the trip, he occasionally alluded to our "marriage" which told me I'd have to face it and make a decision, but the one I made was to set it aside until after the cruise.

I couldn't believe I was actually in China when we stepped ashore in Dalian. Our tour guide showed us People's Square, a Kindergarten (they're proud of their younger generation) and Labor Park where I used a restroom and learned that you don't actually sit on a toilet bowl. The user has to squat over a hole in the floor which has an enamel seat. In another city, the women in the group lined up in front of one booth because someone had discovered it was "western style." It had a bowl with a seat where the user could sit down. Later, we found out it was the "disabled" booth.

We boarded a bus in Xingang to view the Ming Tombs and walk on the Great Wall. In order to reach the Great Wall, we had to labor up a hill from where the bus had parked. At the top, we reached a terrace and a set of stone steps. George opted to wait for me. Before climbing the steps, I succumbed to the sales pitch of a lady vendor and bought a tartan-patterned wool scarf and am glad I did. It came in handy on the trip and later back at home. The stone steps led to a landing with more stone steps and at the top of those, I stood on the Great Wall.

Our guide took a picture of the group before turning us loose. I walked slowly along the wall, struggling to absorb the fact that I was really and truly on it. The portion I could see snaked through the mountains and disappeared, a tremendous piece of engineering, stretching about 5,000 miles originally and built over decades by

300,000 men. It undulates with the land and is lit up at night. Tears overwhelmed me. The little girl from Cumberland was on the Great Wall, a memory that can still evoke deep emotions. I ached with the desire to keep walking but time limits sent me back down the stone steps to George and the descent to the bottom of the hill. We sat for a short while in a little café until it was time to board the bus and return to the ship.

Having run out of superlatives, I'll just say Hong Kong lived up to my expectations. We docked on November 5th and walked through the Flower Market, listening to the caged birds that are sold in the neighboring Bird Garden. The tour provided lunch which meant sitting in a tram that crawled to the top of Victoria Peak. The young man next to me at lunch had grown up in what was once Czechoslovakia. I wish I could remember all of the stories he told me, in his excellent English, about his country. We both agreed to the wish that we had more time to talk but George and I had to stay with the tour. Down again in the city, we visited Stanley Market, an open-air, shopper's paradise, where I bought a cashmere sweater. We enjoyed a boat ride around the bay before we headed back to the ship..

The next day, lunch was in the Raffle's Hotel in Singapore. The city itself has been restored after being used, variously, during and after World War 11, as a center for British refugees, quarters for Japanese officers and a convalescent center for released prisoners-of-war.. Its splendor is back and you can still get a Singapore Sling in any of the bars. It's a vibrant, exciting city that lives up to its allure.

About halfway through our cruise, on November 7th, we became *pollywogs* as we crossed the Equator for the first time. King Neptune, in a long robe, wearing a crown and holding a trident, declared us to be *shellbacks* - seasoned travelers who had crossed the Equator, another tremendous thrill for me.

Our stop at Bali, Indonesia, was cancelled due to a recent bombing. Instead, we were given two days in Fremantle, Australia, a pretty little city where I stepped inside an Anglican church on the city Common while George waited on a bench nearby. Episcopalians are an offshoot of the Anglican tradition. That little interlude of being in a familiar place pleased me.

Australian men are good-looking, the women attractive and all are friendly, easygoing and irreverent. I fell in love with their country, in spite of the fact that they drive, as the British do, on the left-hand side of the road. From Fremantle, we motored up the Swan River to Perth which is a lovely city, especially as viewed from Memorial Park. Traveling back by bus, we were thrilled to see black swans on Lake Monger and a magpie in a tree. Our cruise continued with a visit to Adelaide and Cleland Wildlife Park where I was within petting distance of the free-roving kangaroos. I didn't pet any but took several pictures of them as well as a koala asleep in a tree in their fenced-in area.

I loved Bondi Beach in Sydney and longed to go swimming but could only walk on the beach. However, our mooring spot in Sydney harbor – almost under the bridge, with a stunning view of the Opera House – made up for it, along with a short visit to the city center to browse and buy a t-shirt. The following day, in Brisbane harbor, after seeing Mt. Cootha and Kangaroo Point on the Brisbane River, I watched regretfully from the railing of the Amsterdam, reluctant to leave Australia.

Northern California weather isn't exactly similar to that in New Caledonia so it's possible I'll never wear the sarong I bought but who knows? On that island, we rode up La Ouen Toro Hill for an overview of the city and discovered a gun placement left over from World War 11 when the city of Noumea served as an Allied base.

We found Fiji, our next stop, to be proudly independent and basing their economy on tourism which is a good idea because the climate and shoreline are superb and the round, thatched-roof buildings built on piers out over the water look inviting. The Fijians no longer indulge in cannibalism so we were safe and, according to the pamphlets, they only ate their defeated enemies anyway. We viewed the instruments in a museum – cannibal forks hand-carved from wood and polished.

On November 26th, I picked up the day I had lost as we once more crossed the International Date Line, making me officially age eighty.

Before reaching Samoa, we crossed the equator again and watched the crew *pollywogs* being "sacrificed to the Gods" by being lathered in cream and tossed into the pool.

Robert Louis Stevenson made his home in Apia, Samoa - a paradise of white sand, a warm climate and cultivated fields - because he suffered from tuberculosis. We rode in a rainbow-colored bus to his house - Villa Vailima. It's large and white, with a wrap-around porch and a view of the hills below the imposing front lawn. His books are displayed in a covered bookcase on the ground floor. In another first, during our stay on Samoa, we drank out of coconut shells.

With the tide turning and the danger of the Amsterdam becoming grounded, we couldn't go ashore at Christmas Island, our last stop before Hawaii. On December 2nd, we cruised into Honolulu. The Christmas decorations in the Royal Hawaiian seemed out of place to my New England eyes but interesting in that tropical setting. Once more, I took my bathing suit with me and swam at Waikiki while George sat under an umbrella and watched from the beach.

We tied up at San Diego on December 7th, my eyes still shining from the extraordinary cruise. Could life get any better?

AN OLD GUY LIKE ME

CHRISTMAS THAT YEAR AND the advent of 2005 seemed anticlimactic after two months of cruising halfway around the world. We allowed the days to carry us into January, hoping for some quiet time. We had it but not as we had expected.

On the 4th, the flu hit both of us. For a few days, neither George nor I had any appetite but I suddenly craved food one day and slurped up a bowl of soup. That night, I barely made it to the bathroom before losing the soup. I rinsed and dried my hands and mouth and turned toward the door but soon wondered why I was staring up at the underside of the basin. Dehydration had struck again. I gulped some water and dragged myself into bed, but quickly realized my pillow felt wet. I switched on the light, saw blood all over the pillow and darted into the bathroom for a towel. I called 911 and woke George. "I fell in the bathroom and hit my head," I told him. "Call Darcy, please."

The ambulance came for me and I left him sitting on the edge of the bed. About an hour later, Cliff poked his head around the curtain in the Emergency Room. My eyebrows shot up. "Where's your father?" He pointed toward the curtain.

"My dad called and when I saw him I knew he had pneumonia so he's right beside you."

Following my diagnosis of bronchitis, I stayed for four days. George, after being transferred to Alta Bates Hospital, stayed for seven days. We both had care-givers at our homes. That gave me lots of time to think and to miss him terribly. One thought in particular zinged through me. If I hadn't passed out and Cliff hadn't seen his father, George could have died of pneumonia. It was time for me to make up my mind.

We kept in touch, of course, and on January 24th he called to say, "My live-in care-giver had a family emergency and I'm alone. Can I stay with you?" Even though I didn't have my full strength back, I wanted to have him with me. Together, we grew healthy again and decided we liked living together. "It's time to sell my house," he told me. Cliff, Hillary and I helped him clean it out, give away or otherwise find homes for his furniture. Some of it came to my place. By May, it was ready to go on the market and sold easily.

During those days, he gave me one of my dearest memories which hasn't faded with age. He turned and gazed somberly at me for a few seconds before asking, but not really asking, "What's an old guy like me doing with a pretty girl like you?" I had no answer but could only blush and smile and feel loved.

Before I passed out in the bathroom, I had been scheduled in January for a cornea transplant in my left eye to correct the blurred vision left by a cataract removal. The doctor rescheduled it for May. Before the date, the ophthalmologist, Dr. S., asked me to come to his office. "There's a new procedure, *keratoplasty*, which has been done successfully and often in southern California but is just becoming known in northern California," he explained. "If you agree to have it done, you'd be my first patient. Are you willing to take that chance?" I had come to know him well and trusted him completely, but wanted more details. "It replaces the tissue between the cornea and the eyeball," he said. "It's done on an outpatient basis and the recovery time is much faster than with the cornea transplant. The tissue comes from an eye bank in Atlanta." I told him I was game. George drove me to the hospital on the appointed day in May.

As it turned out, Dr. S. didn't like the first tissue he received, causing him to delay my operation by a day and making me his <u>second</u> patient. Once again, George drove me to the hospital in the morning and took me home in the afternoon. The doctor was right. My eye healed within a few weeks rather than a few months and my post-op appointment with him showed my eyesight to be 20/20. It has stayed good ever since.

Some time later, he asked whether I'd be willing to be the "specimen" for a group of ophthalmologists. I agreed to that, too, and told Dr. S. about their amazed and complimentary remarks as they viewed his handiwork through the refractor.

With that behind me, I published "In the Village of Lonsdale" in October of 2006. Darcy designed the cover which received many compliments. My first-ever book signing, which was held in San Leandro, a city very close to Alameda, didn't go well. The only person, besides George, who came to it was Gretchen, my friend from Writers West. She dropped in to encourage me and that helped. Learning as I went along, I found in order to sell my books, I'd have to do a lot more in the way of publicizing. I contacted the Cumberland paper, the Valley Breeze, for instance, and did an interview over the phone with their editor. I emailed and phoned book stores in the Rhode Island area surrounding Cumberland and was able to place several copies in one of them. St. Mark's Thrift Shop in Foxboro accepted and sold several and the Foxboro Reporter helped me advertise them. Eventually, my efforts produced sales of over two hundred copies. I celebrated silently the fact that I was not only a published author but a published author of a book. I wished often that my high school teacher could be in on the wonderful news but I wasn't sure where to contact him.

Life took a turn away from my writing in January of 2007 after I had assumed the every-day driving. I dropped George off in front a local supermarket while I searched for a parking space. A few minutes later, I walked through the door to find him leaning on the handle of a shopping cart. Before I could reach him, he slipped down, his arms entangled in the handle. A man coming in yelled, "Do you need help?" I nodded and between us we lowered George to the floor. The clerk at the Customer Service counter called 911. While we waited for the ambulance, I knelt beside George and stroked his head.

At the hospital, I called Cliff who said he'd be there as soon as possible. George was eventually diagnosed as having *old-age leukemia*, also known as *anemia* and was put on a regimen of blood transfusions.

Once a month, I drove him to the Alameda Hospital, settled him in a wheelchair and took him to the Fusion Department for his transfusion and a discussion with the doctor. He recovered but slowed his pace and social life.

The episode scared me and gave me the push I needed. For whatever time we had left together, I wanted to be his wife. I removed the last period from my life and said, "You're right. We should get married." He beamed. We found a calendar and set the wedding date for Saturday at 2:00 P.M. on October 7, 2007. Both Darcy and Cliff were happy to hear the news and agreed to be our attendants – the Maid-of-Honor and Best Man. I called my cousin Barbara and asked her to give me away. Fortunately, Cliff and Hilary said they'd host the ceremony at their house in Orinda.

I made another decision - to drop Dean's name and become just plain Violet Grayson. George understood when I explained my reasons. I had changed my name twice and wanted to "keep it simple" and have the name I started out with in the first place..

He suggested picking out a ring at a Kiwanis friend's jewelry store in San Leandro, giving the final decision to me. I found a gorgeous one with three diamonds which we both loved. I could hardly wait to see it on my left hand and be able to call him my husband. The night before our wedding, we treated Darcy and my three nieces - Jan, Marilyn and Ann, as well as their husbands - to dinner at the Pasta Pelican restaurant in Alameda. We included Katy and a friend of Darcy's, Stephanie. Except for Darcy, they had all come from out-of-town to be with us.

On a spectacular October day, with sunshine filling the valley below the house in the East Bay hills, we stood under a flower- bedecked arbor in Cliff and Hilary's yard, in front of thirty friends and relatives. George, at ninety-seven, looked splendid in his best suit and a red carnation in his lapel. Darcy had helped me, the eighty-two- year-old bride, find a lovely white and gold dress at Macy's. We asked a minister, the Reverend Betty Lue from the Alameda House of Truth, to marry us. I furnished copies of the Episcopal service from the prayer book and some Jewish prayers I'd found online and Betty Lue blended them seamlessly and beautifully.

The ceremony began and I listened to the lovely words. It was neither fright nor doubt but simply the size of what was happening that overwhelmed me when Betty Lue asked, "Will you take this man to be your lawfully wedded husband?" I couldn't speak. I tried to open my mouth but nothing came out. In the silence, someone chuckled and the sound broke through my muteness.

I said, "I will," and the ceremony continued. Cliff, in the Jewish tradition, furnished a paper bag with a glass* in it for George to break.

At the precise moment Betty Lue said, "I now pronounce you husband and wife," and I kissed George, a squadron of Blue Angels flew overhead. Everyone looked up in surprise and awe and someone jokingly asked, "How did you arrange that?"

George shrugged. "Friends," he laughed. Actually, it was Fleet Week in San Francisco and the planes had timed it perfectly on their way over the East Bay hills. I never questioned it.

The guests congratulated us, hugged us and admired my ring before we all headed into the dining room and the buffet luncheon. We carried our plates to the tables set up on the lawn. After we ate, we filed back inside for the cutting of the cake but before we started, our guests clamored for us to dance. George took my hand, I hummed a tune to give us the beat and we did a few swing steps. Everyone applauded.

Eventually, our guests left. We thanked Cliff and Hilary, I snipped a flower from the arbor to put into our wedding album and the newlyweds, with the remains of the cake, went home. Once more, that night, George gazed at me and asked, "What's an old guy like me doing with a pretty girl like you?" filling my heart with joy and love and happiness.

---

* There are eight or so reasons given for this tradition but I found one I like the most. A broken glass has been forever changed. Likewise, the two people have been forever changed and together have taken on a new form. Also, Cliff confessed to me later that the bag actually contained a light bulb to make it easier for George, who didn't know, of course.

OVER THE BOUNDING MAIN

S HOULD AN EIGHTY-TWO-YEAR-OLD BRIDE and a ninety-seven-year- old groom go on a honeymoon? Why not? George, with his doctor's permission, booked a cruise on the MS Ryndam that began on January 6, 2008, and ended on February 5th.. He wisely opted for idyllic islands in the South Pacific – Hawaii, Bora Bora, Tahiti, Moorea and Nuku Hiva. On board the ship, our newly-wed status didn't remain a secret for long. One day in the elevator, I made a comment about it and the only other passenger spoke up. "Oh, you must be the honeymoon couple." We laughed as we nodded, pleased to acknowledge it.

Memories remain of the Hawaiian ports George and I visited – Hilo, Kona, Lahaina, Honolulu and Nawiliwili - and the boat trip on the Wailua River as well as having my picture taken with the Opaeka Falls in the background. I recall the fruit snack we enjoyed in Raiatea in the Society Islands and the thatched-roof buildings in the center of town. Bora Bora enchanted me. I wanted to lie on the soft beach but a busload of passengers sat waiting to go to *Bloody Mary's* for refreshments. In another picture, I'm standing next to a *tiki* – a carved Polynesian god - on the grounds of the Gauguin Museum in Tahiti. We peeked at the grotto with a stream running through it where Gauguin liked to swim. Papeete, after the tranquility of the beaches, appeared to be bustling but was also charming. On our last stop in the Society Islands, the tour bus driver stopped beside a field of pineapples growing in Moorea. The guide pointed toward a distant mountain. "That was used as *Bali Hai* in the movie, *South Pacific*," she said and we all hurried out to take a picture.

Aboard the ship again, we crossed the equator for the third time, watching but not participating in the initiation ceremony. The last stop, Nuku Hiva in the Marqueses, had once been a French Possession which interested me since I had never heard of it but loved its tranquil atmosphere. Boats lay at anchor in a crescent-shaped cove with aqua-blue water and sandy beaches.

San Diego came into view much too soon, it seemed. We left the ship but the warm glow of the trip and of just being together stayed with us.

Life didn't stand still at home. We took advantage of a thoughtful and perfect wedding gift from Darcy and my nieces – a weekend in a hotel in Sausalito in San Francisco Bay. The view of the harbor from our room added a delightful touch. We browsed through the stores or sat on a bench in the sun or snapped a few pictures. We did settle down somewhat after that, though, visiting friends, driving around Alameda, eating lunch overlooking the Estuary and just enjoying each other's company. I smiled each time he introduced me as his wife and we shared a happiness that went beyond describing.

In order to spread that happiness around, on April 9th at the Marina Community Center in San Leandro where George's Kiwanis group had held their Crab Feeds, we hosted a delayed wedding reception for one hundred and twelve friends. Of course we had to have a band so everyone could dance and have fun.

A month later, we flew to Santa Barbara for another wedding reception, this one honoring Katy and her new husband, Andy. Marilyn arranged for a Landshark Tour for all the guests - a ride on an amphibious craft through the streets and out into Santa Barbara harbor. At the reception, held on the top floor of the Ronald Reagan Center which gave us an unparalleled view, we did some more dancing, much to the delight of the younger guests. Just by chance, they learned that George, at sixteen in 1926, had played one season with the Brooklyn Dodgers, making him the center of attention for a while.

To catch our breath, we hung around Alameda for the rest of 2008, filling our days with ordinary but delightful happenings and welcoming 2009 before the urge to cruise hit again. Two months prior to George's ninety-ninth birthday, on March 14th, again with his doctor's permission, we embarked on a thirty-eight-day trip around South America, flying to Miami to change planes for Rio de Janeiro.

Jan, who worked for American Airlines, met us in Miami with Ann by her side, another treat. "I've arranged for you to sit in the Admiral's Lounge," she whispered, "That's for VIP's."

She brought drinks for us and said, "I'll check on your plane's departure time." The look on her face when she returned told us something had happened, even before she gave us the news, "The plane has a mechanical problem and can't leave tonight so I've booked a room for you." We thanked her and assured her it wasn't a catastrophe since the MS Amsterdam wasn't scheduled to leave Rio for three days and we had planned for a tour of the city, anyway. A knock on our door at 6:30 A.M. the next morning announced the arrival of a young man with a wheelchair for George. Later, by 5:00 P.M., we were aboard the ship.

During our thrilling stay in Rio, our bus tour took us past Copacabana Beach in Ipanema. I had trouble believing I was really looking at that famous beach, the one I'd seen in so many movies. At Mt. Corcovado, George waited on a bench at the foot of it while I rode a train to the top to stand and gaze up and up at the imposing statue of Christ. On another day, the breathtaking panoramic view from Sugarloaf Mountain enthralled me. Three days was scarcely enough time to cover all of Rio's grandeur but it would have to satisfy us since we had to cruise on to Uruguay. That country proved to be much prettier than I had imagined and I especially liked its far-reaching, sunny and sandy beaches.

In Argentina I admired the soccer stadium and the government buildings in the downtown area. After dinner that evening, we watched an erotic tango performance, joking that they danced almost as well as we did. George had been to the Falklands so he agreed to remain on board while I went alone with the tour. I said I'd meet him on the Lido Deck but I stayed longer than I had intended. When at last I walked through the door onto the Lido Deck, two new shipboard friends sitting with George hailed my entrance. "He kept asking us to go to the gangway and see whether you had checked in yet," they laughed. "He missed you and thought something had happened." My heart swelled once more with happiness and love.

Though George decided otherwise, I wanted to be out on deck when we rounded Cape Horn but I had underestimated the velocity of the wind that whipped across the deck as we left the Atlantic Ocean and entered the Pacific Ocean. Fortunately, another person who shared my wish helped me push open the door. The wind sent us both scurrying for the railing to keep our footing. It caused me to wonder how Darwin and his crew, in a much smaller ship, survived it. Exhilarated, buffeted by the wind and taking in deep breaths of the cold air, I managed to get some precious pictures. A kind woman offered to take my picture at the rail. To get back inside, again I needed another person to help me pull open the door. Each time I look at my pictures I can feel once more the force of that wind.

We docked at Ushuaia, Argentina, to board an excursion boat to see the endearing sight of a colony of Magellan penguins strutting on Hammer Island in their tuxedo-like plumage. From Ushuaia, we crossed into Chile to go ashore at Punte Arenas and spend the day strolling the area and admiring its scenery. Later that day, we cruised past the Amalia Glacier and glided through the Darwin Channel.

The air was warmer in Valparaiso and Arica, Chile. There, in an open market, I bought a wooden plaque for Darcy that had an etching of Tierra del Fuego on it. I liked both Chile and Peru because of their welcoming atmosphere and modern look among their ancient ruins. I'm still wearing the alpaca wool coat I found in an open-air market.

A nut factory on the side of a mountain in Manta, Nicaragua, fascinated us. The workers carve jewelry, among other things, out of the ivory-colored meat of tagua nuts which resemble horse chestnuts.

Though I had been in Costa Rice on my Panama Cruise trip, I was happy to see it again, even briefly. As we approached the end of our cruise, we had the joy of watching the divers plunge off a cliff in Acapulco and of touring that lovely city. Our last stop at gorgeous Cabo San Lucas gave a grand finish to our trip which ended in San Diego on the 20th of April.

One more celebration awaited us. – George's 99th birthday on May 11th. I considered him to be invincible, a truly unusual and fearless man, one who never let his age get in the way. I admired and loved him deeply and felt thankful once more that he had come into my life and trusted we'd have as many years together as possible.

EPILOGUE

WE HAD BEEN MARRIED for a year and nine months at the time in 2009 that we received our yearly invitation from Loretta, a friend I met in the Christ Church choir. Her sixth floor condo made the perfect spot for viewing the 4th of July lighted-ship parade on the Estuary and the fireworks in the hills beyond. The time passed pleasantly as we laughed and chatted with other friends included in the invitation while we *oohed* and *aahed* at the small and large boats, outlined in lights, gliding by and the rockets tossing their brilliant hues against the dark sky. The evening ended, we said our goodbyes and stepped into the hall. Accidents never announce themselves. George tripped on a rug, fell and couldn't get up, even with our help. Loretta called 911. The Emergency Room doctor confirmed that he had fractured his right leg and wouldn't be going home with me.

A few days later, he began a three-week stay in the nearby Alameda Care Center that, we were told, would be followed by another three weeks at home, with physical therapy, before he'd be able to walk unassisted again. I visited him every day, looking forward to the time I could sit next to him and hold him once more. At last, on July 25th, he came home. Cliff hired a male nurse for the daytime and suggested I sleep on the floor near the bed at night to avoid accidentally kicking his leg and in case he needed anything. I agreed, happy to have him at home. On the third night, I disobeyed because I wanted to be next to him. We held each other before it came time to turn over and fall asleep. The next night, I crawled in beside him again and held him again and gave up my place on the floor.

The next morning, four days after he had come home, I served him breakfast while he sat on the edge of the bed which pleased me because it appeared he was recovering rapidly. We talked for a while and I tucked him back into bed and puttered around the house until lunchtime. I was having a quick bite to eat before preparing his meal when the nurse yelled, "Violet!" I rushed into the bedroom to find George with his head thrown back, not breathing. "I'm sorry," the nurse said. Devastated, I threw myself across him, calling his name and sobbing wildly, but he was gone, taken by a blood clot.

It's always hard to remember everything you do when you're ripped by grief. I know I called Cliff and Darcy. As the nearest, she came immediately to share my sorrow and Cliff and Hilary arrived as soon as they possibly could. Somehow, the day passed, George was taken away and that night I sobbed, alone in our bed, unwilling and unprepared to face the reality of his death.

As hard as it was to do, Cliff, Hilary and I planned a funeral home visitation to allow friends to say their final goodbyes. Shortly after that, at a private funeral, the family – Cliff, Hilary, Stephen and his wife, Anastasia, Jason, me and Darcy – stood at George's grave to watch his casket being lowered into it and to individually say a few prayers.

Alone again at home, I dragged myself through our small place, whimpering child-like, wondering how I could go on without him. Friends called to check on me and sympathy cards piled up in our mail box. Minute by painful minute, the hours passed, adding up to days and months and I emerged from my depression with one thought. "I want to celebrate his life." The thought energized me. I checked the calendar. "I'll have it on the 29th of October at Willow Park," I told myself, thinking of a place in nearby Castro Valley where we had danced many times.

Small, unforeseen obstacles blocked my way – I had difficulty contacting the right person at Willow Park, the one who could help me, for instance. Frustrated and confused, I called my psychic friend, Aann. "Why can't I just talk to someone and make the plans?" I ranted.

"George has been trying to help you," she answered, "He has a question. *Why are you going so far?* That's his question." I smiled in understanding. I had considered holding it at the Grand Pavilion in Alameda which had once been Bay Fairway Hall, the site of our first date in 1995, but for some vague reason I thought Willow Park might be bigger and more centrally located. If I needed any proof that the message had come from George, I found it when everything fell into place from the time I made my first phone call to the Grand Pavilion and had no trouble reaching someone.

The night of the Celebration, I asked Cliff to share his thoughts about his father, prompting several of our friends to step up and pay tribute to George with their words and it was just as I had dreamed it would be. I asked Rabbi Bennett from Temple Israel to say a few prayers for George, someone he had never met. He listened to the tributes and did a perfect job. After everyone had spoken, I added my own comments, speaking at times through a sorrow-choked voice.

The guests gathered around the buffet table and the mood relaxed before the evening ended and I thanked our friends as they bid me goodbye. I stood in the empty hall to take one last, long look. It had been the perfect place and George knew that. I thanked him for his guidance. "You were my bonus," I whispered. I called him that because he danced into my life when I thought I had already lived it to the full and he added his gift of love – a love I thought had died with Dean. He took me on a wild ride, as a friend once said, and added a grand flourish to my life.

By early afternoon in northern California, the sun has risen above the trees and the neighboring house to find the large window in my living room. That allows me to relax on my sofa or in either of two comfortable chairs and bask in its rays. Sitting in the sun, its warmth embracing me, I let my mind wander, reflecting on memories of having loved deeply and been loved in return, of having obstacles tossed in front of me but solutions appearing when I asked for help. I also remember the sharp turns that took me along dark and dreary paths, causing me to wonder whether I'd ever feel joy again but I found it in abundance, time and time again, in a life not expected.

HISTORY

GASPEE POINT – King George III imposed trade laws and sent the HMS *Gaspee* to Rhode Island waters in 1772 to enforce the law and prevent smuggling. Under the command of Lt. William Dudingston, the *Gaspee's* crew harassed shipping and delayed ships that had been cleared through customs inspection in Newport. One, the sloop *Hannah,* left Newport for Providence. Lt. Dudingston ordered the *Gaspee* to follow her. *Hannah's* Captain Lindsey deliberately lured the *Gaspee* across the waters of Namquid Point (now Gaspee Point) and the *Gaspee* ran aground on a sandbar, unable to float until the tide came in.

Captain Lindsey reported the event to John Brown, a prominent and respected merchant in Rhode Island. John Brown sent a town crier out to invite all interested parties to meet at Sabin's Tavern. Under the leadership of Abraham Whipple, a small band of patriots rowed eight longboats with muffled oars to the stranded ship, removed Lt. Dudingston and his crew and put them behind bars. Once that was accomplished, the patriots burned the *Gaspee* to the water line. The English officials immediately sent orders to arrest those involved but no one remembered having seen them. ("Nope. Didn't see a thing.") Lt. Dudingston and his crew were sent back to England.

KING PHILIP – The second son of the Wampanoag chief, Massasoit, and known as Metacom or Metacomet, he assumed the English name of "Philip" due to his father's friendship with the original Pilgrims. Massasoit welcomed the Pilgrims and helped them survive through the first winter in Plymouth. Philip succeeded his father but complained when new arrivals from England encroached on the Wampanoag lands. He was forced to sign a new peace agreement asking for the surrender of Native American guns. The final straw came when officials in Plymouth Colony hanged three Wampanoags for the murder of a Native American who had adopted Christianity. King Philip's war ensued and the Wampanoags were successful at first but eventually they and their Narragansett allies were almost annihilated.

His name was well known in the area where the ballroom was located since some of the action took place in the town of Wrentham which was settled in 1661 but burned down in the 1675-1676 King Philip's War.

FOXBORO – The town seal shows the legal spelling – Foxborough – as do the signs at either end of the Common but to its residents it's just plain Foxboro, named for Charles James Fox, a British statesman who opposed the Boston Port Bill which precipitated the Boston Tea Party in 1774. He also defended the stand of the American colonists when they rebelled.

According to information I found in *This Was Foxborough* by Mr. and Mrs. Clifford W. Lane, the land was once part of Wrentham, Walpole, Stoughtonham and Stoughton in Suffolk County. As far as I can determine, that parcel of land was bought from King Philip of the Wampanoag Tribe in 1636. The book reveals that the first white men walked on what would become Foxborough between 1630 and 1635. That area was later renamed Norfolk County.

An overland route called the "Roebuck Trail" stretched from Boston to Dedham, running east of the villages of Norwood and East Walpole, and almost parallel to the present Route 1 as far as Walpole. Known as "The Old Post Road" and the most traveled road of its period in America, it cut through the future town of Foxborough over Mechanic, South and Cedar Streets to North Attleboro.

The house of William Hudson, the first settler, was the only residence, until 1716, on land that was still part of Wrentham. During the King Philip War, the residents of Wrentham were forced in 1675 and 1676 to leave their homes and relocate to Dedham in order to be safe. All buildings in Wrentham were burned down. After the war, settlers moved into what would become Foxborough and the town grew. In 1763, they put up the frame for the first meeting house and applied for incorporation as a town. After several petitions, and with four hundred fifty residents, they were granted incorporation during the fourth year of the Revolutionary War on June 10, 1778.

REFORM OF THE MENTAL HEALTH SYSTEM – In the middle 70's, reform became an issue, with state hospitals being labeled "warehouses" for the mentally ill. Many patients, especially those with the problem of retardation who could be employed in simple jobs, were encouraged to be more involved in their own treatment with some moving to smaller group homes or subsidized housing. Outpatient psychiatric care in more modern facilities arrived. The mental institutions, especially the smaller, less-used ones, gradually emptied of what they called their *clients*. Those Foxboro clients who weren't able to care for themselves went to Taunton State Hospital, a larger facility in the city of Taunton.

ALAMEDA – After the Miwoks came the Spanish, beginning in the 1500's. The first census (name, age and sex of each colonist) taken by the Pueblo of the Mission San Jose shortly after it was established in 1777, included the name of Babriel Peralta, along with his family. That included his son, Spanish-born eighteen-year-old Luis Maria Peralta.

Luis spent forty-five years of his life in the military at San Francisco and Monterey and fifteen of them as Commander of the Pueblo of San Jose. In 1818, two years before he retired, he applied for a land grant, asking for a thirty-five-square-mile piece of land on the eastern shore of San Francisco Bay. In 1820, it was granted and he named it "Rancho San Antonio". It now comprises parts or all of El Cerrito, Berkeley, Albany, Oakland, Piedmont and Alameda. The Alameda section lies seven miles across the bay from San Francisco and was originally known as Encinal de San Antonio or simply Encinal because of its many live oaks.

It became Alameda when William W. Chipman and Gidean Aughinbaugh approached Luis Peralta's son, Antonio Maria Peralta, after his father's death, to purchase some land. Luis Peralta refused to trade with the Americans because he didn't like them but Antonio sold a portion of the land to them in 1851 for $14,000.

Alameda was located on a peninsula of Oakland with a mile-wide neck of marshy land between the two. In 1902, a Tidal Canal, now known as the Oakland-Alameda Estuary, was dug in the marshy land to allow ships to sail into the Port of Oakland, making Alameda an island.

The literal meaning of Alameda in Spanish is "a grove or lane of poplar trees." It's uncertain whether this choice of name was poetic license or ignorance of the meaning of the Spanish word.

ALAMEDA NAVAL AIR STATION – Fill from the dredging of the Estuary was used at the western end of Alameda to form what would become Alameda Airport. The name was changed to Benton Field in 1930 to honor Lt. John W. Benton, an Army Air Corps pilot from

Shasta County, California, who died in a plane crash during the 1926- 27 Pan American Airways Good Will Flight to Central and South America.

Pan American Airways, beginning in 1935, used a yacht harbor next to Benton Airport as the California terminal for *China Clipper* trans-Pacific flights. By the following year, the airport had been ceded to the United States Government and the yacht harbor renamed "Seaplane Lagoon." The terminal itself received a designation as California Historical Landmark #968. Pan American Airlines moved to Treasure Island, an artificial island built in San Francisco Bay for the 1939 Golden Gate Exposition. A year later, on November 1, 1940, the Alameda Naval Air Station opened. A year and thirty-six days later, the Japanese bombed Pearl Harbor.

The bombers for the April, 1942, Doolittle Raid on Tokyo were put aboard the USS Hornet CV-8, an aircraft carrier based at Alameda Naval Air Station, to be taken within bombing distance of Japan.

That carrier was sunk during World War II. Its 1943 replacement, USS Hornet CV-12, also saw a great deal of duty during the war but survived. In 1969, it picked up Neil Armstrong, Buzz Aldrin and Michael Collins when the Apollo returned to earth after landing on the moon. Rescued from becoming scrap metal, it's now the USS Hornet Museum and fittingly moored at a pier on the former Alameda Naval Air Station, now known as Alameda Point.

MY WRITING CREDITS

10/86	CAT FANCY - *The Cat That Didn't Want to Move*
12/86	BYLINE MAGAZINE - *Spinning Your Wheels*
May/Oct '88	THE FOXBORO REPORTER - *I Remember...* (12 personal experience stories tied in with the history of the town of Foxboro, Massachusetts)
09/88	WORCESTER TELEGR AM & GAZETTE, SUNDAY MAGAZINE - *It's a Hurricane*
12/88	CANADIAN WRITER'S JOURNAL – *Memories for Sale*
12/88	HOME LIFE – *Christmas Comes Again* – also taped for the blind and visually-impaired 12/89
08/ 89	THE FOXBORO REPORTER – *A Blue-Collar River*
08/90	BLACK STONE RIVER TOUR ISM COUNCIL – *A Blue-Collar River*
11/91	YESTERDAY'S MAGAZETTE – *I Remember Pearl Harbor*
04/92	READER'S DIGEST – anecdote
02/93	REMINISCE – *Short Memories*
08/93	THE FOXBORO REPORTER – *Rubbing Elbows With History*
Nov/Dec 93	WRITERS' OPEN FORUM – *Your Cookies or Mine?*

Winter '93	GOTTA WRITE NETWORK MAGAZINE – *Focusing on Senior Markets*
10/94	ALAMEDA JOURNAL NEWSPAPER – *Why I Love Alameda*
Winter '94	GOTTA WRITE NETWORK MAGAZINE – *Capturing the Essence of Flow*
Jan/Feb '95	W R ITERS' INTER NATIONA L OPEN FORUM – *It's the Thought That Counts*
09/95	SHOW AND TELL MAGAZINE – *Where the Sidewalk Ends*
11/95	GOOD OLD DAYS SPECIALS – *I Remember the Mittens*
07/96	MATURE LIVING – *A Silver-Gray Box*
09/96	GOOD OLD DAYS SPECIALS – *No Privacy*
May/June '97	I LOVE CATS – *A Cat of a Different Color*
Fall '97	THE LUTHER AN DIGEST – Reprint of *A Silver-Gray Box*
May/June '98	DOGWOOD TALES MAGAZINE – *Toby or not Toby*
06/98	GOOD OLD DAYS – *Skunked*
10/98	MATURE OUTLOOK – *A Repotted Life*
2006	*In the Village of Lonsdale* – book of personal experience stories
2011	*A Gossamer Cord* - book of fiction
1/28/12	GUIDEPOSTS – MYSTER IOUS WAYS (Online) – *A Pot of Hope*
2013	*Jeremy's Cottage* – book of fiction
Feb/2016	GUIDEPOSTS – *Continued* feature

www.ingramcontent.com/pod-product-compliance
Lightning Source LLC
Chambersburg PA
CBHW020436130626
46549CB00001B/162